CUSTOMER TO HUMAN

ADVANCE PRAISE FOR THE BOOK

'In today's VUCA [Volatility, Uncertainty, Complexity and Ambiguity] times, the only constant is the importance of customer experience or CX. There are books about CC [Customer Centricity] from an academic perspective and then there are books like this, penned by an industry veteran like Murali who has been there and done that in the trenches with a rich diversity of roles and experience. He draws on these to offer some real nuggets of experience in an easily digestible format. This is highly recommended reading for everyone who believes CX is central to the enterprise and wants to learn from real-life experiences'—T. R. Ramachandran, Group Country Manager (India and South Asia) at Visa

'Great reading and guide for those striving to move from customer loyalty to customer advocacy'—Shyam Mani, Managing Director and CEO at TMF Holdings Ltd

'This is truly the author's reflection of his passion, namely the human touch that binds the customers and employees of an organization's wide ecosystem together. It sets out to explore a collage of possibilities across a variety of scenarios in a vast swathe of situations and settings, and then connects these experiences into analytical and actionable building-blocks, through a framework built around data and logic. It strives to discover patterns and weave a story around them that will compel the attention of any reader who deals with customers, irrespective of the industry setting— banking, telecom, airline digital services medicine or education. A terrific combination of historical events and personal anecdotes add to the appeal of the narrative'—Abhijit Sen, Ex CFO, Citibank; Corporate Advisor and Board Member

CUSTOMER TO HUMAN

The *CX Factor* in
Modern Business

MURALI BALARAMAN

PENGUIN
VIKING
An imprint of Penguin Random House

VIKING

USA | Canada | UK | Ireland | Australia
New Zealand | India | South Africa | China

Viking is part of the Penguin Random House group of companies
whose addresses can be found at global.penguinrandomhouse.com

Published by Penguin Random House India Pvt. Ltd
7th Floor, Infinity Tower C, DLF Cyber City,
Gurgaon 122 002, Haryana, India

First published in Viking by Penguin Random House India 2021

10 9 8 7 6 5 4 3 2

This book is a work of non-fiction. The views and opinions expressed in the book
are those of the author only and do not reflect or represent the views and opinions
held by any other person.

This book is based on personal experiences and a variety of sources, including
published materials and interviews and interactions conducted by the author with
the persons mentioned in the manuscript. It reflects the author's own understanding
and conception of such materials and/or can be verified by research.

The objective of this book is not to promote, advocate or profess the preferability
of any particular business model, idea, technique or approach over another.

ISBN 9780670095650

Typeset in Adobe Garamond Pro by Manipal Technologies Limited, Manipal
Printed at Replika Press Pvt. Ltd, India

www.penguin.co.in

To my dad and mom

Contents

Preface

'Who must be satisfied for your organization to achieve results?'

—Peter F. Drucker

'If your business can induce the same excitement that sports does to its ardent fans, you will not be short of customers.'

—Unknown

Every business has customers, big or small, and they are your most important asset. Whether you are a start-up or an established business, there is something for you in this book. The book is all about invaluable stories on inspirational customer experiences (CXs) that are universal in nature regardless of the industry you belong to.

Stories allow all of us to see concepts in much clearer light, help us clarify, customize, and implement accurately. Matt Parker, a mathematician and author of the book *Humble Pi*,[1] explains it beautifully. While million, billion and trillion are just numbers with added zeroes that don't make much sense till you interpret it in an quantifiable manner, if we use time to explain these numbers, a million seconds is eleven days and fourteen hours, a billion seconds is over thirty-one years and a trillion seconds later would occur sometime during the year 33,700 CE (that's more than 31,680 years away if you are reading this book in 2021).

CX is all about people—customers and employees. It is important for management to share a sense of the challenges that they are facing using pictures, numbers and stories. Only then can the CX solution demonstrate why it is needed. This is the first step in the CX solution getting embedded into the organization in an effective manner.

In this book, examples are drawn from common sense, personal examples and with empathy towards the customer. When woven intricately into the fabric of the organization in a customer-oriented manner the impact is phenomenal. It's akin to a series of brush strokes in a painting where the individual brush stroke is just a 'pixel' in the overall picture, but when it works in harmony with thousands of other pixels, the impact of the painting is that of pure joy.

It is well established that more than 80 per cent of CX investments go waste. This book aims to reduce that number significantly by showing examples of best practices across industries in order to increase the impact of these CX investments. My experience shows that organizations struggle to find a way of 'how to'. Some stop thinking because they have landed themselves in a situation where the problem looks unsolvable. Most answers to problems are actually quite simple. Businesses avoid change by merely stating examples of failures and sticking to the 'don't change it if not broken' principle.

The book is filled with ideas, execution frameworks, concepts, methods, measures and benchmarks to accelerate your success, while keeping you connected to the human side of CX.

It's important to remember that the most important lesson in CX is to always be pro-active. This means that you need to be willing to go beyond customer service in order to handle the demands of both service and complaints.

At International Business Machines (IBM), I understood the value of insights from other industries while competing within your own sector. I was also introduced to the concept of a T-shaped person, i.e. a person who is a specialist in one area while being a generalist in another. CX in your organization is also T-shaped. You will deepen the expertise you have in some areas, while you outsource or remain a generalist in others.

As an example, Apple's core focus is on design, customer experience and intellectual property while outsourcing a majority of its manufacturing. In one of its public videos,[2] Apple explained how a single 'Yes' emerged from a thousand 'Nos' to help define its CX culture. They continuously redefined baselines and took risk to get closer to their customers. Examples of this include–popularizing touchscreen on its phones, no Flash in its browser to propagate HTML5, dropping the 3.5mm headphone jack, adopting a reversible Lightning port as standard before USB-C, and so on. The lesson from this that you need to remember is that your baseline should always evolve in order to sharpen your approach towards your customers.

Another important aspect of CX has been highlighted by Richard Branson who once remarked, 'Every airline has a Boeing or an Airbus; how you turn that into an experience proposition will make all the difference.'[3]

If you are in your 'Year 3 or more' of business, congratulations! You possibly have more existing customers than potential ones you will acquire in the current year. This means that your energy needs to be channelled towards your existing customers as much as acquiring new ones.

CX shall be the underlying differentiator in the next decade and this skill is an essential one to embrace. You can read the entire book or pick up valuable lessons by just reading a few pages. The choice is entirely yours. While it took me over twenty years to piece it all together, I am asking for just a few hours of your time. The book has been written to find a special place in your mind and in your hands.

'A single book written well, read many times, will give many different inspiring experiences each time you read it.'

—Tamil Poet Thiruvalluvar, fourth century BC

Introduction

I earned two professional degrees involving a deep dive into numbers, facts and figures as part of my formal education to become a chartered accountant (CA) and a cost and works accountant (CWA).

It is during this training period, which also involved an apprenticeship with an audit firm as industry experience, did I realize that the joy from learning about the ways a business operates would enthral me more than working with numbers.

Over the next twenty-five years, I have had the privilege of working with, consulting and transforming some of the world's major organizations. I have used the experience I have gathered as the foundation for this book.

The companies I interacted with during my career placed great emphasis on the day-to-day challenges of running a business. I soon realized that customers are the fulcrum of any business and the companies I worked with spent a large amount of time discussing how best to serve them. To capture the gist of my practical lessons, I began to keep a journal (or more of a scratch book). My personal insights would also find its way into this journal. Whenever I would find myself in a pickle, the scratch book became my sounding board for ideas and to test my hypotheses.

After my apprenticeship, I joined Citibank, one of the most reputed foreign banks in India—and saw how management graduates and CAs alike would compete to make it to this global company's rolls. During my time, Citi's unique positioning in the banking market revolved around innovation, technology and customer experience. It wasn't just due to this stable framework, the bank also earned its reputation because of a bunch of really smart people who worked together to create this environment. My journey there enabled me to learn valuable lessons from a really smart bank.

Over the years at Citi, I picked up different ideas, strategies and tactics that revolved around customers. I worked in its various divisions, including operations, sales, product and customer retention, both in the corporate and consumer bank. This widened my understanding of the models concerning business-to-business (B2B) as well business-to-consumer (B2C) operations.

At HDFC Bank I noticed immediately how differently it managed its customers, and took upon challenges that Citi considered difficult, even impossible. After all, I was in charge of the product and marketing divisions, and supervised the entire customer journey within the bank.

As I moved from the business end of things to IT services and consulting at Polaris Software, and later at IBM, I learnt that industry agnosticism was the best approach for a steeper learning curve in one's career. I picked up lessons from other industries to augment my journal. This shift was a little different, as I was now working on B2B more deeply while pushing the boundaries of my prior knowledge. In the meantime, I also managed to travel extensively and in the process picked up global lessons. One such revelation involved how two different businesses on opposite ends of the globe did the exact same process very differently, even though their customer segments were alike. These interactions involved my deeper connect with chief executive officers (CEO) and chief experience officers (CXO) of large corporations, which further strengthened my customer experience (CX) journey.

At that point in my career, new technologies, products and processes were being introduced globally as the markets were maturing. The time to play catch-up was shrinking as well, and a fierce competitiveness in the market became the norm.

By the time I made partner at Ernst & Young (EY), I had been a part of several corporate boards and management teams, advising them about transformation in complex CX processes. This became equally important in my later journey as an adviser at a Middle-Eastern conglomerate. As I gained more inter-business experience, I no longer needed the crutches of a single industry, and lessons from other enterprises became equally important with regards to customer experience.

During this journey, I also spent time doing research and observing best practices in CX. I continued to travel, and the journal that I filled up with the lessons I learnt along the way would make anybody a proud owner.

My journal became the basis for this book.

It is a true reflection of the famous saying by Chinese philosopher Lao Tzu:

The journey of a thousand miles begins with a single step.

As this book was taking shape, we were struck by an unprecedented black swan event—the breakout of the pandemic of COVID-19. The pandemic brought to light a different CX need—metamorphosis through adaptation in response to a once in a lifetime event. These kinds of occurrences have always left an indelible mark on the way business is conducted. But what's more intriguing this time is that the distress from COVID-19 is combined with another type of global crisis—a 2008-style recession, which looks inevitable as the book is readied to make its way to your hands. I felt that it's crucial to talk about this, and have included a chapter, 'Customer Experience in Times of Crisis', as a result.

The real benefit from the book that will define its success will be in the practical application of the lessons through acts of doing and showing. This is entirely in your hands.

Within the book you will also find a section called 'Facts and Figures' that incorporates terms and charts that may help you navigate the book better.

SECTION I

CONNECTING THE DOTS

One

C for Customer, H for Human

YOUR POINT OF VIEW (POV)

In my twenty-five-year-long journey as a CX practitioner, I have learnt various lessons, both through personal experience and by example. By sharing those lessons in this book I hope that some of these will eventually make their way into improving individual CXs in your business. Selfishly, I also stand to gain as a customer!

One of those fundamental lessons is having a strong POV. I have noticed that when my clients had a strong point of view they had a much higher chance of success. In most cases, these strong points of view were developed through intensive preparation and greater attention to detail. It is noteworthy that sometimes these strong views came from customer-centric employees regardless of their position in the organization's hierarchy. The strength of these employees to show their teams and seniors their points of view drove innovation and execution.

One such example of POV that I learnt very early in my career is to 'simplify the way you do business'. In my first corporate role, we embraced 'the 3-ring rule' to answer the phone. Customers started to recognize our responsiveness and this practice embedded itself into the fabric of the organization. The company leadership drove that commitment which was the result of many years of digging into facts, speaking to customers regarding CX and a belief that things could be improved. The 3-ring rule was supported by publishing turnaround times, quality commitments and internal process simplification. All of these good practices required training and investments into process modifications and technology but the investment was worth it as it enhanced both customer satisfaction and employee confidence.

Another lesson I have learnt over the years is that you should be willing to change your POV when you realize you are wrong. Over the last several decades, the primary focus of the largest corporations has been of 'Shareholder Value', i.e. delivering the best return on investments to shareholders. However, in recent times we can sense that there has been a shift in this approach. In a recently concluded event with nearly 200 CEOs participating, including the likes of Apple, Pepsi and Walmart, the order was seemingly reversed: customers first, followed by employees, suppliers, communities, and, at dead last—shareholders. This fits neatly into something rather simple that I have discovered in my role as a consultant. If you can get your clients, customers and their employees to succeed, there is always a deal on the table. The key to getting this right is actually quite simple and if I were to describe CX success in one word, it would be 'consistency'. Delivering CX consistently is a sure-shot way to guarantee success.

Once you have a firm point of view, all you need to do is what the Nike slogan says: 'Just do it'. And, of course, 'Just do it' consistently.

BACK TO BASICS

At HDFC Bank I re-learnt the value of basics. The focus to get the fundamentals right provided us the platform to innovate and expand. We kept a keen eye on CX and combined this with a focus on profitability allowed our programmes and policies to have a real impact.

The bank started building on savings and current account balances before they ventured into complex products like credit cards. The cost of funds was critical to the profitability of the bank and since only 1 per cent of Indian customers had credit cards at the time these products were of lesser priority.

As the bank grew, it was open to innovation and changing its CX focus which led to the evolution of different points of view to grow their customer base. Today the bank prides itself on loans issued in twenty seconds which became a reality over time through relentless focus on CX. Having recognized the difference between a Mercedes-Benz buyer in Bathinda, Punjab, Hyderabad and Telangana allowed them to become a leader in auto loans in India.

The bank would look at many solutions implemented by other banks globally and choose those that balanced CX with profitability. Take the case of ATM withdrawals. Long queues and wait times at ATMs resulted in the introduction of the 'quick cash' option where the last recorded withdrawal amounts of customers were stored for repeat transactions. This CX solution resulted in quicker transactions being made by customers and cut down on waiting times for everyone else in the queue. By picking out a needle from a haystack, the bank found that one solution that made all the difference.

Though I left the bank to pursue other interests, I kept in touch with their progress. The lessons they offered expanded my knowledge and helped me understand CX better.

Success in CX needs to be intertwined with profitability. To take an example, the first apartment that I purchased was through Alacrity Housing. I made that commitment based on the strong ethics and foundation for CX that the company had. Alacrity Housing built reliable and well-designed houses for the middle class and provided excellent CX. Yet, they went bankrupt because of their lack of focus on profitability. The important lesson here is that balance is an important survival criterion for any organization.

Another important factor that I have recognized throughout my career is the presence of headwinds and tailwinds. If you don't take cognizance of tailwinds, all previous gains you have made will dissipate quickly and others who take advantage of them would now be miles ahead. Likewise, if you did not recognize headwinds, you may go out of business. Take the case of Apple and BlackBerry. Apple rode the change in customer mindset for a touchscreen phone, while BlackBerry failed to recognize headwinds from the change that was in the offing.

DOING THINGS DIFFERENTLY

In 2005, we embarked on a journey to expand my employer's footprint into Chile, Latin America, with one of the country's largest retail chains. Their chief business officer (CBO), chief technology officer (CTO) and an adviser/consultant travelled from Santiago, Chile to Chennai, India for a few days. They wanted to familiarize themselves with our company and its culture. The CBO and the CTO understood only a bit of English, but the consultant was fluent due to his American upbringing. The chairman of my organization was excited as it presented a great mutual opportunity to create value.

At our meeting, they discussed details of the solution they wanted to take to the market. The discussion was in Spanish with the consultant interpreting. I didn't understand a word of Spanish back then but had a background in German (which, like Spanish, has a Latin origin), and a strong cards and loans background for me to follow the discussion. In one instance, the consultant interpreted the conversation differently to my reading of the Spanish conversation. I immediately offered a clarification and they concurred with my interpretation of their comment. While we had a great approach and solution that fit their requirements, they were impressed with that incident. We spent the rest of the afternoon understanding their success in running one of the best-known multi-product supermarket chains in Latin America.

The next day they were to meet our chairman at the Park Sheraton in Chennai, but we saw one of the biggest downpours Chennai had experienced for decades. The roads were flooded but our chairman kept good his commitment and reached their hotel for dinner. They were suitably impressed with our effort on both days.

We were excited about this potential partnership to enter Latin America and to expand on their financial services proposition. It marked many firsts for us: for instance, customer centricity and integrating an extensive data mart that housed transaction level data. We won the bid against fierce competition in the end.

They later told us that it was our human touch combined with a perfect product solution that did the trick. The human factor is always key to doing business.

Cards and unsecured loans presented highly profitable business ventures for banks and I had experience in this field from helping India's premier private sector bank establish both their cards business as well as expand their Visa and Mastercard franchise. Customers typically got their cards and loans approvals over days but that was about to change. Their model also speeded up the process of giving cards (within a twenty-minute window) to housewives who did not earn a separate income. The credit policy too was adapted for housewives.

The Chilean retail chain first floated the proposition—come to shop, and pay with your private label credit card. Later they adopted the Visa and Master franchise as well. We had the record for what the customer had purchased previously. We also knew about slow moving perishable products at certain times of the day and days of the week. Combined with transaction level knowledge we could discount the price to sell before the products perished. The local market took to it while the foreign banks struggled. Customers were delighted and the supermarket margins doubled.

As a team we gained a lot of knowledge about customer centricity and the Spanish language during those three years. We learnt to appreciate Latin American culture while understanding a different way of doing business. The retailer learnt to deal with his data much more efficiently. The contract for our services continued to be extended and this provided our company revenue beyond the initial implementation.

These lessons and examples provided me enough inspiration to learn about failures and successes in the light of CX.

'GOOD CUSTOMERS' ARE SCARCE

Over the years, I have come to recognize that fresh perspectives can emerge from different quarters. Sports, for instance. I cheer on as India continues to churn out various world-class sportsmen. I realized that the journey of our Olympic athletes started with a big dream to succeed as young boys and girls, often from a remote area in India. Through their hard work and perseverance, they overcame setbacks and improved their technique with strong mentors and coaches. A few arise through their ability and courage to get into national teams. A fewer among those go on to compete at the Olympics, and fewer still win a medal.

I realized that many a time, 20 per cent of my customers gave me 80 per cent of the revenue. That led me down the path of accepting that 'good customers' are scarce.

Your 'real' customer set is very finite, and are supremely pampered by things that are already out there. It is a real effort to get their attention. And when you do get that opportunity to make them your customer, you just can't afford to lose them.

At IBM, I worked closely with TELCOS and consequently developed an appreciation for their business models. Let's use TELCO as an illustration of the point I am trying to make.

India's population is over 1.2 billion, and we have a billion mobile phone customers. The average ARPU (average revenue per user) for an Indian TELCO (for example, Vodafone) was around Rs 120[1] (< US$2) as per the Telecom Authority of India (third quarter, 2018). The average global monthly ARPU was around US $17.5, derived from GSMA figures for the same period. The Indian ARPU was declining 12 per cent quarter on quarter.[2] The cream of the crop, post-paid ARPU, stood at Rs 348[3] (~US$5) during that same period, yet account for less than 10 per cent of the entire subscriber base.

With a steady migration of customers from post-paid to prepaid, it presented significant concern to the TELCOS.

During my many years of running marketing campaigns, I would need to extract the customer database for groundwork purposes. A data set of 2,00,000 customers would quickly narrow down to 35,000 customers after taking away ineligible customers, do not disturb databases, recent contacts, uncontactable numbers, etc. Campaign costs would thus escalate quickly. The risk staring at us was a poor campaign response rate of 3 per cent against our desired benchmark of 25 per cent. The bottom two layers of many customer segments represent laggards, who don't respond to campaigns very well. Suddenly, millions of customers are actually whittled down to a small fraction.

Water covers over 70 per cent of the earth's surface, yet fresh water (including frozen in glaciers, ice and snow) accounts for less than 3 per cent of the earth's water; 97 per cent is saline.

As a consultant, I learnt to absorb these CX lessons from other industries. One of the companies I actively followed was Nike. They have a set of superstar endorsers who are paid very heftily to represent the brand. Nike needs to get players from every conceivable sport they represent to push their products to those categories of customers. They are celebrities with huge endorsement potentials and targets for Nike's competitors. Nike's brand appeal gets a shot in the arm from such endorsements and they are in short supply. Without them, their customers will be a much smaller fraction.

Over the years I found an interesting way to look at competition. A recognized leader, is the one you compete against to be 'one up'. If you are on the journey to the top, others seemingly look like allies. And, if you do in fact have it all, you only stand to lose right?

All I am saying is that you need to build sensitivity to acquiring the right set of customers, and it's harder than you think. You need to find a way to respect those customers who have walked through that elusive door of yours. The more you recognize it, the better it gets.

WHO IS YOUR CUSTOMER?

'A customer is the most important visitor on our premises. He is not dependent on us. We are dependent on him. He is not an interruption of our work. He is the purpose of it. He is not an outsider of our business. He is part of it. We are not doing him a favour by serving him. He is doing us a favour by giving us the opportunity to do so.'

—Mahatma Gandhi, South Africa, 1890

The answer to 'who is your customer?' is harder than what appears at the surface.

When I started building business plans, I would simply take the number of customers desired and multiply that with the revenue per customer desired to arrive at the total revenue. Not much thought would have gone in into 'who that customer really was', and, of course, if we did not have enough customers 'we really fell short'.

Over time, I recognized customers as individuals, human beings with a latent or a potential need for your product or service because it could change their life. Individuals have choices, aspirations and moods that evolve and are influenced by many things. They are willing to pay 'reasonable price' for those services. Individuals differ in age, creed, ethnicity, race, upbringing, financial and non-financial backgrounds, choices, aspirations, moods and influences.

Let us take an example. My family of four goes on vacation. We need to go on an airplane and stay at a hotel. The airline or the hotel sees four customers. Yet, only I actually purchase the ticket while my wife and I may ultimately decide which airline to take, or which hotel to stay in. The airline or the hotel needs to focus on these two people out of the four to drive decision. But if the two non-decision makers are unhappy, the buyers may not travel on that airline or stay at that hotel again.

In the Chile retail chain example, the actual buyer was the housewife, while the sponsor was the spouse. The retailer's fundamental proposition revolved around providing 'value' to housewives.

While doing sales, our customer estimation was much more scientifically established by demand forecasting techniques and geography distribution, while benchmarking this to competitive information for a reality check.

My work at several public-sector Indian banks, led me to another stark revelation. Our largest Indian banks had customers with an average age of 40+ years, inching upwards every year. We arrived at the conclusion that the banking sector needed to attract customers below forty years, especially in the eighteen to thirty-five age group in order to stay relevant. The banks had fathers as their customers, but needed their sons to continue to bank with them. The average age of an Indian is approximately twenty-seven years, and continued focus on 40+ customers would only make matters worse. Another thing was important too, while our average stood at twenty-one years in 1950, it would become thirty-seven by 2050, representing the need to gradually shift over the next twenty-five years.

Another revelation that emerged from data was that the focus was on attracting borrowers for mortgages, personal loans or vehicle loans between the ages twenty-one to forty-one. And, customers beyond twenty-six also started steadily building their savings.[4]

Hence 'who is your customer' is really dependent on the 'value on offer'.

CX VS USER EXPERIENCE(UX)

I often encounter people who are confused between the terms customer experience and user experience. Some regard them the same or to be similar, at least. Embracing both concepts together, helped me better deal with understanding CX in the real world. Think of CX as being the elephant in the room and UX being its tusks.

User experience happens when a person perceives or responds to a product, system or service. For example, when you use a website, the delight or annoyance is UX. It includes emotions, beliefs, preferences, perceptions, physical and psychological responses, behaviours and accomplishments. They occur before, during and after use. The focus of UX is on elements like Visual Design (what you see), Information Design (what you understand) and Interaction Design (how you respond). User needs, usability and content become critical subsets of UX.

UX is a subset of CX. CX includes engagements with a customer across sales, marketing, advertising, customer service, channel and technology. Additional dimensions like creativity, innovation, vendors, partnerships, people engagement and processes all fall under CX.

CX is about the sum of all experiences over the course of the lifecycle of a customer. Therefore, CX matrices involve hard and soft measures. Hard measures are like number of customers, average timelines with you and profitability. Soft measures include elements of trust and advocacy influenced by competition, price, expertise, brand, emotions and referral. If any of the subsets go wrong, CX takes a beating.

UNDERSTAND YOUR CUSTOMER'S TEMPERAMENT

Initially, when we established new businesses, we had only demographic information about potential customers. Over time, we realized that similar demographic customers behaved very differently. This is where we shifted our focus to 'the mind over matter'.

The best way to describe this shift was popularized by Everett Rogers, a professor of communications, through his theory 'Diffusion of Innovations'. In a simple way he defined customer adoption over five basic categories—Innovators, Early Adopters, Early Majority, Late Majority and Laggards by using a bell curve.[5]

He explained that only 2.5 per cent were Innovators (risk takers) who took early advantage of a differentiated product. As word spread an additional 13.5 per cent jumped on the bandwagon as Early Adopters. Early Adopters are the influencers and thought leaders, active on social media, and who could create reviews around their likes and dislikes.

Products then start to get a mass-market appeal and the Early Majority (34 per cent) customers start to adopt the product. Some are in no rush to adopt, and wait to read about the great experiences of others—the Late Majority customers (34 per cent). These customers are naturally risk averse. Laggards (16 per cent) don't specifically want to change and may continue to use something that's not trending. They are likely to be from an older age group. A customer database segmented by these clusters would add immense value to enhance your success criteria.

Beyond adoption, I quickly became aware of four personality types and the way that influenced their decision-making—

- Aggressive people like to take charge and are sure about their decisions. They need facts and details. They are to the point, direct, and don't like to be taken around in circles.
- Analytical people are thinkers, they research in advance and still wants facts and details.
- Expressive people are extroverts. They are friendly and like compliments. They are emotional, which could affect their buying decisions.
- Passive people keep to themselves. They like personalization and need to be able to relate to the product or service. They don't like to be pressurized.

Over time, I have also recognized that no individual falls squarely into one bucket, but has a mix of personalities, and could lean towards a trait more strongly than others. By mapping our client's customers into these four buckets we got closer to unlocking value.

UNLOCK VALUE

One of my clients came back to us with a problem statement. They recognized that they had onboarded a set of customers different from their target segment. The result was that profitability, margins and product cross-sell became an issue. That led us to the questions—'What business are you in? Who ought to be your customer? Are you attracting your potential customer with the right value proposition?'

We recognized and validated these questions by talking to a target customer set that they did not get the right value. As soon as the client made amends, they got more of their desired customers. The steeper the value, the more the number of customers.

Dwelling a bit on photography, my other passion—Tamron competed with Sony to make lenses for the Sony FE mount. They launched a lens in the 28-75mm range for their full-frame set-up. They priced the lens affordably at almost 40 per cent reduced rate of Sony's costs, yet managed to keep image quality comparable. The result was an absolute sell-out in the first six months with backlogs. The success was so big that they launched another lens, 17-28mm, with expectations of another success, and are seeing similar results.[6]

Note here that we are not talking about profit, which is measured by the price charged against the cost of operations. The value provided might actually exceed the price charged making this unprofitable.

Time and time again, organizations have proven to me that 'common sense is not so common'.

As organizations understand the perceived value, some get greedy marking up prices to be in the premium range. At a certain cut-off point, there are simply no takers. This explains why luxury goods have such an exclusive market.

Sony's full-frame cameras have taken on a premium positioning in terms of price, but Tamron has broken that by providing infinitely better value. The market noticed.

Luxury brands use attraction. Take Apple, which creates queues before a new product is launched outside their stores using this attraction.

As a regular visitor to Kuala Lumpur, I got introduced to Haidilao, a popular hotpot Chinese restaurant. A hotpot is where the diners cook their own meat and vegetables in a boiling broth placed on their table, and the focus of the employees of the establishment is to greet, serve and entertain. A Haidilao employee buffs and paints nails, for free, while the diners enjoy their food. Its success is reflected in its long waiting list for reservations. The customers love this Chinese hotpot chain—there's even a free shoe shine service while you wait.

A big part of today's businesses, involves the value provided that extends well beyond the sale. Take cars for example, where the car servicing operations are also lucrative over time, and equally important to the manufacturer. Another example is that of software services industries that have moved from one-time sale to subscription-based models, that allow customers to use their latest software, only for a small fee per month.

My lessons from all of this is, 'You can provide value to customers in different ways', including convenience, design, brand, risk reduction, or reducing costs. Yet competitive pricing is a quick solution that organizations resort to many a time.

Digging deeper, I realized that my client's customers reacted differently to different values. The client's success was based on their ability to gauge their customers' perceived value to each of the above dimensions (convenience, design, brand or status, price, etc.).

A third dimension that affects perceived value is 'trust'. My customers gained trust through interactions and doing their research. Their trust was upheld or broken based on my say–do ratio. Ideally, all organizations should do what they promise. As trustworthiness builds, the customer's human nature unfolds for repeat engagements.

SAY–DO RATIO

As an early bird user of Microsoft software, I got introduced to the term WYSIWYG—'What You Say Is What You Get'. The same principles apply to business, and it's called the 'say–do ratio'.

When your organization focuses on sales and marketing its thrust is on 'say'. When it backs this up with great employees, with the right attitude, efficiency of operations and providing a positive customer experience, it focuses on 'do'. Being able to keep up your 'say–do' ratio creates trust. A consistently positive 'say–do' ratio ramps up your customer base while deepening your pockets. Organizations focused on only 'say' benefit in the short term, but suffer in the long run. Their customers start to speak ill of them and the bad publicity ruins their reputation.

As an avid traveller, I follow Boeing and Airbus. The recent case involving Boeing 737 Max provides a great CX lesson.[7] An airline's fundamental commitment to individuals is of trust—'We will take you safely from point A to B.' Nobody questions trust till its broken. When two airplanes crashed within six months (Ethiopian Airlines and Lion Air), it caught everybody's attention. The aircraft type was grounded because of passenger-safety reasons. Even after these concerns are fixed, customers will continue to have considerable reservations. Passengers will now look at aircraft type before they book their flights. With a long waiting list, the Boeing 737 Max now has an uphill task to restore faith. The second crash created cause for concern centred around 'consistency'.

I take away three important lessons from all of this:

1. Past success is not a measure of future customer experience.
2. Inaction or lack of initiative destroys trust and consistency which in turn destroys top line and bottom line.
3. Pilots were not informed or trained about the changes, leading to inability to respond to complex changes in flight path.

If your organization is going through poor brand or customer experiences, your ability to quickly unwind from that impact can positively influence CX. When Samsung had a lithium ion battery exploding issue, the matter rapidly escalated resulting in a huge clampdown by airlines.[8]

We have spoken on elements that are par for the course. Like you won't enjoy buying last year's gadget when companies manufacture more advanced ones, your competitive value diminishes every year if you don't re-invent yourself.

FOCUS ON DELIGHT

Whenever there is a 'sale' going on, the only thing I don't like is the crowd. Yet the delight of a good bargain always takes me back. I am not the only one who is delighted when organizations go the extra mile for its customers. I have travelled Virgin on business, and have consistently felt it is a cut above the rest. As I followed their CX journey, I came across an interaction that clarified my observation. A nine-year-old wrote to Richard Branson requesting for a customized menu at Virgin's trains. Virgin responded by serving a breakfast of her choice. It's these little gestures that create the brand and these little things that turn customers into advocates.

CX is a journey. Your evolution around CX is your own story over the years. Consistent improvement is perhaps the most important indicator for your business.

I quickly came to the realization that you will evolve as you tap into the energy surrounding your customers when they develop a special liking towards you, your culture and the ethos. Organizations thus create an individual style with which customers associate immediately. All leading CX organizations are described with that individuality in mind.

In my extensive travels to the US to meet my clients, I got introduced to Nordstrom. Their story is quite remarkable. Their success has been built around simple customer service principles. The results speak for themselves—they are said to have one of the highest sales per square foot performance in the retail industry. The entire customer service handbook has been streamlined to their one rule—'Use good judgement in all situations.' The Nordstrom salesperson rarely points, they simply walk you there. Good CX demands 'show', not 'tell'.

Their good judgement expands into three pillars—

- Why are they doing this in the first place?
- How does the customer need to feel at the end of that experience? and
- How should one go about accomplishing that experience?

When organizations provide employees with autonomy to go the extra mile without compromising their standards, it goes a long way to add that human touch.

Your designation is inconsequential—you are either serving the customer directly or are part of the value chain that does. Once you understand that linkage of C for Customer and H for Human, your path becomes clearer.

Nordstrom has been in existence since 1901, starting off as a shoe retailer. You shop there, you get a personal experience by and large. They stride with the times, by using technology to streamline experience. For example, you can pay and checkout anywhere within the store, and avoid waiting time at the sales counter. Constant innovation and strategizing, without losing their core ideals, are fundamental to Nordstrom's customer service principles.

Many big lessons came to me through the power of observation. I have spent considerable time at hospitals and nursing homes for a sick family member and a friend. During those moments I recognized that patients are core customers for the health care provider. The latter's engagement and display of empathy combined with physician loyalty are the foundations for building trust and positive patient experience (PX). A rock-star surgeon alone cannot create great CX.

They need a competent team focused on a 'patients first' policy combined with safety and compassion.

By travelling on British Railways, I recognized their privatization efforts through the likes of catering and train services, but their single biggest 'pain point' was disappointing punctuality. Delight cannot come at the cost of basics.

Having extensively travelled on Indigo, India's leading carrier, their tagline caught my attention, 'To be on time every time.' While generally reliable, they suffer from a shortage of pilots often leading to multiple flight cancellations. Consistency was their major challenge.[9]

Many of my clients took refuge in technology to provide a breakthrough. Today, that technology takes shape in the form of cognitive and artificial intelligence, to capture and gain a holistic view of customers with an ability to learn and adapt in real-time. Human interactions, conversations, and sentiments play a significant role in such technology. While still at its infancy, the potential to provide a personalized human experience is no longer a dream. To stay ahead of the curve, and given the complexity of information created and collected, organizations are significantly investing into data sciences.

Each of these examples and lessons led me to conclude that there are possibly five key components to improve your CX:

1. Understand your customer
2. Unlock value
3. Keep up your say–do ratio
4. Focus on delight and
5. Create advocates

We focused on the first four till now, but the real fruit of labour is in our ability to create advocates.

CREATING ADVOCATES

Delighting customers consistently creates advocates. Advocates bring in more customers.

My pick of organizations that have gone through this journey include Amazon, Apple, Starbucks, Ritz Carlton, USAA, Virgin, Harley Davidson, Disney, Netflix and Nordstrom.

Most organizations, keep getting stuck at Step 3 (ensuring good say–do ratios). Step 4 involves innovation, R&D, change, new people and disruption. It's a path for the brave. Solutions being tried and tested is not enough. Traditional banks have been there for centuries, yet challenged by the likes of digital banks, non-bank finance companies, Internet players like Amazon and Alipay. While traditional banks have begun to accept partnerships as a way forward, the important questions here are: 'Is your product or service good enough?' and 'Can you continue to woo your customers?'

DOWNWARD SPIRAL

Many stalwarts that I looked up to for CX have lost their pedestals. Yes, I am referring to Xerox, Polaroid, Motorola, Kodak, Nokia, Blockbuster and Blackberry.

If I were to describe their loss of relevance in three words, they would be, 'changing human aspirations'. This disruption may come about within a period of six to nine months, and sometimes it becomes difficult to regain your position in the marketplace even after you have caught up.

As an ardent Apple fan, I have owned several Apple products over the years. My defining moment came on 29 June 2007[10] when Steve Jobs announced Apple's first iPhone. It changed aspirations, perspectives and competition forever.

I took four valuable lessons out of all of this:

- They were your customers yesterday, not necessarily today or tomorrow.
- If you don't follow individuals' choices and aspirations carefully, that rug under your feet might not exist.
- Advantages are temporary, and ignorance is not an answer to many threats.

- When someone pivots to respond to a threat, they improve and quickly adapt.

It wasn't that Apple got everything right always. They have misjudged affordability and reliability issues that have proved costly many a time. Bad news related to unicorn companies travels much further and faster.

Apple II computer for homes met with a resounding success. Apple was encouraged to launch Apple III in 1980 aimed at the business user. Unfortunately, it had buggy hardware and software, and was priced very high (price range of US$4,340–$7,800). IBM saw an opportunity, and in 1981 launched its PC at US$1,565[11] with no software or hardware issues. Customers jumped ship. Apple tried to regain customer confidence by relaunching Apple III with improved specs and a lower price. Customers did not buy into that offer.[12]

I learnt five things from all of this:

- Don't rush a product or service to market.
- Gained trust vanishes with bad experience.
- Higher the price, exponential service is the expectation.
- When IBM delivered the expected 'trust' at a much lower price, customer trust improved towards IBM, while hampering Apple's trust quotient.
- Negative brands create negative memories even if they are fixed afterwards.

It's important to take course correction measures earlier when things start to go wrong. While great customer reviews boost sales, bad ones hurt you even more. One bad customer can undo the work of forty happy customers!

These days I see some organizations trying to fool us by just putting out positive customer reviews on their websites to increase their customer advocacy. I have consistently looked to do my own research on the Internet from multiple websites. When my investment is high, the intensity of the research just increases. Negative feedback from other websites does greatly impact my trust at such times.

When my clients want to launch a new product, my question to them is, 'Is the product that you are proposing something that you genuinely want for yourself?' When my clients have profitability or cost issues, which can be attributed to products, my question would be, 'Is the product still relevant?'

When 'once champion products' become meaningless, sometimes my clients are still emotionally attached to them. My clients have kept them alive by just looking at the lifetime value of their product, while the product's year-on-year impact continues to decline. Product replacements are often caused by radical changes in the company's board and management. At IBM, I learnt that organizations need to be extremely strong in finance and forecasting, as much as in innovation and R&D. When they see margins decreasing significantly over the medium term they offload some of their businesses to other organizations that can possibly do this better. China has specialized on this business model but it requires a completely different standard for sustenance.

THE POWER OF HABIT

A doctor once told me, 'If some patients had reacted to symptoms and created healthy habits long before they succumbed to the disease, they would be in a significantly different position.' To me that sums up 'habit'. Getting close to customers is a healthy habit. Habit is like a muscle that requires regular exercise to gain strength.

I have often realized that gut is a better reminder than numbers. By the time all numbers come in, sometimes it is too late. Some signs that amplify that things are not too good include, poor communication, disengaged employees, employees turning to competition rather than to collaboration, high employee attrition, poor Net Promoter Score (NPS) or Customer Satisfaction Scores (CSAT), significant increase in customer attrition, or a drop in repeat customers. Listening to your gut is a great habit.

The urge to act is another very good sign to win the battle. After I have deliberated, when I start my actions and decisions, I have always felt that half the battle is won. My customers' reactions have more often than not told me whether I am doing well or not. The outliers are the first to leave, then there is the larger exodus. I realize that trust is the last glue to hold the customer. And, actions are the best way forward for creating healthy habits.

I realized that you just need to act 'one degree' at a time, and before you know it, you would have brought in a sea change to your impact on the customer.

As a movie buff, I like Marvel movies. They released their *Avengers: Endgame* movie which grossed a record-breaking US $1.91 billion in their first ten days becoming the fifth highest grossing film of all time.[13] In 1986, Marvel was in a different position. The theatrical venture *Howard the Duck* earned them a reputation of the most expensive box office flop.[14] Within a decade they were forced into bankruptcy under Chapter 11. By the time the new millennium dawned things looked brighter with their release of Spider-Man and X-Men. The change? One degree at a time.

GOOD TO GREAT

I have often wondered what makes an organization great. Through some introspection I found that reactive organizations don't make the cut. Sometimes being first and easy to replicate just puts the competition ahead of you. When ICICI Bank launched India's first Gold Credit Card in 1996, we just improved upon it and launched in quick succession removing their first mover advantage.

It made me realize that the difficulty to replicate is one big deterrent you can build in. That could be the result of a credible supply chain that took many years to build or a significant amount of work that went into product research with a patent. Products requiring a multi-year payback or cost recovery model require deeper investments, which keep away competition.

Over time as I became an Apple fanboy, I noticed that Apple was hardly 'first to market' for many of their products. Their investments in innovative products integrated through a complex supply chain combined with years of research separated them from the rest. They increasingly put their efforts into moving from Step 3 (say–do ratio) to Step 4 (focus on delight).

Considering the risks, many new products are launched after consumer research and 'early adopter feedback', before full-scale rollout. With the rise of social media, the reviews are even more visible. Customer ratings matter for acquiring new customers or repeat business. Riding on social media, I noticed that even established companies have adopted crowd funding techniques. Social media gives quick feedback from potential customers. Take Gillette's attempt to create a new line of 'hot' razors for its customers.[15] It saw Indiegogo (a crowd funding platform) as the way to support this new initiative in 2018. It helped them test customer advocacy.

While I worked in the credit cards business, we often used 'Champion–Challenger' tests. We used these control tests to validate the credit card company's hypothesis. During the survey, the tested category is often named Champion, while the other set of customers who are left untested and are called 'Challenger'. The test is usually with one criterion, to have clear results. When these results are inconclusive, larger sample sizes with a more restrictive sub-criteria are used to provide better answers.

I also realized that keeping your focus on potential customers was critical. Potential customers are just a click away from sharing experiences. Hence your product launches need to be handled carefully. Since more than two thirds of purchase decisions are based on recommendations, this part is important.

There are many stories in this book which repeatedly show how profit and customers go hand in hand. The focus on profit alone, to achieve short-term goals, will destroy your business model and shareholder value. To maintain a balance between profit and customer is the only way to go. When a customer does not perceive value, they will shift. Many of my clients have misjudged their customer base. Their business model did not meet customer expectations. Getting your business model right for mass or sections of the customer base is critical. Investments need to be fine-tuned to cater to such demand and supply.

I loved flying the Airbus A380, and was sad to read the news[16] about their recent failure. It was being sunset despite being able to carry between 555–853 passengers. First and Business Class passengers travelled in extreme comfort, but represented a small percentage of passenger volumes. Passenger traffic was seasonal in some sectors, which left too many empty seats. Fuel economy in air transport is critical. A380 ranked lower in fuel efficiency per passenger. Airport infrastructure including runways had to be changed to accommodate the weight of these double-decker aircraft. Additionally, with the economic and financial stresses, filling these giant aircrafts with enough passengers and freight was challenging. As a result, airlines operate 777 on sectors during the lean seasons. Airbus increased its dependency on Emirates to sustain their business model. When Emirates also started to cancel orders due to unsustainability, the impact to Airbus was severe.[17]

Coming back to Apple, it launched its watch with extreme fanfare. Its premium offerings with gold and ceramic had limited appeal because of its higher price points. A separate assembly line to create these products just added to the cost of the entire manufacturing process.[18] Apple realized that a majority of customers accepted the product for its 'function' rather than 'form'. This eventually led to the phasing out of these premium offerings in their later editions.[19]

WHAT CAN YOU LEARN FROM START-UPS ?

At its core, a start-up has to provide 'superior value' at 'an affordable price'. Their proliferation and the threat from them became the reason for my clients to either 'embrace a start-up culture within their organization' or 'partner with to provide their end customers with value'. Innovation increasingly came from technology, which also popularized Robotic Process Automation and Agile, to stay competitive.

Despite this, I observed that a few start-ups actually succeeded while most failed. My search for a good reason for this also led me to read Peter Thiel's book, *Zero to One*,[20] where he described what made start-ups actually succeed. He elaborated about the start-up mentality by emphasizing the need for creativity for organization survival. Organizations embracing start-up mindsets have rejuvenated themselves from the shackles of 'me too'. He goes on to explain that serious competition creates winners. Winners also need to start looking at differentiators as a means to success, rather than just look at what has succeeded with customers in the past.

The four key pillars to succeed in any business are:

- Focus
- Passion and motivation
- Commitment and
- Willingness to see or listen

Start-ups are money hungry. Hence, they are susceptible to cash in too quickly for additional capital. They need to strike a fine balance between mentors for great advice and supplementing domain knowledge on one hand and delays in raising capital on the other.

Once investors and promoters start to work together, their focus shifts rather quickly to getting their offerings out into the market and working on profitability.

When I was a part of a strategy-led product company I learnt many lessons. Though they had a fairly large customer base they still exuded a significant start-up mindset, full of energy and ideas with an entrepreneurial culture and employees who grew along with the organization.

Yet their modest beginnings as a services company provided customers what they needed or wanted, without product or design considerations. So, while initial costs were lower, the customers soon started to feel the lack of flexibility and configurability. As a lesson, we gradually moved towards a product roadmap, but that journey was extremely painful.

Every company beginning a new journey needs to take a step back and take cognizance of this issue. If there was a way to rewind, many companies would take such a route to become more structured and methodical. They would invest their first six months to concept and design before the actual build-out and putting the product in the market. Though these lessons came from the Indian software industry these challenges are faced by many start-ups.

SHOULD START-UPS PUT CX AT THEIR CORE?

I had the privilege of setting up many banks for my clients in India and overseas. They had some form of financial services business but needed a significant recast to become a bank. In a way this is nothing short of a start-up, if you define a start-up as 'the action or process of setting something in motion'.

The process required a different approach and culture, the 'start-up culture'.

Three important pillars for success emerged:

- Innovation from new product and services
- Speed of expanding their product sets into their existing customer base, while growing a new customer base and
- Scale to compete with the big boys

But none of these three pillars made sense without customers at the centre. Over the years I recognized that many of my clients kept looking at incremental changes, as a complete refresh was simply too expensive and laborious. That became the mantra for many of my start-up clients since it requires much lesser effort. Re-engineering was a complete nightmare for too many existing organizations.

I found that established companies got around this problem by creating 'silos' or new companies.

The focus on the customer came from four areas:

- Their buying habits
- Unboxing thrills
- The support they are going to receive, or
- The touchpoints that they will experience along the way

As a big crowdfunding supporter, I noticed how that interaction provided a fantastic avenue to enable both funding and customer acknowledgement. One such company I have supported is Peak Design, who always had a good story to tell.

Peter Dering went on a holiday with his camera. He hated carrying his DSLR. It pained him so much that he started the company[21] 'Peak Design' out of San Francisco and quit his job. His first invention was the capture clip which he tested out through a Kickstarter campaign. Over the years, he found the crowdfunding model to be enriching for his company. With more than nine Kickstarters[22] under their belt having raised US$25+ million over the years, they have through each campaign got much closer to their customers. They now have more than 100+ products in their stable. Each time he acknowledges the role of the customer and the importance that Kickstarter played.

They are now truly beyond their initial start-up pangs, with thirty-four full-time employees and catering pretty much to a global population. Their products are easily available at leading stores, and supplemented through website sales and e-commerce players like Amazon. They acted on customer feedback and improved their product with Gen-2 and Gen-3 versions. By expanding their product portfolio but staying within the travel and photography community, they solved other problems their customers faced. From a product positioning perspective, their focus was always on quality that the customer wants and needs, with 'functional design' at its core. Their products are always positioned as aspirational with great value.

As you can see, the focus has been to put the customer at the centre, rather than look at the service design in terms of customer service.

THE MINIMUM VIABLE PRODUCT (MVP)

My clients have often focused on opportunities to either save cost or increase revenue. One area that I have always loved to look at is their 'products and services'. Often that provided me with answers to what was the state of their business.

When a product is not loved, it becomes an orphan. A product that is loved, but too expensive to acquire, is unrealistic. The sweet spot is a good product, at a reasonable price point. You could arguably call it a minimum lovable product.

As time went along, I increasingly came to the realization that MVP was not really a 'product', but a process. A process that helps you think in a certain way. That process still needs to solve the 'core' problem, yet the customer needs to 'love' the outcome. Hence, the word 'minimum' clashes with the word 'viable'.

The critical question of MVP is—what does the customer 'really' want? And, understanding that takes time. Take Peak Design's case for designing a carbon fibre tripod. The idea and the initial sketch was made on the back of a napkin about five years before it was launched. They took five years to get the idea from a rough sketch to a consumer acceptable proposition. This is a company with a good history.

Their challenge:

- They had never manufactured a tripod before
- Their customers did not yet associate them with tripods and
- They were competing with the gods of tripods like Gitzo, Manfrotto, Vanguard, Sirui and 3 Legged Thing.

To understand their customers better, Peak Design decided to test it through a crowdfunding programme.

Building MVPs is an iterative process to get the ingredients right. All design elements to build a product need to be considered for customer endorsement. That's why some products take more than a year to launch, in fact over three years in some cases. Your outcome (product) cannot stay stagnant, it evolves over time, hence the benchmark for 'minimum' goes up.

While this term is linked quickly to a lean start-up methodology, it's even more relevant to sunset, no-longer viable products. Sometimes, products with poor initial acceptance can be tinkered to create a great product, but with a different branding.

Many a time, I get asked, 'How often do you need to revisit your MVP proposition?' The answer always is, 'As frequently as you perceive the customers choices to get disrupted.' While Apple has annual product releases, they keep working on the MVP proposition continuously. As soon as the year finishes, they put through established improvements into their next manufacturing cycle.

THE POWER OF OBSERVATION

My biggest asset to learning about customer experience came from the power of observation. I have always believed that one can learn from others' experiences. Great examples also make great guidelines towards being exceptional on your journey to the next peak.

I have travelled on business to many countries and met many clients with different requirements. On one of my visits to Tokyo I took the initiative to explore the city on a Sunday with a colleague. We were booked to stay at the Marriott there.

We agreed to head straight out after breakfast to visit Disneyland and Akihabara (Tokyo's electronics district) later in the evening. We headed to the travel desk to enquire how to best plan our day. The lady at the desk promptly pulled out a custom-printed map explaining the stops between the hotel and Disneyland. The map listed out the

Metro stations, the fares, written in both Japanese and English. We were impressed, and I pressed on to see how good she was. We asked her if we could go to pick up some traditional Japanese clothes. She didn't flinch. She took out another map that explained how to get from Disneyland to that destination. I then went on to ask her how to get from that destination to Akihabara, for which she pulled out yet another map that explained my question. I was really impressed with the whole experience. While it may be common sense to have all of this for tourists, I had not experienced this in other cities.

This was a rather pleasant surprise from Marriott and the lady who showed how a seemingly normal experience can be turned into an exemplary one.

Sometimes CX 'aha!' moments come across as obvious, yet blindsided due to various circumstances. Think about situations where you have had to repeat what you already said to many call centre executives.

IN SUMMARY—ONE

As Steve Jobs once said, 'Stay hungry, stay foolish.'[23] By narrowing down your real customers, staying true to basics, keeping promises, unlocking value, providing delight, living your dream as a start-up and creating a habit out of all of this, you can find your true advocates. Don't forget to stay consistent.

Two

Get Closer to Your Customers

WHY DO CUSTOMERS BUY?

'Just having satisfied customers isn't good enough anymore. If you really want a booming business, you have to create raving fans.'

—Ken Blanchard

I am always intrigued by what nature can teach us about CX. For instance, bumble bees instinctively know which pollen to collect. Although they have ample choices, these bees are attracted only to sweet flowers and can fly back to their favourite flowers time and again. I realized quite early in my career that the bumblebee analogy works perfectly when thinking about our customers. Our customers are surrounded by an incredible array of choices for every buying decision and the question that we need to always keep in mind is this: 'Is my solution sweet enough?'

In my experience working with various clients who put out products and solutions for their customers, I paid attention to the nature of stimuli and customer responses. Viktor Frankl explains this aptly in a quote:

'Between stimulus and response there is a space. In that space is our power to choose our response. In our response lies our growth and our freedom.'

—Viktor E. Frankl

Let me illustrate this by giving an example. I was booking a flight from Mumbai to Singapore and had many questions before making a decision:

- Day flight or a night flight?
- Ample leg room?
- Too near a toilet?
- Baby that might disturb my sleep?
- Flat bed?
- A380, 737 or 777?
- Indian food?
- Will I make it for the morning meeting?
- In-flight entertainment?

. . . and the list goes on.

There were at least half a dozen airlines with Airbus or Boeing configurations that flew to Singapore around the same time. As a frequent traveller, I am well versed with the differences between airlines serving the route and had clear preferences. From my flying history, my preferred airline, Singapore Airlines (SIA) knew about my choices and preferences but not necessarily about my decision-making process (or the space in-between as Frankl puts it). On the Mumbai–Singapore route SIA offers flyers the option to travel both premium (on the flagship SIA) or budget (on its subsidiary, Scoot). Like many other flyers, on shorter routes, I have shown clear preferences to trade-off price with comfort and over years of travel, I have noticed how SIA has paid attention to this and introduced four travel classes: Economy, Premium Economy, Business and First. Certainly, data analytics has helped them bridge that gap between preferences and the decision-making process.

Another fact I recognized was how negatively influenced I was when a great customer experience was followed by a sub-standard one. For instance, flying factors like reduced leg space, poor in-flight meals and flight delays made a massive difference to my satisfaction. If an airline moves from a good experience to a great one, the customer's response is that of real delight. If things go the other way around, the customer starts looking for alternatives really quickly. I see this as an interesting upshot to Viktor's quote.

I always treat social and business events as occasions to enjoy a great experience and I frequent restaurants for this reason. The occasion could be my wedding anniversary, catching up with friends, introducing a special guest to great food, business meetings or my kid's birthday. Sometimes the food is great but the service falls short. That's when I discovered that it's not just the food that matters but the whole dining experience. This is only true not only with my experiences at restaurants but all other personal services. For example, my dentist accommodates me with a late evening or a weekend appointment to keep up with my schedule, thus putting my (the customer's) needs first.

The idea of a great experience isn't just for complicated products, but even for things as mundane as my toothpaste choice. As a child, I was swayed by my parents' choice, later in life I made choices based on colour or flavour, and then I realized that my teeth sensitivity decided my choice of toothpaste. So, for any marketing professional one of the most fundamental questions to answer is, 'Why do customers buy?' This is the first step towards providing great customer service and ensuring complete customer satisfaction.

> 'All great things are simple, and many can be expressed in a single word: freedom, justice, honour, duty, mercy, hope.'
>
> —Winston Churchill

In my corporate career, I quickly recognized that my customers bought a solution, not just a product or service. A solution that made life simpler. They chose our company over others because our product or service was better. I also realized that communicating this in a simple way had a profound impact. Simple is often confused with easy but they are actually quite different. Easy requires very little time to do, while simple just means you have removed the noise and the clutter.

I am reminded of Steve Jobs' knack for simple communication and easy understanding. It saddens me to see Apple struggling with simplicity in the last few years. Its technology jargon has replaced the simplicity of Steve Jobs. It was Jobs's simplicity that held the audience's attention. Today, audience reactions to faster chips and more megapixels fail to convince them that they could become better photographers even when they buy an Apple product that comes with a better camera. Microsoft, unlike Apple, seems to have learnt the lesson of simplicity better and this has resulted in a significant boost to its brand over the last few years.

One of my prime lessons in this regard comes from financial services and I will use a mortgage example to demonstrate this point

Anna (my customer) wants to buy a house. She looks for a good builder and an apartment to suit her needs. My bank (and its financial product) is incidental to the entire workflow. Yet, as a banker I introduce six additional steps to slow down the process of letting her realize her dreams. If I provided her with a seamless underwriting experience she would be delighted. I could have pre-qualified Anna long before she came to me. I could have had properties pre-evaluated. I could have had partnerships with builders. Then the process would have been much smoother. Over the years as I moved from banking to consulting, I have noticed that banks have improved. Turnaround times have moved from hours and days to minutes and seconds making the mortgage process less painful for customers. Yet, the one place where banks still fail miserably is in customer retention. They are good at getting the customer onboard faster, but their processes are still slow in fulfilling customer requirements. Simple things like an address change, card PIN generation, upgrade or a card replacement still takes ages. To me, this is akin to a bucket orchid that traps bees with its aroma!

The lesson here is simple—Anna needed to buy a house. We know that a house purchase creates great emotional bonding and the bank can only create frustration in the customer if it does not participate in that emotional journey. Places where banks can make a difference are driven by convenience, simplicity, transparency and competitiveness.

Another area where I have seen massive CX change over the last decade is in food deliveries and take-aways. As it became a staple component of a busy work schedule, brands like Starbucks and McDonald's have been forced to adapt to customer needs. Starbucks launched a mobile-based guest checkout programme and learnt more about 'non-members' without the need of a prepaid wallet. McDonald's customized its food offerings to cater to different markets with their franchisee model that now accounts for nearly 95 per cent of its restaurants and includes healthier foods with fewer calories for certain markets. This has spawned the growth of food delivery services like Swiggy, Foodpanda, Zomato and Uber Eats as viable business models.

Till the early 1990s public sector banks enjoyed a lion's share of the Indian market as well as the mindshare of customers like me.[1] Foreign banks were still regarded as an elite sub-group. The introduction of a new breed of private-sector banks like HDFC and ICICI raised the bar as they introduced innovation and service standards at an affordable price to the common man while also offering a much wider branch network. We are now seeing a similar wave of disruption with the entry of private-sector banks as microfinance and non-bank financial companies have obtained banking licences and have penetrated many un-banked and underbanked customer segments and will lower costs even further. Existing private sector banks will have to find new ways to stay competitive.

My professional interactions with the four influential Australian banks—Westpac, NAB, CommBank and ANZ—has given me a great deal of insight into the evolving global banking sector. In the last few years, these banks have faced threat from online-only banks like ING and RaboDirect. The challenges faced by brick-and-mortar and online-only banks are quite different from each other. While the former seek to retain market share through offers for significant savings and discounts, online banks face challenges with no human presence at cash deposit centres.[2] To an elderly person, online banks provide little by way of personal interactions or providing confidence and trust, while the average millennial has taken to them as if it was their second nature.[3]

All of these examples have offered me a realization that can be captured in a simple statement, 'Customer profiles shift and so do their buying behaviours.' If we don't realize and adapt, our customers are simply going to walk away.

THE CUSTOMER PERSONA

My clients often have large supply chains. This can create confusion in CX as the 'customer' could mean different things at different stages of the supply chain. The key here is to nail down the 'primary customer'. It is the primary customer who is the key influencer of the value chain and needs better CX.

Let's take an example from the fast-moving consumer goods (FMCG) sector, and look at the business of 'soap manufacture and sale'. Soap is sold through distributors to shops who sell it to customers like you and me. While we are the primary customers, the distributor is a catalyst and needs to be motivated and incentivized. An influenced shopkeeper pushes the product to you and I, but ultimately, it's you and I who create the demand for the product and ensure their success.

Broad brushing all customers with the same yardstick would make a product generic and satisfy no one. In the Australian banks' example, we spoke about differentiating between customers—an elderly person and a millennial. That's where a specific 'customer persona' comes into play and helps narrow down customer preferences. The first step is to define an illustrative primary customer based on interests, goals, behaviours, attitudes, emotions, interactions, frustrations and motivations. This helps create positive experiences for a customer who broadly falls into this illustrative primary customer group.

While the persona itself is fictional, you can identify customer segments based on these homogenous characteristics. Customer segments are real people. If you don't define the customer persona well, your sample sizes for such characteristics may be too small or too large for decision making. To narrow down characteristics, you need to identify the personality, needs, wants and opportunities before, during and after the sales cycle. I started using these principles and identifying customer segments early in my career in order to deliver 'value' to them.

When I started using personas and their interactions in my design for products and services, their emotional state, the touch points and attention span became sharper.

Even in later years while I engaged in more complex B2B conversions, the understanding of client personas led to fruitful engagement with organizations that wanted to become banks, grow a certain portfolio, or improve their brand presence in a certain product area like 'Wealth Management'.

How my clients responded to stimulus (to go back to Viktor Frankl's quote) and obtained 'freedom' is best described by an empathy map. Their reactions were based on how they thought and felt, heard or saw, what we said or did. It also revolved around our understanding of their pains as well as their gains. In all, this provided us the opportunity to serve them better.

When we engaged, our initial task was to understand what the customer was trying to accomplish (the problem statement) and link it to their thoughts and their feedback, while noting how they were feeling (using language and diction).

Having used the persona and empathy map in our own engagements with clients, we also utilized the same to identify client solutions for their customers.

We often realized the impact of the right brain (the emotional half) and the left brain (the rational half) in buying decisions. This was true both for our clients as well as their customers.

The emotional side presented delight of connection or promise. The brand, trust, convenience, confidence, recommendations, surprise, or an accomplishment added to that delight. The flipside was when the product became un-affordable, it created disappointment. More often than not such decisions were made from pure gut instinct. I also noticed that as one grows in the leadership ladder, the gut instinct has a higher significance than mere statistical results. This was often forced because of the lack of statistical data. Gut was primarily driven by the freedom of 'feeling significant'.

Once we had the right brain on our side, the left brain often provided the justification—the value for money, the promise of delivery or just a satisfaction of needs. Supporting this decision with firm execution provided delight and repeat sales. However, when we failed to provide the necessary value, we met with significant disappointment.

We worked extensively with small companies as well as big ones. Smaller companies focused more on emotional factors to provide the right impetus in the absence of a perfect brand reputation. Our focus was to create an impact following client acquisition by prioritizing delight, which in turn created advocates for the product. An eco-system of advocates eventually built the brand. A great example of this is Apple, which started out with a single product but demonstrated value and managed to get subscription from customers towards their expanding stable of goods and services. A more recent example is the start-up I had mentioned earlier called Peak Design.

Once a company acquires a significant brand presence, even a 'not so great' product drives customer endorsement if they continue to make their customers feel significant.

The science of left brain versus right brain leads us to another question. Does being left handed make them right brained? If this is the case, does this present an opportunity? That according to cognitive specialists is a myth as the right brain for left handers is only used to process language.

As I got more entrenched into CX, I developed a skill to help my clients personalize their product offerings. I learnt about the role of cognitive technologies in improving experiences, and also how adaptive online experiences provided better experiences than fixed structure websites. I also saw how my deeper understanding of my clients (and their customers) led to superior engagements and loyalty. As cognitive technologies evolve and becomes mainstream for all companies, customers are even more likely to enjoy personalized CX.

Of all the things that I learnt in customer buying habits, two of them deserve mention:

1. Longer and deeper engagement with customers always delivered value to me financially;
2. Most engagements with potential clients were at a subconscious level and that could only be achieved by constant engagement.

WHY DO CUSTOMERS WALK AWAY?

In my first job, I saw that my organization's sole focus was towards getting new customers. Within the organization, there was a tendency to ignore faults of the sales department in customer acquisition, even when the customer did not really want or need the product. In essence, we had taken our eyes off our existing customers. Over a few years, we started bleeding, losing more customers than we would acquire that year and ended chasing our own tail. We created an atmosphere of indifference and our customers were invariably leaving us for our competitors. Over time we woke up, started looking at the numbers and put in place a set of actions to improve CX.

As I engaged with new businesses, I realized the difficulty in getting new customers. However, looking back I realize that it's a bigger pain when your existing customers are leaving you. Later, as I started working with more established organizations who were sitting on a gold mine of customers, I noticed that they were afraid that somebody would take their customers away from them.

In all of those adventures, the point around H for Human stuck out quite a bit. That factor mattered the most when customers decided to stick on or not. In most organizations, customer retention teams provided new offers and prayed that the customer stayed on. At the same time, the customer service team would collect feedback from customers and try to learn from their poor experience, but the root cause would remain. It dawned on me that CX is not just a customer service problem.

To give an example, my bank's relationship manager (RM) calls me twice a year to check up on me. The RM tries to woo me with new products and services, but I know that the call was part of a bring-up in his diary and he would forget about me as soon as the phone call ended. When I went to my bank a couple of times with a problem regarding a basic banking transaction, it took days to fix. This re-iterated my understanding that organizations that fail to see H for Human are likely to fail faster. The bank failed to realize that it is extremely difficult to mend bad or poor experiences that could have been avoided in the first place. In its pursuit of creating RM's for more and more customers, the bandwidth of each individual RM becomes too narrow to create meaningful relationships. This leads me to Dr Robin Dunbar's[4] conclusion regarding social relationships. Based on his extensive research, he concluded that you can have 148 meaningful social relationships in your lifetime and no more than five of them form the critical top layer of relationships. By allotting a single RM to over 200 customers at the lowest investment tier, or 75 customers at the highest wealth-management tier, you are immediately putting your customer relationships at risk. The only way around it is to marry these metrics with significant amounts of technology, but the result is that banking is becoming highly impersonal.

It took most of my clients and their customers many years to build trust. The reward of years of work in building trust is paid in full through their spending with you. As you can see, the return on my investment with my clients (and my clients with their customers) took a long time to recoup. Yet, this was worth every moment, but under many circumstances I have noticed that in order to ream short-term benefits, we often cut corners. Many industries such as banking, insurance or automobiles can't monetize such relationships in a single year. In cars for example, the relationship goes beyond purchase (often through a down payment) and other expenses such as fuel, finance charges, insurance, maintenance, repairs, tire changes, and others, quickly follow. All of these service providers want your business: your fuel station wants to see you back; your bank hates it when you transfer balance to another bank (whether it is a loan or an investment) since they had spent quite a bit of money getting you in the first place (and a transfer within an effective lifetime value actually dents their profit and loss account); insurers are worried about repeat premiums; and the dealer is interested in providing after-sales service (or maybe even finance).

Let me illustrate this using an example. When I speak to e-commerce retailers, they tell me 40 per cent of revenue is created by only 8 per cent of their customers. This 8 per cent were repeat customers and they made their operations profitable. What's interesting is that just by making their second or third purchase, the likelihood of these customers coming back increased by 50 per cent.

I have also realized that there is more wisdom to be found when it's the other way around. If the customer didn't want the product in the first place, they would leave. If I didn't step in to fix the issue at its roots, I possibly lost the customer and not a sale. This symptom is called 'Buyer's Remorse' in the credit card industry and this frustration is caused due to incorrect or lack of information from the salesperson.

I also quickly found out that as a customer, if I did not get a basic level of service (and that was true irrespective of the type of customer I was), I would leave. I would be hurt by inequality, especially if there was no price premium attached to it.

In the last few years a new kind of trend has emerged which is changing CX. Convenience has taken away another set of customers from their original organizations. My local delivery person takes orders for fresh milk, eggs and other grocery items before 10 p.m. on a given day to deliver by 6 a.m. on the next day. The IOS or Android app through which I would order these goods put my neighbourhood 7-Eleven store out of business.

The other day, I threw out my last remaining audio cassettes and compact disks. This made me recognize the revolution in the music industry brought about by Apple Music and TIDAL by making music available in an electronic format, downloadable at the click of a button. Even within the market for high resolution audio, there remains a niche that is catered by companies like Astell&Kern that manufacture portable devices. However, most customers have largely accepted poorer quality music (MP3), when compared to Compact Disk, as a trade-off in favour of portability and the option to have access to millions of songs.

The movie industry has similarly been undergoing a similar revolution that is leading to the slow death of traditional formats like video cassettes, VCDs, DVDs, Blu-rays and 4K disks and players. Portability offered by online streaming services like Netflix, Amazon Prime, Apple TV+, Disney and others have changed viewing preferences completely.

The player that has successfully disrupted the industry in convenience and emerged as the undisputed leader in changing customer preferences is definitely Amazon.

This leads me to an important question. What can industries like banking, real estate, automobiles, insurance, healthcare, etc. learn from the online streaming industry in order to adapt towards and create disruption through convenience in their own sectors?

Over the years, and as elaborated in many examples in the book, it became obvious to me that it's easier to convert a repeat customer than a new one. Many industries have established that it's as much as six to nine times easier to do this. They further add that along with repeat orders, the customers' average order size also goes up. This became the fundamental basis for one of my clients to focus on as much as 90 per cent of existing customers to drive their profitability upwards.

In my professional career, I have also been exposed to many false presumptions. My clients (including me) initially thought that you can increase customer stickiness through a loyalty programme. We became aware that such programmes have little use to many customers and do nothing to undermine their motivation to leave. Other factors like indifference, long queues, convenience, etc. had a higher priority. Moreover, given that when the customer cashes in on a loyalty programme, it drains the organization's revenue, many organizations are quite relieved if the customer doesn't encash. This meant they didn't really want a working loyalty programme, but it was merely a box-ticking exercise.

One of my big realizations has to do with customers becoming increasingly impatient (including myself). I no longer wanted to stand in long queues The abandonment rate is greater than 80 per cent if you had a few items and stood in queue at a supermarket or a retail outlet.

Another realization is that I find many industries (let alone organizations) putting in very little to no investment into R&D or innovation. Although in their personal lives they yearn for the latest car technology or mobile phone, people in leadership roles in many organizations don't realize the true impact of innovation. This leaves their back exposed to a disrupter who will change their fortunes quite abruptly.

Let's take the example of the traditional camera industry that was shaken up when the iPhone was launched in 2007 and had to keep pace with Apple as it upgraded its camera technology year after year. With Android joining the bandwagon, things got even worse and the consumer camera market saw a significant decline. Although the number of photographs taken has grown exponentially, many camera print stores had to close shop. Professional photography was largely relegated to the sidelines and soon got confined to niche areas like real estate, small budget movie making, aerial shots, 360-degree shots, high-definition video, action cameras and the like.

What I am saying here is that I feel industries need to stay focused to stay relevant. Today YouTubing is become a career choice for many in the Western world overtaking traditional work. This will obviously provide additional avenues to camera manufacturers and their ability to repurpose will enable their survival. Even in the prosumer and professional market, the lack of innovation and drive to move from DSLR to mirrorless has hurt both Canon and Nikon pretty badly, while the disrupter Sony, is waltzing in the park. Therefore the imminent question is—if you had to disrupt your own industry, where would you start?[5]

I find that competitive information is much easier to obtain than earlier, and your product or service remains in the forefront till your competitor launches their counter. But not reacting or facing that competition has led to the demise of many a company. Take the lack of understanding of Amazon's playbook by online retailers who have established themselves in India. For a customer, as he embraces and moves on, they have already assumed a new identity for themselves, which causes these once established organizations to disappear. Trust me when I say that the goliath PSU banks are already feeling the pinch with the shift of millennial customers away from them. It would be their bane, if they don't adapt quickly.

I grew up using Nokia phones but switched despite the desire to cling on to an old operating system. Nokia failed to gain customer acceptance as they could not innovate and their eventual re-incarnation came too late for their survival. Apple, Samsung, Google, LG, Sony and some other low cost phone brands like Xiaomi, Huawei and Vivo have happily absorbed that market share.

As I travel for work and pleasure more frequently, I often bump into airplane staff who have been very cordial and would try and answer some of my questions. During one of my trips, I asked a pilot on his preference of aircraft between flying Boeing versus Airbus. He was quick to respond. He said, 'Airbus is far more modernized, especially in the cockpit; they have less noise, and have far more comfortable seats specially to deal with pilot fatigue.' If I ordered my next set of airplanes for my airline, and if the pilot did influence buying decisions, which aircraft type do you think I would choose?

WHY DO CUSTOMERS KEEP COMING BACK?

Most of my clients accept the fact that many of their CX turn out to be neutral. That seems acceptable to them. Yet when I ask them how many of those neutral customers end up doing repeat business with them, there is usually pin-drop silence. That's when I explain to them that if their customers came back for a second transaction, their spend would have seen a 67 per cent uptick.

At this juncture I can't help highlighting some pertinent points that Malcom Gladwell[6] made in his book *The Tipping Point*. He says, 'little things make a big difference'.

In the book, he focused on three considerations:

(a) 'The Law of the Few': He basically expands on the word of mouth principle where information known to a select few gets amplified across a crowd. How many times have you had a great conversation where your potential client highlights your reference to another customer? After all, the world has just six degrees of separation. This can also have negative consequences as we saw in 2008 when there were strong rumours that ICICI bank was not sound, there was a sudden rush by customers to withdraw money from the bank.

(b) 'The Stickiness Factor': There is a maxim in advertising where an advertisement has to be seen six times before anyone remembers it. This maxim justifies the spend of giants like Nike or Coca-Cola on advertisement. In this context, Gladwell explains the need for creating opportunities to create 'contagious impact'.

(c) 'The Power of Context': Gladwell makes a case for the influence of the success of a book or a movie based on initial feedback from early adopters.

Probably the biggest takeaway from the illustration from *The Tipping Point* above is that it was built on differentiation as the critical factor. I have noticed that when my products or services had little or no difference with the competition, I didn't get noticed. It wasn't about trying everything with everyone. But with an added focus towards gaining loyalty towards my target segment, I had to build that loyalty with differentiation. As I look back into the DSLR camera market, Canon built its loyalty with its differentiation in colour science and lenses. Sony built its loyalty with advanced features in its mirrorless range. Interestingly, one is emotional (Canon), and the other is matter of fact (Sony) in its customer approach. So, while Canon builds out better functionality in its cameras and its mirrorless range, Sony builds improvements into its colour science, and makes better professional grade lenses. The take-away for me is that it is important to personalize value towards building your customers to 'the tipping point'.

Over time I discovered something else, that interactions to make a connection and loyalty were quite closely interlinked. And customers even had preferred choices for engagement, interaction, communication and education. Essentially, while many of us use social media to make personal connections, businesses have also caught on to Facebook, Instagram, YouTube and WhatsApp as marketing platforms.

Businesses however need to be wary of novelty. I see many of these new restaurants springing up in the neighbourhood. I have noticed a phenomenal rush to taste their food. This buzz goes on for a few weeks, and then the crowds start to taper. So, when you go to your nearest McDonalds or KFC, start to notice that besides the classic favourites, you always find some new menu item like a dessert or a drink that shows up. Though it evokes interest, it stays as a novelty and they invariably roll it back when the novelty factor vanishes. This is again a misinterpretation from a business that is looking to woo old customers back or acquire new customers. Coming back could just be a temporary phenomenon.

As businesses grow and expand, things backfire, or they succeed. When my bank got acquired by another bank, its core system changed to that of the new bank. The Internet banking platform changed as well. Their lending policies changed, their customer service capabilities changed. As banks grappled with their own internal integration, staff became unsure of their jobs. Quality suffered, and I jumped ship. As a customer, I got increasingly uncomfortable with the new experience and value that the new bank gave back to me. While this isn't something new to me as a consultant, I didn't have the patience that the bank demanded. I have seen a similar behaviour with my clients' customers when they are undergoing any significant change—a merger or an acquisition, a software change, a transformation, a restructuring or a layoff, or any redefinition of a foundational aspect in the organization. Customers and employees tend to shift based on such changes.

I once had the opportunity to advise a community bank based in the US, and it was competing very well against big banks like Citibank and Bank of America. Their customers and employees were very loyal. One of their key differentiators was to stay relevant to its community. They hired from the community, and had customers from that community. Some of these banks find donating a portion of every sale or doing a good deed as a way of connecting while doing business. Still others have found a way to engage the customer in the product development process and ensure they feel good about you.

As I read on the two deadly Boeing Max crashes in the news within a period of five months, I started to follow the story. One news article pointed out to the whistleblowing by a certain group of employees, and the failure to take corrective action to prevent such catastrophes.[7] While I don't know the congressional hearing details in the case, what I can say from a CX point of view is that by not listening to your customers and employees, we are just waiting for bigger disasters to happen. In the case of an airline, a single crash can set back airline profitability by many years, and two can force the airline into bankruptcy.

I had bought a piece of solid wood furniture from a wood manufacturer. Imagine my pleasant surprise when I suddenly received a thank you note, and a small gift from the manufacturer several months later on for my anniversary. It did go a long way for me to recognize that the organization cares. These days I get a lot of customer satisfaction survey calls, and that indicates organizations care about the action it needs to take in several circumstances. Even more so as every interaction has the potential for a customer to switch camps, various Net Promoter Score (NPS) surveys are undertaken to understand the customer satisfaction for that immediate interaction. More often than not, loyal customers are given freebies or invited to special events to show gratitude.

Given the sudden interest in YouTube by millennials, I have been intrigued by the platform's business model and what attracts the younger generation to them. One of the key habits of YouTubers that I recognized is that successful YouTubers posted relevant content (on a single topic) to provide value to their viewers. Additionally, they posted twice a week. A combination of both habits gave them incredible success.

Its staple for me and my wife to visit an IKEA store on our trips overseas. One of my friends explained this concept to me with regard to 'the IKEA effect'.[8] Apparently, IKEA discovered that customers placed a cognitive bias towards high value products they partially created. Assembly created a sense of involvement in its customers, and it evolved to the extent that customers created hacks to different uses of the product that IKEA did not originally envisage. I certainly am very fond of those products and carry them when I shift houses.

Why? IKEA's quality is certainly competitive, and I have to also put in a significant effort in creating the end product.

Another company I am quite fond of is Waterfield Designs popularized by its brand of bags called SF Bags. I bought a product from them and I am quite happy with it. When they asked their customers to design their wallets, they got an overwhelming response with different ideas, which they used in their final product. For good reason, many customers came back to pick up that final product.

Another business that has taken off in India is MTR—an instant meal that can be boiled or mixed with hot water. This was born out of the desire to have Indian food quickly anywhere around the world. Interestingly, I see these packets all the time at Indian grocery stores anywhere around the world. I also see that expat Indians keep buying these packets from time to time for a quick fix if they have busy schedules. My customer experience lesson out of all of this is the simplicity of execution that results in pleasure (taste).

I was visiting Singapore for business and I checked into one of the premium hotels there. At the check-in the staff greeted me by my name, knew of my preferences, including my pillow choice, and the newspaper I read, my cuisine and beverage choices and my choice of a non-smoking room. They also knew whether I usually took a hotel cab or hailed a taxi from outside. While it's not difficult to do this, I did notice their attention to be personalized and they engaged with their customers. Obviously, they were using real-time analytics. They were not alone, companies like T-Mobile, Royal Bank of Scotland and Informatica focus on making the customer feel special.

I have been repeatedly enamoured by any organization that is able to track their existing customers. Earlier, when I visited shops, restaurants or banks I would be asked for a specific loyalty number to trace me back into their system and extend the same benefit. These days, they have all got smarter. It's just your phone number. Given that it's become an integral part of your life, it becomes the key to carry. While I advised the large retail chain in Chile, I discovered how their social security number—RUT or RUN—became an essential to buy or sell their apartments, cars, open a bank account, get a phone, a passport or a driving license. While this seems standard in some countries, and now getting standardized in India, this has been in place in Chile well before 1990. India is still discovering how they can use the civil ID Aadhaar effectively in different business situations.

TIMING

'Time you enjoy wasting is not wasted time'

—Marthe Troly-Curtin

Observation provided me with the ability to get a deeper understanding of customers. I noticed that in the first four months a customer either adopts the product or service or gives up on it. Trending products sell. Products past their prime tend to fail. So, timing is everything.

The Competition requires only six to twelve months to catch up even for new technology trends. That became my lead time. Figuring out a differentiator took me years sometime, but within months I would know my results, and a few months later competition would replicate if it was successful.

After Blackberry launched its smart phone in 1999, competition followed with physical keyboards. Apple disrupted that trend in June 2007. By September 2008, Android came out to compete.

The way we do business has changed significantly. Today's mantra is all about speed to market, quick wins, early return on investment, agility and sprints, early detection of setbacks and risks, or smaller failures. Technology had to keep pace. They introduced Agile Methodologies to that effect.

If I look back in blocks of six months, I may not feel much change in customer experience, but if I reflect back in blocks of ten years or more, the world has changed so significantly. You could call each change atomic, yet the sum of it all is formidable. My current self takes a number of things for granted—24x7 mobile, customer insights by channel, virtual businesses, virtual reality, cognitive, artificial intelligence, social media and much more. If I woke up after a ten-year sleep, my first reactions would be of utter shock or delight.

I also learnt from my fair share of mistakes. When I launched products much ahead of time, markets were reluctant to adopt. General Motors launched EV1—their electric vehicle in 1996,[9] but was phased out three years later. Apple launched Newton, their portable computer, an expensive and a non-reliable handwriting recognition, that faded away.[10] Microsoft launched the Spot watch. Many have dabbled in the wearables market but it was Apple that got it right.

Some companies have ignored changes by calling them 'fads'. This has relegated their success to pages in history—Kodak, Nokia, Xerox or Blackberry.

BUILDING A BUSINESS PURELY ON PRICE ADVANTAGE

When we didn't understand how to compete on value, we dropped prices. Quickly we noticed price was just one dimension and attracted bargain hunters who ignored loyalty. Loyalty demanded other factors like quality, differentiation, ownership pride, and motivation to continue with us.

I noticed that once customers bought a product based on a relative price, the price point was often ignored, and customer complaints revolved around loyalty factors highlighted above.

We learnt that price wars benefitted no one. Quality reached a point of steady decline, till all players got burnt out. Even if we would get many customers, the service would just not be profitable enough to sustain.

When we launched credit cards in India, we noticed the trend of zero fees that attracted customers like bees, but the industry struggled to keep the lifetime value of the customer up. Customers would hop across banks and take their balances with them through balance transfers. Banks bled, portfolios got consolidated, and we now have a smaller number of cards from where we started.

The airline industry in India with Jet Airways, Kingfisher Airlines, didn't learn from that debacle, and they continued on the same footsteps, hurting their margins. Jet Airways finally succumbed as they couldn't burn cash anymore. In finality, the price wars did not help anybody.

Promotions are at best tactics for a short burst of time, to get rid of old stock or attract new customers but they are not sustainable.

So while these wars were going on in banking and airlines, another industry—mobile— decided to follow on similar footsteps since their launch in 1995 in India. Their game was—gain market share by reducing prices. Competition was fierce. By 2018, nobody is really winning. Indian TELCOS have terrible ARPUs, unsustainable for the economics for new technologies like 5G. The only strategy that seems prevalent is to revert to minimum pricing and weed out customers without a minimum ARPU. Mobile penetration has already peaked, and therefore expansion will see further consolidation in the market place.

As I absorbed these lessons, it taught me ways to sniff out anomalies when I saw them. During a transformation engagement with one of the largest banks in South East Asia, I noticed that a certain credit card product was being sold with a very high feature set, but with low cost. What happened next? You guessed right. The product got restructured to make it far more viable to sell. By giving away too much, they were effectively competing on price but at what cost?

POSITIONING FOR ADVANTAGE

All products make a promise, if the customer endorses, you have a sale. If the customer agrees after the sale, that milestone marks fulfilment, which in turn demonstrates value. Repeating these steps creates the brand. Customers differ in aspirations, expectations on quality and price. So, customers have choices. A customer ranks different products in their head based on its perceived value. This engagement inside the customers head is what Al Ries wrote in his book *Positioning: The Battle for Your Mind*.

These different behaviours, motivations and goals combined with customer demographics allowed us to demarcate different customer sets. We started calling them 'customer persona'. This way of thinking provided more structure for us to position things to the right customer set.

When we get real customers based on our perception of customer persona, we start to notice differences between individuals. Some individuals are likely to pay a premium for additional value, and some may not. That leads us to introduce tiered products within each segment. For example, a MacBook Pro customer is likely to pay more for a faster processor, additional RAM or storage.

When customers reach a certain peak of exclusivity, they demand it. No two cars manufactured and handcrafted by Rolls Royce or Lamborghini are the same.

I constantly use a positioning map to reflect pricing and value that may attract specific personas.

If the price was high, compared to value, the perception that immediately followed was, 'inferior product', 'a rip-off', or 'an overpriced product', giving the customer an immediate sense of discomfort.

If the price was too low, you would move from 'cheap' or 'discounted' to great value for money. This is the positioning for the price war category that we spoke of earlier. 'Cheap' has a mass following but not for brand reasons.

However, companies like DJI (drone manufacturers) have managed to build a sustainable business by providing consistent value at a different price point. That is a technological breakthrough.

If the price and perceived value was higher it became an 'aspirational' or 'premium' item.

The space in between is 'middle ground'.

What determines these perceptions is only known by talking to potential customers. When other products start to compete in the market, your rank on value and price may differ because of competition. With time, your high-end 2017 product may slide downwards in a 2019 ranking.

Based on your business's spot in the positioning map, you can identify your competition. As you move to the edges, your focus position starts to change. For example, as you move from aspirational to premium, your brand value and innovation starts to take precedence over function. So, while Honda the car manufacturer, competes on aspirations, Mercedes tries to compete on premium offerings.

If you notice, premium brands have managed to maintain dominance. Let's dive deeper here—take the eyewear industry for example. You would have noticed that your glasses are getting more and more expensive. If you look closely into the industry, you will find a few brands like Luxottica (an Italian company with high quality manufacturing capabilities) and Essilor (a French multinational) control most of the market. You will start to notice that they own most high street fashion labels. John Lewis Opticians in the UK, Ray-Ban, Lens Crafters in the US, Sunglass Hut, Versace, Donna Karan and Prada are all owned by Luxottica. Essilor in turn owns Crizal, Varilux and Transitions brands.

It's no different for premium corporations like LVMH, who are spread across segments. If you look at wine and spirits, they own brands like Chateau Cheval Blanc and Mercier, and in selective retailing Starboard Cruises and Sephora, fashion brands like Berluti, Fendi, Bulgari and LV, and in the watch segment Hublot and Tag Heuer.

Creating brands within companies creates the ability to make inter-industry offers at a later stage.

Middle ground is an unstable territory, and you have only three directions to move in (cheap, premium or aspirational) for survival.

The sweet spot for a high CX, is the middle to upper end of the aspirational block, and the premium segment. As soon as the customers perceive it as over-priced, they will start dropping off. An example is the price increase of Adobe in its CC line of products, where they have doubled prices. Customers are starting to flee, since some don't see the value for the premium they will end up paying.

I noticed that a start-up is quite unsure of its positioning and follows a scattergun approach. What follows is not encouraging—they fail to connect with their customer set and finally don't really get the customer personas they aspire for.

If you flip the positioning from selling to buying, there is a similar approach with the 'purchasing chessboard'.[11] AT Kearney popularized this framework to address every type of purchasing situation. They built this using 500+ case studies and expanded it from a 4x4 matrix into a full-fledged 64 square chessboard.

THE ART OF PERSONALIZATION

'It takes 20 years to build a reputation and five minutes to ruin it. If you think about that, you'll do things differently.'

—Warren Buffett

'If you don't care, your customer never will.'

—Marlene Blaszczyk

'The aim is to go from segment to individual.'

—Ginni Rometty

As my customers matured, they picked me on the trust that they felt I cared. I also saw that their approach to marketing and personalization changed quite a bit. When they did too many mailers, they failed to connect to even the most needed customers. By personalizing, they managed to bump up their sales figures by as much as 20 per cent. They understood one rule though—'Don't send out too many mailers.' It distances the customers.

The auto market became very competitive in India over the years providing many choices to the customers. Customers wanted to know their options in terms of brands and models, insurance, finance and aftermarket accessories. Their behaviour confirmed the *Forbes* finding '44 per cent of consumers stay with the brand after a personalized shopping experience'.

This war on personalization has led to a scary question—'How personalized is *personal?*' When I look at one of my clients with 220 million customers, creating 220 million options isn't feasible. The criterion here is 'personal enough'.

Innovation was a great way for immediate association with customers. My first employer convinced me regarding this by staying first in the market, and putting out market leading products consistently. Ultimately, though, I learnt that it's the feature set or the benefit that appealed to those customer personas. So, the thumb rule is—be meaningful, valuable and innovative.

Sometimes, our inspirations come from global markets.

When you have a global market, and you want to launch a really innovative product, how do you go about it? Recent evidences came from crowdfunding:

- FirstBuild, a subsidiary of General Electric, raised $2.8m on Indiegogo in 2015 for their Opal Nugget Ice Maker[12] and
- Gillette pushed its hot razor campaign on Indiegogo, which got successfully funded.

Again, experiments in innovation were tested out in the real world:

- Amazon Go, the physical store for Amazon, that got rid of checkouts with technology, proved popular with many return customers.

- Facial Recognition technology at retailers[13] like Tesco, ASDA and Sainsbury was a way to identify customer age and prevent selling age-restricted products to children. Tesco took it a step further to identify individual customers and personalize advertisements as they reached the cash register.
- When L'Oréal personalized their Makeup Genius[14] app, it allowed women to try on L'Oréal's products in real time.

Another experiment was in looking for ways to engage customers through Gamification.

- Heineken used an interactive beer bottle[15] with accelerometers, bright LEDs, and a microprocessor, that light up the whole bottle when people are cheering or taking a swig, that can also be synchronized to music.
- Pepsi[16] did an augmented reality campaign during the 2014 World Cup with users playing football with the world's leading players.
- Nestle partnered with Shazam to interact with KitKat[17] customers and join the Breaker Party that provided an opportunity to customers to win 'the break of a lifetime'.
- Rebecca Minkoff[18] personalized the fitting room with smart mirrors and self-checkouts at its boutiques. Why? Since shoppers who use fitting rooms are seven times more likely to make a purchase!

Closer home, a lot of the personalization came from providing convenience:

- Big Basket, India's largest online grocer, personalized the mobile grocery store on wheels.
- The dabbawallas from Mumbai personalized food delivery by delivering your home-cooked food, and has been a famous case study for Harvard Business School.

- And finally, Mygate personalized security for apartments and gated communities in India.

These examples are just a tip of the iceberg on personalization from innovation.

As we began building products with our customers, I realized the unique perspective of India's demographic. We have an average age of the population in their twenties. These millennials want a feeling of discovery and personalization, but core values are still integral.

Using those principles, Amazon and Netflix push up their sales by as much as 30 per cent[19] by providing recommendations. I like the Netflix perspective of looking at each view as a different product, and each recommendation is based on the product that the customer had consumed earlier.

Innovators don't need to change business models. They could just rethink campaigns. Coke's campaign in 2012, 'Share a Coke'[20] replaced the soft drinks logo with consumer names, encouraging customers to spread the brand message.

Recent trends with my customers showcased that even traditional sectors like banking have joined that band wagon. Singapore-based DBS and UK-based Atom Bank have apps on digital initiatives attempting to create unique customer experiences. Interfaces can be customized to create individual personalization. ATM queues were a significant bane for many of my banking clients, till they discovered that the Quick Cash trigger at ATMs solved that problem by remembering the last withdrawal made.

If you notice, personalization does not have to be expensive. It could just be a business innovation or a campaign with very little additional outlay.

Whatever the mode, businesses are increasingly trying to learn more regarding their customers. Some prefer to connect their current understanding and overlay that with personal information from Facebook, Twitter or LinkedIn, or by using recent technologies like Bluetooth.

The recent Bluetooth V5.1[21] which has the potential to bring in directional location-based services to include the Angle of Arrival (AoA) and the Angle of Departure (AoD) can potentially have the same impact as GPS in outdoor positioning.

All of these personal intrusions have led regulators to look into corporate behaviour regarding collecting customer data or improving children's safety. Consumer data protection guidelines like the European Union's General Data Protection Regulation (GDPR) seeks to regulate trust with regards to this, and the American regulators have been pushing for stricter guidelines to regulate YouTube viewing for children.

In the retail giant Target's case a new purchase triggered a 'pregnancy prediction score' and customers were surprised with special deals on baby products, which led to a significant PR disaster.[22]

So when it comes to personalization, there are many options, but as a corporate, it's becoming increasingly intricate as a subject.

THE BUSINESS OF 24/7

The biggest seismic shift I have been a part of in my corporate career is the business of 24/7. With the Internet, cloud and digital services, outsourcing and mobile phone apps, this is here to stay. With 24/7, our patience has shrunk to the size of an ant. What we want is immediate access and instant gratification.

To give you an example, my bank sees me more than twenty times a month but doesn't take my permission to call me anymore, and our email inboxes are filled with junk messages that we never read. Even the local grocer (BigBasket in this case) receives orders lasting only a week or less and my neighbourhood 7-Eleven is slowly but surely struggling to keep up with this emerging trend. Some of my friends or relatives work midnight to 8 a.m. shifts and a human voice service interface is available at our beck and call at all hours. Banks are trying to appease customers by sanctioning a loan in seconds.

Beyond our own borders, people are discovering new products to go along with it. For example, Nike introduced Nike Apps for its customers to stay connected to their ecosystem.

There are examples from other industries as well. Cars can now be driven in, exchanged or sold, and new cars acquired at an instant. Along the way banks are finding new ways to sell you insurance and also give you great deals on car accessories. The bundling of goods and services is something quite new and technology has made 24/7 more realistic than ever.

On a business trip to Sri Lanka, I noticed that the Sri Lankan Central Bank was thinking innovatively about its payments infrastructure, and I witnessed that the Indian initiative with National Payments Council of India (NPCI) followed quickly thereafter. Our remittances system (immediate payments system or IMPS) runs 24/7 without holiday or weekend restrictions. Other product innovations within the India banking system like Unified Payments Interface (UPI) are of great interest to other South Asian countries due to their success.

I can't think of an industry that hasn't been affected by 24/7. Examples include retail (Amazon), manufacturing (through shifts), emergency and critical care (ambulances and hospitals), music (Spotify, Apple Music), movies and videos (Netflix, YouTube), books (Kindle), transportation (Uber), and the list goes on.

The question that I often ponder upon is, 'How are businesses making it work?'

That has led me to three answers: 1. digital technologies and automation has helped the process; 2. In areas where human intervention is necessary, costs are finding their way back to end customers—for instance you pay more for a cab ride at night or during peak hours; and 3. Outsourcing has enabled higher margins coming out of lower cost locations or smaller sized vendors.

Let me give you an example from my own life. As a camera enthusiast, I follow B&H—the camera store in Manhattan, New York, USA—quite closely. They seem to have found a sweet amalgamation between the physical store and its digital platform. They follow 'office hours', while their ordering services are up pretty much 24/7. Additionally, they confirm upfront holiday closures like for Sabbath from Friday afternoon to Saturday night or National holidays.

To manage that gap in service hours, they have trained their staff to highlight product functionality rather than cost implications as well as staying authentic to the B&H brand and its values. That honesty has given the retailer respect and encouraged interaction with their customers. What I really appreciate is that they are frank in their responses to queries or concerns. Additionally, their activities on social media and masterclasses at their store enables them to stay connected to their community. Through this, they have been able to generate a huge social media following on platforms such as YouTube, Facebook and Twitter. They don't sell if they don't have to, and that earns them their customer's trust. B&H also actively asks their customers for reviews for products that they have sold and customers are also encouraged to provide feedback on their website.

As I see it, the B&H example demonstrates how you can create your own version of a 24/7 model that works.

I have another example from my own professional experience. While working in Santiago, Chile, we used the time zone differences pretty well to maximize productivity. I worked onsite with the client, while my team worked offshore, while the client was sleeping. Emails in the night were magically answered by the morning and updates or corrections were pretty much seamless. The end result was that the customer always felt things were moving pretty fast.

BEYOND VERBAL

'The more advocates you have, the fewer ads you have to buy.'

—Dharmesh Shah, founder Hub Spot

I have always been intrigued by business models that don't really advertise their compelling products, yet gain a staunch following. My neighbourhood tea stall is one such example.

I grew up in the by-lanes of Calcutta, where I was exposed to Maharani, my neighbourhood teashop that had a dedicated clientele. At any given point in time, from 6 a.m. to 10 p.m., thirty to fifty customers would spend around 10 minutes sipping tea there before moving on to their next job. Maharani's neighbouring business was a fast-food snack joint that was created by the tea stall owner who had made an extra dime for himself.

What intrigued me was why customers came back repeatedly to the teashop. The business did not advertise its products yet its value proposition spread by word of mouth. When I thought about the business model, I realized that it had many unique selling points (USPs). It's products were affordable, it satisfied the immediate needs of the customers and it had become a tradition to have tea there and have intellectual conversations with peers. The business was thriving for years on end and the quality never deteriorated all this while. The tea there was really special and it wasn't quite the same experience in another neighbourhood. The only other parallel in terms of the overall experience I can think of is the India Coffee House on College Street.

I observed that customers left their perceptions about their purchase at the stall using different verbal and non-verbal cues which the tea shop employees took note of and responded by adapting their products to suit the customer's preferences.

To use another example, if you look at Tesla, Elon Musk strongly felt that his focus on engineering rather than marketing would lead to success and followed through with that thought. He felt that word of mouth publicity is all that matters and interestingly that simple belief has a lot of meat to it.

While I was at IBM, I got introduced to the science of unstructured data, customer sentiments and emotions, and fatigue and frustration. This science has since matured into artificial intelligence (AI) and machine learning which help predict and monitor complex situations such as chronic diseases. These techniques have become so powerful that we are finally being able to analyse the complex question of why customers buy!

A scientist, Dr Albert Mehrabian, developed a communication model famously called the '7–38–55' rule. He demonstrated that 7 per cent of what we communicate consists of the literal content of the message, 38 per cent is taken up by the tone and volume of one's voice and 55 per cent of communication is made up of body language.

Maharani, the tea shop, developed its goodwill from the 55 per cent body language component exhibited by their presence, while the 38 per cent component was filled in by people having healthy conversations regarding the latest news and sports events. So, while these factors controlled 93 per cent of the entire customer satisfaction aspect of the business, the customers themselves did the remaining 7 per cent through advocacy amongst friends, colleagues and family.

Overall, since Maharani was a relatively simple enterprise, it understood its business without the use of any computers or modern technology. However, it stayed true to the all-important element in CX, 'H is Human'.

Dr Mehrabian's model also provides insights on how a face-to-face interaction could help understand customers better. While we tend to think that there is definite benefit in inserting this model into customer-facing businesses, it's equally applicable to digital channels, call centres and physical stores. Dr Mehrabian's model can improve call centre efficiencies, corporate messaging as well as online interactions through chats and clicks.

While the world is moving to digital, traditional platforms are still relevant. A vast majority of banking customers visit their bank's branches at least once a year. From research, we know that though 20 per cent of customers access their digital channels at least ten times or more during a month, they prefer to visit a branch when it comes to seeking advice. To take this further, studies also indicate that customers are keen to have access to both physical and digital channels. As digital technologies mature and gain the trust of customers, we are likely to see a further reduction of around 25 per cent of volume on physical channels. This trend was evidenced when I met a number of global banks who were mulling over the proposition to downsize their branch footprint a while back.

This is a tricky area for banks as the demand for branches comes from customers who believe branches create a sense of trust and likeability. Both of these are values every bank aspires to create.

It's not just banking that is grappling with the tussle between digital vs physical. Amazon, the global online merchant has invested in Whole Foods, a high-end American multinational supermarket chain, to indicate that the physical store is going to be relevant in the foreseeable future. I find this an interesting proposition for a company like Amazon as an interaction with a knowledgeable store associate just keeps customers coming back for more!

Another critical factor that has emerged in the business of 24/7 is that technology has allowed customers to shift their loyalties with just a few clicks. In my reading, over 80 per cent of customers have shifted loyalties due to poor customer service in the last year alone, and what is significant is that 90 per cent of them don't even complain, while the other 10 per cent tell 'many other people' to make matters worse. This seriously highlights how much corporates need to start paying attention to non-verbal cues of their customers.

'A complaint is a chance to turn the customer into a lifelong friend. I say that seriously, not as some press release baloney.'

—Richard Branson

'The most important thing in communication is hearing what isn't said.'

—Peter F. Drucker

So how do you communicate with millions of customers directly without saying a word? The answer lies in 'product signalling'.

Let me give you an example to illustrate this. My dad got me a pair of Nikes on one of his overseas trips and, for me, this became a synonym of aspiration during my school and college days. As I grew up, I discovered Nike's humble roots—they were known as Blue Ribbon Sports and changed their name to Nike only in the 1970s. But this change in brand name was accompanied by its instantly recognizable swoosh logo which helped the company reposition itself as a premium footwear company. It changed its brand image from premium wear into a lifestyle statement by creating the now famous tagline, 'Just do it'. The tagline empowered its target audience and that's probably also what connected me with Nike in the first place. Nike continued to create aspirational value by working with 'winners' like great athletes to create customized products. Bill Bowerman, the renowned track-and-field coach who co-founded Nike, is one such example when a 'winner' created a 'winning product', the waffle outsole.

I realized that it's not just the endorsement, but the entire process where winners work with the brand process. In such cases, the logo itself becomes an advocate for customer experience. To continue with our non-verbal cues, customers become passive advocates by not uttering a word but flashing a credit card or wearing a product that they choose to endorse. Furthermore, talking about these products as influencers on social media platforms creates the right product signals. This kind of customer-led recommendation moves away from traditional brand endorsement with a celebrity at the centre of the sales pitch. It is no wonder that this is becoming an increasingly popular technique amongst brands wanting to create an associated identity.

Another recent example that comes to mind is that of the tennis legend, Roger Federer, who left Nike after twenty-plus years of endorsements in order to 'work together' with Uniqlo, and play a role in the design process to look good, feel good in his clothes and ultimately play good tennis.

Product signalling is not just about working with celebrities or brand ambassadors. Apple, for example, took a different approach. They endorsed the colour 'white' to signal the brand—white earbuds, white wires, white iPods and the like. They extended it to other forms of product signalling like the Apple watch, where the wearer just flicks his wrist to see the latest alerts.

As our businesses become more and more complex, data analytics starts to play an important role. With all the firms I have worked with, I have seen that they have taken advantage in analysing organized information for customer insights. At IBM, I got introduced to non-verbal cues with the possibilities of unstructured data. The potential of the data that can be captured is immense as it can be gathered when a customer walks to a certain kiosk to collect a pamphlet, adds stress in his voice when expressing concern or even a simple notepad capture of a tele caller on customer feedback fed into the system. Such information would traditionally remain untracked, but IBM used it to understand it's customer and improve CX. Despite examples of early innovators like IBM, the surprising fact is that over 80 per cent of our data stored is actually unstructured, and, increasingly, over 20 per cent of an organization's time is spent analysing and interpreting such data.

The data that is captured has hidden gems regarding customer perception of value and issues regarding a company's products and services. I had the good fortune of working with Capital One on one of my engagements a while back and have been following their growth story ever since. Their advances in using machine learning and other advanced algorithms to serve their customers better as well as prevent life-changing events such as fraud is fascinating.

Over the period of my long professional interaction with call centres, I have noticed that they are increasingly focussing on customer interactions and investing in areas like first call resolutions. The focus on unstructured data helps guide call centre executives to keep their composure and steer away from conflict. Unstructured data-like voice modulation are language or industry agnostic and help deliver better CX which in turn develops trust. When customers get comfortable with transaction platforms involving the web or mobile interfaces, their call frequency or store visits also reduce.

Given that call centre executives develop skills to handle specific emotions pretty well, it has also become a norm to route customer calls to the agent who has the right skills to deal with the specific customer. The communications services company Vonage uses this quite effectively.

Linked to unstructured data is the science around text and voice mining for sentiment analysis using natural language processing combined with AI and machine learning techniques. It has been scientifically proven that your voice exhibits a deeper fingerprint than what might be discernible at the surface. The voice pitch, pauses between words and sentences, listening vs talking rate, among others, provide different biomarkers that can be used for various purposes. Organizations like BeyondVerbal, IBM and Sonde Health are expanding the use of data gleaned from voiceprints beyond CX into areas like medical sciences in order to detect early symptoms that warrant intervention.

In addition to the factors discussed above, letters from customers, tweets to gauge public opinion or Facebook posts all give you information regarding what the customer is thinking.

The use of voice has become even more important with the emergence of virtual assistants. The role of Alexa, Siri or Google assistant is increasingly becoming mainstream. Initially they are just doing simple tasks like checking balances, ordering an Uber or checking meeting room availabilities. But their capabilities are increasing exponentially and are likely to handle many more complex tasks in the near future.

To summarize, human emotions like joy, anger, frustration are not merely simple words. They bring with them a bundle of information and if tracked well, they can yield significant positive results for businesses and improve the final CX.

IN SUMMARY—TWO

Real customers have specific emotions during both their buying or their walking away process. The value you provide through price, innovation or feature set has a direct bearing on success. In today's world, the emotional communication with your customer will be well beyond verbal cues as you are likely to be interacting with them 24/7. In all of this, your customers want you to deal with them personally and offer tailor-made solutions. So what does that mean to your business model? Does this mean you stay the same or does your business need a rejig?

Three

Customer Experience in Times of Crisis

When any new crisis looms, I have noticed that people generally start to react to it with denial. Since organizations are built for the long term, the question for them is not 'if a crisis comes' but 'when'. That leads us to the situation that all brands are exposed to crisis and the need to recognize a customer experience crisis management plan. Throughout my career, as I experienced different circumstances that could clearly be classified as a crisis, I acknowledged the importance given to a crisis management team, and a crisis management plan.

But before we talk about crisis management, it is essential to understand what a crisis means and includes.

WHAT IS A CRISIS?

According to the Oxford English Dictionary—

Crisis: A time of intense difficulty, trouble, or danger

A natural fallout of a crisis is a huge gap between potential future income and existing costs, combined with a change in consumer response. So, there is little surprise to say, that this has a definitive impact on the organization, individuals and customers and the way they respond in trying times.

Having been a witness to different forms of crisis over the last twenty-five years, I would broadly classify them into the following seven types:

1. A Natural Crisis
2. An Economic Recession or a Financial Crisis
3. A Brand Crisis
4. A Crisis from Organizational Misdeeds
5. Crisis from Errors in Judgement
6. Service Disruption, Legal Entanglements and Public Relations Nightmare
7. A Technology Crisis

Let's quickly derive some examples here, shall we?

The COVID-19 outbreak is first and foremost a human tragedy, affecting thousands of people. But within no time through its growing impact on the global economy it resulted in a period of struggle for many industries—travel and tourism, airlines, manufacturing, hotels and resorts, cruise liners, auto parts and equipment, and oil and gas to name a few, caused by the contagious nature of the epidemic and the need for social distancing.

Before the coronavirus epidemic, banks had already been struggling with some legacy issues of the 2008 crash. The virus further compounded the situation due to intense economic pressures from this natural crisis.

The abrupt halt in the global economy as a result of this is definitely pushing the world towards a global financial crisis. With job losses and earning capacities deeply affected, especially within the economically vulnerable parts of society, areas like debt collections are deeply affected, and countries, through lockdowns, are forced to suspend economic activities or go slow till the pandemic subsides.

A little further back in history, between October and December 2015, the Centers for Disease Control and Prevention (CDC) reported over sixty cases of E. coli related poisoning linked to Chipotle, the Mexican grill joint, the cause behind a brand crisis resulting from a severely damaged consumer confidence.[1]

In the chapter 'Going Above and Beyond', we talk about an epic fail for Volkswagen, causing a crisis emanating from organizational misdeeds. Volkswagen is not alone in this, others have had their fair share of failures. Subway, for example had hired Jared Fogle as the face of the brand after he lost 200 pounds in the early 2000s eating only Subway sandwiches. But fifteen years later, in 2015, they had to distance themselves from him after he got sentenced to sixteen years in prison for distributing and receiving child pornography and having illicit sexual contact with a minor.[2]

In the same chapter, we talk about two cases of massive failures caused by an error in judgement—the opening day of T5 in Heathrow and the launch of Starbucks in Australia.

When United Airlines dragged off a man from an overbooked flight[3] in 2017, and followed it up with a letter from its CEO, Oscar Munoz, to its employees describing the passenger as 'disruptive and belligerent', it caused a deep PR disaster, resulting in the CEO having to apologize profusely with a promise to set things right later.

Rather than this being an isolated incident, however, United Airlines[4] has been unfortunately involved in multiple PR incidents over the years.

Sometimes disruptions are caused by unfortunate developments from events like the Deepwater Horizon oil rig explosion that got compounded by BP's[5] failure to stop the oil spill causing an ecological disaster combined with political and financial consequences.

Recent history[6] highlights software failures, ransomware attacks, IT outages and data leakages affecting some of the biggest companies and millions of customers around the world. These include the Heathrow disruption in February 2020, the British Airways IT glitch in August 2019 and CPU hardware vulnerabilities leading to an increased risk of hacking, among others.

CONSUMER BEHAVIOUR AS A RESULT OF CRISIS

We are deeply affected by crisis and it reflects in our cognitive behaviour. Under regular business circumstances, companies have used their knowledge of common events to predict actions. But customer behaviour during a crisis significantly changes in orientation when they are exposed to higher risks.

These cognitive behaviours are reflected through results that show up in business. An example is how banks are noticing a sharp drop in savers with the latter moving to chase higher interest rate products when crisis strikes.

While collective behaviour in general is determined by demography, income or social factors, during a crisis, there is an increased buying consciousness that affects us. I still remember, before buying my house, we read the purchase agreement in its entirety, but when it came to a dispute regarding a particular clause much later, our attention zoomed in on that particular issue. It's the same when crisis strikes. We start paying attention to the fine print.

When we focus on the economic recession induced by coronavirus, we could be looking at multiple scenarios.

One scenario could be of a real recession where there is a market contraction, and there are severe exigencies related to demand or supply. For example, cars could be in abundant supply with fewer takers, while critical care medicines could fall short of demand. This is akin to war or similar disaster-like situations which drastically affect consumer preferences as well.

Another scenario could be related to a policy measure where financial conditions and credit intermediation chokes off expansion. Impacts like these have been felt by, say, the non-banking financial companies in India in the weeks after the coronavirus outbreak.

The final scenario could be a proper financial crisis, where the financial imbalance builds out over time, and disrupts the financial intermediation process and, ultimately, the economy.

Since what proves to be a bane for some is usually a boon for others, irrespective of which storm we are currently going through, some sectors always stand to benefit from it. In the current coronavirus crisis, for example, essential utilities, local pharma, diagnostics, consumer goods and durables, online education, mobile data traffic, etc. have seen a spike.

BUSINESS METAMORPHOSIS AS A RESULT OF CRISIS

As the reality of any crisis begins to dawn, the first question that comes to mind is: 'When will this come to an end?', quickly followed by, 'What will the world be like after this crisis?'

I started my career in banking at a time when the Indian stock markets were hit hard by a scam in 1993. The resulting lessons came from a much stricter governance and scrutiny mechanism across the industry to ensure that financial paper was backed by adequate underlying assets. I see these lessons repeat, showing us that adversity will change the way business is conducted.

It's not that we are facing the outbreak of a disease for the first time. Seventeen years ago, after the outbreak of SARS, the e-commerce business experienced tremendous growth.

Another case in point is the pressure on the supply chain in China during this crisis is causing organizations like Samsung electronics to shift its production of premium flagship phones to Vietnam.

For India,[7] it's giving a fresh relook into shifting manufacturing from China to India, a boost to its already successful pharmaceutical industry.

The opportunity brings about a call for investment, economic policies, bilateral agreements and faster governmental clearances.

Business rebounds are likely to be of 3 different types.

1. The classic economy rebound—a V-shaped curve with a shock followed by eventual rebound in growth.
2. A slightly different twist to this scenario is a U-shaped curve, where growth resumes but there is some permanent loss of output. This looks more plausible in the coronavirus recovery path. This means that some customers may also sign out of existing products and move towards a different way going forward.
3. There is however a different curve, that will see an ugly light, and is likely to impact us for a longer term. Certain products and industries are likely to experience an L-shaped curve. A curve where there is significant structural damage to existing industries, products and services, and the shift will mean a move towards something entirely new. For example, we could be seeing telemedicine spawn off as an attractive industry and will be regarded as a first line of defence. This could see patients from around the globe consulting doctors about diseases online and seeking initial opinion before going to a local clinic to get treated. This becomes a win-win for both patients and skilled doctors who would get to widen their client base.

The US is believed to be suffering from high unemployment levels of 14.7 percent, the highest since 1940. Discouraging as this may seem, companies are still hiring. This mismatch and shift has pushed Verizon and Accenture towards a collaborative effort called People+Work Connect, allowing for companies and employees to work together to bridge the gap for businesses with an urgent need for workers.

TURNING CHAOS INTO OPPORTUNITY

As we head deep into the coronavirus epidemic, connecting with family and friends across the world became critical to check-in on their well-being. In one of my conversations with a family member in Hong Kong, the word crisis written in Chinese, 'Wei-ji' came up.

As John F. Kennedy had said, 'When written in Chinese, the word crisis is composed of two characters. One represents danger (wei), and the other represents opportunity (ji).'

This immediately reminded me of the story of Soichiro Honda, founder of the Honda Corporation and the maker of Honda cars and motorcycles.

From 1938, Mr Honda, a student then, had a single minded pursuit to sell and manufacture a piston ring for Toyota Corporation. After years of effort, he showed his prototype to Toyota but was rejected. Instead of getting disappointed he pursued his dream, which was accomplished a few years later.

With great difficulty he built his piston factory at the brink of World War II, but bombing by the US destroyed it completely. Instead of giving up, he found a way to use scarce resources to build a motorized bike to ferry him to the market and back. With tenacity, he refined the bike to create a product that Mr Honda could stand by.

For me, this is a great lesson on how to thrive during chaos.

In another example, as cinemas temporarily closed in January 2020 due to the coronavirus outbreak in order to stop social contact and virus transmission, Huanxi Media Group, a media company producing movies in China, turned the crisis into opportunity by tying up with an unlikely partner, ByteDance, for film distribution. This is the same company behind the blockbuster app TikTok and a number of native Chinese apps like Douyin, Jinri Toutiao, Xigua Video and Huoshan Video. The challenge for TikTok was that it was built around a 15-second view platform, and the Huanxi Media Group's movie *Lost in Russia* was over two hours long. ByteDance, however, agreed on the partnership, which got inked in less than 24 hours, and the movie met with unprecedented success. It got more than 600 million views and this profited both Huanxi and ByteDance as advertising revenue was being shared by the two companies.

We usually design our customer experience assuming business as usual, and everything is stable with predictable outcomes. As Benjamin Graham, the famous American investor to whom Warren Buffet looks up to, once said, 'Price is what you pay, value is what you get.'

In the early 2010s much of the Arab world experienced a series of anti-government protests, uprisings and armed rebellions. This presented a situation completely opposed to a business as usual operating environment. Egypt was not spared either and it was struggling under unprecedented chaos. This presented a real life crisis for Unilever, which was operating in that market. Unilever was presented with infinite hardships in a situation with no government, no president, no constitution, no operating banking system, no satellite TV and even no Internet connectivity. But opportunity comes from understanding how to drive value in such a crisis. Since the food business provided over 50 per cent of Unilever's business in Egypt[8], the company focused on value for supermarkets and to the consumer. To re-invent the non-functioning traditional supply chain, Unilever teamed up with the Army to bring in food supplies after curfew hours and also worked closely with competitors like Nestlé and Procter & Gamble.

As we head deeper into the coronavirus crisis, we are faced with severe shortages of ventilators and masks. Stepping in to help, unlikely heroes are emerging. In the US, Ford and GM are racing to build ventilators, and Apple is making face shields. In India, Maruti, Mahindra & Mahindra, Tata Motors, Hyundai India are pitching in, while in the UK, Dyson has stepped in.

Beyond pure commercial considerations, these events mark an opportunity for a brand to present a deep message to the customers—'we care'.

'Don't wait until you're in a crisis to come up with a crisis plan'

—Phil McGraw

SHIFT IN MINDSET TO GROW

The recent coronavirus outbreak is making businesses think negatively with downsizing, layoffs, survival or something even more drastic becoming the norm. The crisis has changed everything. Agreed that the 4 Ps in marketing, product, price, promotion and place, have all been impacted in the traditional sense of the term, but the real change is that the light is now shining in a different direction. The idea, however, is to adapt to a changed consumer behaviour and create a business model around it.

Let's take some examples,

1. Many people who are genuinely trying to work from home are recognizing that their work from home infrastructure is not up to the mark. This creates opportunities for manufacturers to cater to this growing demand. It could mean sitting–standing desks, printers, coffee machines, software and services.
2. Book publishers around the world are under pressure because of social distancing, and are withdrawing from literary events in the wake of a lockdown. But the end customer has more spare time, can engage and participate more in such activities. The real question is how digital technology and solutions can enable creating an event where hundreds more could attend? Virtual events through platforms like Zoom, Crowdcast and Instagram Live are likely to replace physical events in the short- to medium-term.
3. In the future, touching surfaces are likely to be taboo. So people will hesitate to touch your credit card or the lift button, for example. For financial services providers like Visa and MasterCard, or even for payments fintechs, this is possibly the best opportunity to push contactless and mobile ecommerce within their portfolios. For manufacturers of gloves or plastic, it may present an opportunity to invent the new self-retracting stylus of the future.

4. We still need to respond to customer and client needs. Social distancing will force us to form rapid response teams and help people discover that co-worker and employee talents are relevant—even vital—which could be invaluable under these circumstances.

5. The environment we are working in has grown quieter as a result of the lockdown. This has, for example, helped YouTubers film in quieter environments, have helped product managers to think in quieter environments and agile businesses time to really prepare for events of the future.

6. People will complain that the restaurant business is under pressure. But if businesses notice carefully, they will see that while restaurants are on their largest ever decline in sales, bakeries with very few dine-in tables are busier than ever before.

7. People are growing increasingly conscious of personal hygiene. Tushy, a company that makes bidets and promotes them as toilet paper replacements, has seen their sales rise significantly during this outbreak.

8. Telecommuting may be the most important job perk to ask for after health insurance. Even after the end of this outbreak, companies will find ways to create more opportunities for employees to work from home, which actually might be more productive than before.

9. Footfalls in public places like cinemas and malls has decreased dramatically, but the demand to entertain oneself hasn't. We are likely to see higher consumption of movies digitally, which could be fulfilled by examples similar to the partnership between Huanxi Media and ByteDance for the movie *Lost in Russia*.

10. Schools and universities will be better prepared for distance learning. They will be investing in more equipment and other resources needed to move their classroom online. This creates its own advantages as people will no longer have to stay near their school or university or be housed inside an institutional dormitory. Online classes would also mean that class timings

could vary depending on the time zone of the geography you are based in.

11. Businesses like car manufacturers are getting into different areas to offset the decline in sales during the outbreak. It presents an opportunity for some to stay on in a new line of business. If you take the Internet service provider Gigaclear as an example, they took on the challenge of targeting hard to reach locations with reliable broadband. Last mile connectivity is a more lucrative challenge to solve than it has ever been before.

12. Leveraging an adaptive approach to keep your business growing will be the need of the hour. Huazhu, a Chinese hotelier operating in 400 cities across China, leveraged its internal information platform through its internal app Huatong to make sure that its employees and franchisees were armed with timely information and guidance about the outbreak.

As you can see, the real question is 'How can you make hay while the sun shines?' Yes, you heard me right. The outbreak presents opportunity and forces you to think differently. There are answers out there for you to discover. This is not to say that different sectors may have different recovery speeds, or that you will recognize the need to adapt that recovery strategy depending on location. Nevertheless, an opportunity has arisen to innovate around new needs and spot new consumption habits being formed before others can capitalize on them.

HOW CAN YOU PROVIDE A MEANINGFUL CX

When dealing with a crisis, actions determine their true meaning. Small changes actually don't make much of a difference. Crisis is a clear exposure to fragility. To respond and be meaningful to customers at the end of the day is a very precise balancing act between your own survival and customer empathy.

But what can you do? Well, plenty actually.

Save your Brand

Bad things happen, but then the right strategy makes your company stronger and enables it to face the mess head on and save the brand. In 2009 and 2010, Toyota was the target of adverse media attention, as a result of consumer complaints that eventually led to recalls in order to save face.[9]

Owning up and taking measures to reclaim your quality and safety standards is that key element to save the brand and bring customers back.

Being Pro-active and Respond Quickly

The first thing I always notice is that my customers are increasingly looking for guidance and relief during any crisis. When our customers reach out for help, a fast response is crucial. We need to pay attention to our customers' needs or concerns.

The Indian government made arrangements for delivering essential supplies to homes in demarcated red zones during the coronavirus epidemic. The government also quickly introduced economic measures and the finance ministry gave guidelines to banks to become more human.

Be Human

Chances are that conversations with our customers during a crisis aren't the easiest ones. Being able to express empathy and show them we understand their point of view is crucial. Of course, the first step towards that is to listen.

The Tata Group showed its support for the Indian government's coronavirus epidemic response by opening its doors across Taj Hotels to doctors on duty and donated funds for proper equipment, testing kits and treatment facilities across India. Similarly, United Airlines temporarily eliminated their change fee policy to accommodate customers' needs.

Over-Communicate

Disasters cause displacement that affect both employees and customers. Combined with a certain loss of being able to think clearly, disruptions may affect distribution and delivery or a certain customer aversion related to any of the seven types of crisis, proactive communication takes precedence. Luckily we have email, social media, digital and analytics to keep our customers updated consistently.

Ask for Feedback

Many organizations become reluctant to ask their customers for feedback. All of a sudden, existing customer service and CX measurement criteria just stop functioning causing a bigger harm to both customers and businesses.

Evangelize a Contingency Plan across the Organization

Under normal business-as-usual situations, contingency plans are relegated to the attic. Suddenly, the fire hydrant (contingency plan) becomes the most important tool in your arsenal when disaster strikes. It's during this period that I find that people don't even know where to look for the fire hydrant or even how to use it.

This is where internal communication, strong roles and responsibilities and their follow through should be discussed and actively executed.

Just to re-iterate the obvious, the contingency plan is a living document and its efficiency lies in keeping it updated and reviewed often. The power of your response during the crisis can also trigger customers shifting to greener pastures as the crisis unfolds or immediately after the crisis dissipates.

MANAGING WORKPLACE STRESS AND EMOTIONS

A crisis is not only about organizations and customers. At the end of the day, the employees are the ones who stand right at the centre of it all.

Any workplace crisis also involves stress and emotions for employees while they are performing their work-related duties.

As you have lesser face-to-face interactions and collaborations, understanding instructions can be stressful. At this time, email can be stressful if it's not understood clearly.

The boundary between work and home disappears in many situations, like in the case of work from home during the coronavirus situation. This is also when the demarcation between working and non-working hours become less visible.

When you work in the office, a simple hop, skip and jump to your neighbour's workstation would be all it takes to collaborate. Hence, informality creeps in because of easy access. Under the current circumstances, scheduling appropriate time for collaboration becomes all the more important.

In all of this, it is important to schedule and drive tasks from your calendar, in order to maintain the proper distinction between work and play.

So what does this have to do with customers, you may ask? The answer is simple; unhappy employees can't serve a customer very well.

At the end of the day, with leadership facing stress to keep the lights on, they are also likely to display the same stress. Thoughtful leaders need to exercise hope and compassion to encourage their teams, assuage fear and help team members see into the future. A pretty nice example of this is when JP Morgan and Bank of America gave employees who couldn't go home extra pay and provided them job security. The same was true of PayPal, Amex and Citigroup[10] who announced that all jobs will be safe during 2020.

THE FUTURE OF WORK AND CUSTOMER EXPERIENCE

When we sail into unchartered waters, we often have no experience and don't know what might happen. This was the case when humans first landed on the moon in 1969. The outcome was just like Neil Armstrong's first sentence after he landed, 'One small step for man, one giant leap for mankind.' We didn't fully comprehend the impact of the first email message that was sent over the ARPANET network in 1972, which merely said 'QWERTYUIOP', representing the top row of alphabets of the modern day keyboard.

We have been hit by financial crisis repeatedly. It's easy to forget that we had a crisis in 1980, a slowdown in 1990, a bust in 2000, an economic crisis in 2008, and now, in 2020, a financial crisis is showing its ugly head.

What's important to note here is that 80 per cent of battered companies did not manage to gain back their pre-recession growth rates according to a Harvard Business Review (HBR) Study.[11] Also, only a small 9 per cent of them managed to flourish as a result of a slowdown, outperforming their rivals by at least 10 per cent in terms of sales and profit growth.

Four clear strategies emerge from a crisis,

1. Prevention focus prevention—defensive moves to avoid losses and minimize downsides;
2. Promotion focus—investing in the offensive to provide upside benefits compared to peers;
3. Pragmatic moves—a hybrid strategy that combines preventive with promotion-focused moves; and
4. Progressive focus—optimisation of pragmatism towards end goals.

As the saying goes, 'Strange times require stranger thinking.' Let's turn now to a few examples to understand outcomes of these strategies.

In 2008, Sony focused on cost reduction with factory closures combined with job losses and delayed investments. Though this was clearly focused on a preventive strategy, Sony struggled to gain momentum subsequently. The HBR study referred to earlier also underlines the fact that few companies that follow a prevention strategy do well after a recession.

In stark contrast, Hewlett-Packard (HP) drew ambitious plans at the height of the year 2000 recession. These ambitions strained corporate resources and thinned management attention, and HP found it tough to match the competition from Dell and IBM.

In the early 1990s, the French auto industry was affected by a degrowth in car orders in the wake of the First Gulf War. FAVI, a French metal manufacturer, was affected as a result, but despite the crisis, it supported the livelihoods of around 500 employees.[12] FAVI, at that time, had a number of temporary workers but nobody at FAVI, including their CEO, saw them that way. Within the hour, a new agreement was reached where everybody took a temporary 25 per cent salary cut to support the fate of those temporary workers.

A clear, progressive focus involves challenging accepted perceptions, critical thinking around the business and execution triggers, an actively involved board, a return to a cash method of thinking rather than an accrual method to conserve revenue and drive profits, and driving a change story that your customers are likely to buy into, while not losing sight of quick wins.

The entire second part of this book is dedicated to actual principles and methods that make all of this possible.

The coronavirus has exposed a similar economic fault line that we ignored during peacetime. Our strategies, thus, need to be tailored towards a progressive focus. Therefore, while we create strategies, we can't ignore emerging trends that could re-define a progressive focus.

Two emerging forces from this pandemic are the Internet's big bang moment and the push towards working at the speed of light. Businesses are going through a phase of metamorphosis of their traditional models as an outcome of this epidemic. An example of this is how companies like Apple and Google have started working on the integration of coronavirus visualization on maps leveraging GIS datasets with real-time updates. Workers' health is being brought to the forefront, and prioritization of cleaning and sterilization are emerging as important factors. Another aspect will be that in the future, travel budgets will shrink since companies will realize that it is possible to build a thriving business model with fewer face-to-face interactions.

While many companies have policies to support staff for a flexible work method in the form of 'work from home (WFH)', the coronavirus outbreak is the largest natural experiment that tests WFH and compels us to learn everything the hard way. We are not going back to square one any time soon. Organizations are likely to recognize the forced need for working online and remotely, and notice opportunities towards lowering overhead costs, while developing new skills, comfort levels and better accountability for such employees whilst maintaining and improving customer experience standards. This will lead to looking into opportunities to re-engineer the workplace.

What this, in turn, means for individuals is that there is an immediate need for them to upskill during downtime, so as to be ready and prepared when the uptime swings by again. What it means for customers in the longer run is an improvement in products and services since we are deploying technology and higher skilled workers, both of which are factors that influence better products and services in the longer run.

The coronavirus outbreak is also likely to bring to the surface the concern about technology's impact on the future of work. Historically, we have seen that robots replace human labour in bursts, especially in the wake of shocks when it's more expensive for firms to deploy lesser skilled workers, rather than deploy technology with higher skilled workers.

A serious look at artificial intelligence (AI) and robotics will become more prevalent as businesses look at opportunities to eliminate process redundancies. This will not only be in the services sector, but also in manufacturing and supply chain to support business resilience and versatility.

Various organizations have become heavily dependent on reducing face-to-face interactions and have made a move towards group video calling using tools like Facetime or Zoom. More robust and secure investments are likely to follow in this area after the event has passed.

As millions of students and their teachers have adjusted to remote classes and an online mode of education, universities will possibly find a big impetus in driving online education as a means to broaden their top-line.

Some industries such as the entertainment sector (the film industry, for example) are already witnessing a push towards re-visiting their current business models. A Netflix-like subscription based streaming model is likely to emerge stronger as a result of this re-evaluation of business models.

Supply chains have increasingly begun considering shifts from global to local as a means to de-risk themselves from manufacturing hubs like China. Countries like Japan are incentivising this programme to bring back businesses into Japan.

Companies are also increasingly focused on the business end of the engagement, and in times like the coronavirus outbreak, the balance clearly tilts back into areas that we hadn't given much thought to—science matters. A number of studies and research around social distancing go back to 1918 when the influenza flu pandemic broke out, yet for the vast majority, the current pandemic is proving to be a difference between life and death. Increasingly, we will get people to be attracted towards the cause of science and dedicate their entire life to be useful to the larger society in times of crisis like this. Investments in science and scientific research by companies, for instance pharmaceutical and healthcare, will continue to grow as they realize its importance in long-term prosperity.

IN SUMMARY—THREE

At the very end, it needs to be reiterated that all business models need to be re-thought with the customer at the centre—the customer is, of course, that very person who makes it possible for us to put food on the table.

Four

Going Above and Beyond

I simply couldn't have learnt all my lessons through personal experience. Some of these lessons came from research. Some from my colleagues and others from my clients while we were trying to solve problems. Also, some of my learning were derived from books, magazines and articles that talk about successes and failures.

The challenge for all of us, I guess, is to remember these stories and apply them when making a transformation in our own business or in that of others.

I have cherry-picked a few inspiring stories that have brought success as well as those that have failed either in part or in full. Enjoy!

INSPIRING ORGANIZATIONS

'Everything that can be invented has been invented.'

—Charles H. Duell, Commissioner of
the US Patent Office, 1899

The quote was possibly followed by an unprecedented century of discovery, invention and change. The twentieth century witnessed change at a much faster rate than that the world has ever seen before.

In hindsight, it is quite ironic that at that time, Duell believed that the patent office would shrink in size and ultimately close.

A company that fails to invent could reconcile itself to a similar statement. Market shifts may take time to showcase real innovation but ultimately an outsider will show you the way forward.

'Humility will open more doors, than arrogance ever will.'

—Zig Zigler

INSPIRATIONS FROM RED BULL[1]—'ASSOCIATION' BEYOND MARKETING

I first discovered Red Bull on my long-haul flights. It simply helped my jet lag and I continued to use it without much thought. As I was having a pizza at an Italian restaurant, I couldn't help but keep staring at a Red Bull billboard that was in my line of sight. That experience led me down the story I am about to narrate.

Chaleo Yoovidhya was the owner of T.C. Pharmaceutical and had introduced a drink called 'Krating Daeng' in the Thai market. It became popular amongst Thai labourers and truck drivers. During one of Dietrich Mateschitz's (a former marketing executive for a German consumer products company) flights from Austria to Thailand, he discovered that the drink helped him cure his jet lag. He saw a potential for the drink in the Austrian market and partnered with Chaleo to create a new company. Each invested $5,00,000 in 1984 and launched a new drink called Red Bull that was targeted as a trendy, upscale carbonated drink with a lower sugar content. This resulted in the birth of a new category of beverages, the now ubiquitous 'energy drink'.

Over the years, the Red Bull brand consciously linked itself to extreme sports, marathons, motorsports, skate- and long-board competitions and other non-conventional competitive sports. By 1992, the brand expanded beyond Austria into Hungary and

Slovenia. Now it is in 171 countries putting Dietrich in the Fortune 100 list.

The caffeine-based drink saw a meteoric rise in sales and emerged as an aspirational energy drink for endurance from its original roots of being associated with Thai blue collar workers. In fact, it happens to be among the most expensive non-alcoholic drinks available at convenience stores.

Red Bull attracts customers through marketing campaigns designed to evoke the 'right brain' (or emotional side) of customers. It promotes activities that a customer would desire to engage in or watch. These campaigns focus on athletes and the endurance activities that they have to undertake. In Red Bull's marketing campaigns, the connection link is 'endurance'. In essence, it makes the customer the 'hero' of the story. The brand's target demographic is the 18–34 age group and its slogans are aimed towards the consumer becoming a hero with the thrust of the messaging being, 'If you believe in it, then anything is possible.'

The interesting secret is how it sells the idea of the transformation after you drink it. This is done through a strong association of the drink to the consumer's immediate physical state after they have it.

THE SPOTIFY JINGLE—TIMELY INNOVATION

During my growing up years, I used to record my favourite songs on cassettes to make mix tapes. As technology changed, I did the same with CDs. But then something wonderful happened and a simple MP3 player made it possible to download many more songs in a very small form factor.

But with this technological revolution came more stringent copyright guidelines creating serious threats to digital music sharing companies like Napster, Rhapsody and others.

Spotify, a Swedish music streaming company, came up with a solution in 2008. It allowed customers to download unlimited DRM (digital rights management) protected music. It was the first legal subscription-based service and revolutionized the industry. Spotify never downloaded the files, but merely cached them. It quickly became the Netflix for music.

For the first time you could take your massive music library with you and stream it on any device using virtually every available operating system. Thus, you could make your TVs, stand-along speakers, computers, phones, etc. stream 'your' music. To add to this, there is no friction in switching devices. All of a sudden your CD and MP3 players seemed obsolete in comparison to this service. Prior to Spotify, music piracy was thriving, and Spotify enabled music labels to offer their content through a legal online streaming platform. Over time, Spotify accumulated an impressive catalogue of music and music lovers immediately took to that diversity. Spotify now boasts of more than 35 million songs and covers practically every genre and region. It offers chart rankings, specifically customized and curated content, and suggestions based on user tastes. With their diversity of music, they have become a social network of music, building successful communities of people who like specific content. They have a team that curates this music to user tastes. This humanized music tastes. Users also have followers and friends who can listen to similar music based on their tastes.

Spotify offers freemium services, but their premium service offers much more. Spotify's success got Apple to launch their music streaming business, Apple Music, in 2015 that remains a paid service till date. Spotify Premium allows you to play your playlists better, gives you double the bit-rate, the ability to download up to 10,000 songs to listen to offline and more.

Spotify's business model has been doubted by many. They said 'people won't pay for streaming services'. Besides, iTunes had already been around for five-plus years. But their brilliant execution coupled with 'unlimited songs', and taking full advantage of the music industry's crisis around piracy, proved beneficial for Spotify. With freemium on offer along with their paid service, there were a lot of non-believers in Spotify's business model; yet in seven short years they managed to get over 50 per cent of their subscriber base to pay for their premium services.

One of the biggest success factors at Spotify is their agile engineering culture. When they started off, they started practicing scrum to execute on agile. But too many scrums caused traffic jams and was later replaced by a method they called 'squads and tribes' model'[2] for execution. The squad is a self-functional autonomous team of less than eight people housed together. They build the stuff end-to-end, and the design is executed for a specific mission, strategy or purpose with identified short-term goals. All squads are aligned by strategy or overall goals from the leadership. Loosely coupled but tightly aligned squads allows them to work like a tribe. The entire success is also based on cross pollination of ideas and standards rather than that of standardization and dissemination. The success of multiple squads creates de facto standards, rather than the other way around.

Each squad owns a small system and is responsible for its upkeep and integration. The architecture is integrated by Spotify, providing customers a number of services (through small systems). The basis of its success stems also from its culture of 'sharing' versus 'owning', making the model work really well. Since code is shared where needed, peer reviews are also quite common.

Over time design and standards start to emerge. That becomes the basis for the organization to mature.

Today, Spotify is valued at $8 billion, which says a lot for a great idea with exemplary execution.

FLYING HIGH WITH VALUE

My nephews and nieces introduced me to drones, these small flying objects that became an obsession for them to play with. My interest in photography and videography meant that I had observed many of these gadgets being used in filming. I always wanted to try one out, but the laws in India weren't exactly conducive to go down that path.

Before that, the only time we had really heard of drones was in context of their use by the US military for air strikes in a foreign land.

But the world changed forever with the use of drones in commercial and personal photography as it offered us a completely different dimension, i.e. the aerial shot.

Frank Wang is known to the world as 'the drone billionaire'. His company Da-Jiang Innovation Technology (DJI) controls over two-thirds of the consumer UAV (unmanned aerial vehicle) market and is known to be the Apple of drones. Set up in 2006, it manufactures UAVs for amateurs, professionals and industrial use. The company has also diversified into camera accessories like gimbals and stabilizers.

Wang's own dream was to create a device with a camera that could follow him (the seed for the CX). He found his calling when he managed to build a helicopter in his dorm room but failed at the class presentation. Also, within the first two years of setting up the company, DJI, all his co-founders left him. His first breakthrough came about in 2011 when the cost of manufacturing fell significantly to a sub-$500 figure. Within two years of that, by 2013, he managed to put up their then flagship product, the DJI Phantom, which bundled software, propellers, frame, a gimbal for the camera and a remote control for sale.

Today DJI enjoys a whopping $10 billion valuation, with presence across all major continents and countries. DJI's success can be attributed not just to being 'first to market' as other manufacturers soon hit the market. Its focus on quality and a very low learning curve, cost and capability surpassing competition, coupled with its actual technical complexity (barrier to entry) proved to be the ingredients of its success.

However, if one were to attribute DJI's success to one single factor, it would be the fairy tale dream of a young boy of a drone that follows him wherever he goes and how he converted that dream into reality.

CREATING POWERFUL COMMUNITIES

As part of my experience in technology and consulting, I travel quite a bit. While in the US, I was exposed to one of the best community banks there. This Philadelphia-based bank existed simply because of its strong community connect. Competition in the likes of Citi or Bank of America never managed to wipe out its strong customer base because they were simply too good at what they were doing.

My own lessons on the benefits of a community bank were the elements on which its success was created:

- being locally owned and operated
- creating powerful relationships with the community by
    - o   employing from within the community
    - o   working on community programmes
    - o   supporting other local community businesses, and
    - o   having customers from those communities
- building a sense of trust through personal interactions

Another community bank, the United Community Bank,[3] ranks forty-fifth on the *Forbes* list of top banks. The bank, which delivers services in Georgia, North Carolina, South Carolina and Tennessee, built their success through customer service and experience. It also features among the elite in JD Power US Retail Banking Satisfaction Study. The JD Power study[4] shows strong linkages between satisfaction and community and highlights the factors that play a crucial role in this. These include,

- building communities around digital technology
- providing branch only, and
- offering communication and advice

Another example of my experience around the importance of communities comes from my work in Latin America, which required me to set up a local office. We were just starting off, hence co-working spaces were the best option to begin with. That shared workspace marked the beginning of a deeper understanding within me that businesses built around communities are here to stay. This experience eventually led me to the discovery of the American company that has revolutionized the concept of co-working spaces, WeWork.

WeWork provides shared workspaces for individuals, start-ups and small and large businesses alike, providing them with an environment to build a community. Their philosophy goes beyond infrastructure and brings together high-speed Internet, comfortable workspaces and relaxation zones, printers and refreshments. A connected experience allows you to ask for feedback, recommendations, or just network with people from diverse sectors to expand your professional circle. It also hosts events that enable people to network in order to find work and business opportunities within the network. By redefining workspaces, WeWork managed to create a different business model to office space renting.

Over time, high impact groups have formed within these co-working spaces. By connecting individuals, who might otherwise be lonely in their professional pursuits, WeWork creates communities and helps individual businesses grow. It creates organic connections through social events within common spaces.

Another powerful story impacting communities comes from the Harley-Davidson brand. It has a cult following that would be willing do anything for their favourite company. Though their initial successes came from the deployment of their motorcycles in WWI and WWII, the brand's following became stronger with time due to excellent ride quality and reliability. These factors saw their footprint and following increase beyond the US, into Europe, Asia and Latin America.

The Harley brand was created by capitalizing on '"personality'. Over time, they had to broaden the scope of their unique brand of 'personality' to connect with a wider audience and freedom and power remain core elements of the brand personality statement across the globe.

The Harley-Davidson story, however, isn't without its setbacks. An important lesson for every company is that when your community shrinks, so does your customer base as Harley-Davidson found out the hard way.[5] Its persona was not made for the current crop of millennials and the brand does not have the same following amongst this demographic. This has caused a serious loss of market share for Harley-Davidson in recent years. The lesson here is that when your community starts to morph, you need to adapt.

THINK DIFFERENTLY

In my career as an employee, I had got onto a hamster wheel of doing the same thing again and again. Yet expectation was that 'I should get different results this time around'. The immediate reaction to this as an outsider is that 'this isn't common sense'. As a consultant and independent adviser in recent years, however, I quickly realized that 'common sense isn't common practice'.

This behaviour is not just a problem with individuals. When ninety organizations take a decision to turn right, the ninety-first one will take the same approach. That ninety-first organization will be stuck in the same hamster wheel, with the only differentiation being in terms of incremental improvements for better CX.

If you take the automotive sector, for example, the profit and loss (P&L) of that business is built around petrol and diesel engines. As environmentalists are building considerable awareness around greenhouse gas emissions created by the automobile sector, some of these manufacturers are shifting their focus towards electric cars, electric scooters, electric bicycles and lately electric bikes. The benefit of this, of course, is no emissions once the vehicle is charged.

Yet the final electric mobility product was just a small experiment in the chain for most automobile manufacturers as they feared change.

To break that fear, it took a completely different company, Tesla, to accelerate a sustainable mass market electric car proposition.

Even if you take BMW who have fairly deep pockets, their flagship electric offering, the i8, takes over 2 hours to charge but extends its range as a hybrid car to around 330 miles.[6] Currently, the fastest way to refuel the car is at a gas station as it takes a few hours for the current generation of batteries to be charged. This deficiency in charging has led the industry to focus on three kinds of new battery technologies: solid-state, sodium-ion, and lithium-sulphur, as well as charging technologies like gallium nitride (GaN).

Battery technology will definitely improve over the next 2–5 years, but results are needed in the interim if electric cars are to become more mainstream. A Taiwanese start-up Gogoro,[7] founded by Horace Luke and Matt Taylor, did just that. Since its birth in 2011, Gogoro have been focused on investing in smarter, cleaner sustainable technologies. With the invention of the Gogoro smart scooter (app based and sensor driven), they provided the ability for instant diagnostics to detect maintenance issues and established a network of hot-swappable batteries to refuel in 6 seconds. Over 1,200 Gogoro stations open 24/7 allow you to swap batteries for fully charged ones. They have over 1,00,000 battery exchanges every day, making the playing field fair across gas and electric vehicles. This kind of swapping facility had been offered in other electronic equipment, but is a first for vehicles. There is a station every kilometre in urban areas, making refuelling a breeze. With its partnership with Panasonic, Gogoro has also ensured that its li-ion technology is reliable. This makes them different from the rest of the crowd.

BUILDING BLOCKS TO A MARATHON

Continuing from the earlier story, applying logic, you might conclude that all new business models are built through new companies that have the hunger to succeed. Let's break that myth.

As a young boy growing up in the 1970s and 1980s I played with Lego blocks. My daughter now plays with them in 2020. As a corporation, Lego[8] never posted a loss between 1932 to 1998. It had been a part of the growing-up years of at least three generations of children, and yet by 2003, it looked like it was likely to go under with over $800 million in debt and their internal reports also revealed that the company hadn't yielded value in the last decade. At the time I was quite disappointed that I may not be able to share my childhood joys with my own children.

Lego was given the wrong advice to look at other companies like the US toys and entertainment giant, Mattel. By doing so and diversifying into clothes, theme parks, video games, jewellery, etc. almost did Lego in.

Yet by 2015, their fortunes had reversed. The company continued to remain family owned and made profits in excess of £660 million. They also stayed put on the pedestal as the number one toy maker in Europe and Asia, number three in North America, and overtook Ferrari to claim the title of the world's most powerful brand.

So, what changed between 2008 and 2015? Their CEO Jørgen Vig Knudstorp first dumped things they had no expertise in, and hived off Legoland Parks to Merlin Entertainments. He halved their inventory and encouraged interaction with Lego fans. He promoted adult Lego conventions and events like Brickworld. Lego also promoted crowdsourced competitions for design and content and gave away 1 per cent of net sales to winning ideas.

Their ability to create new toys like replicas of Burj Khalifa, Robie House and the Guggenheim; conduct ethnographic studies of children around the world; build a brand for adults (Lego Architecture); and create a sub-brand aimed at girls, Lego Friends, changed perceptions dramatically.

Their focus on reimagining the brand also resulted in the relaunch of classic successful lines like City and Space. Additionally, they expanded to build programmable robots and began outsourcing, while sticking to their basics—as engineers. That helped the brand create movies, TV shows and partnerships with brilliant people. Their creative teams spent extensive time travelling the world, speaking to children and their families, and participating in their daily lives and activities to understand their customers better. The focus for Lego, has been on the 'kids of today and tomorrow'.

Thus, the once forgotten organization, having lived its legacy for over sixty years, innovated. While listening to its customers—adults and children alike—it became 'the Apple of toys', and the engineer of design-driven miracles.

CREATING MAGIC

When you use the word magic, my mind goes back to Disney World and to all things Disney. I have been continuously exposed to Disney and Disney World as a kid and as a parent. Yet most of my clients can't keep up with that word, when it comes to treating their customers well. That's what led me to dig this story out to tell.

Disney is probably the most recognized CX brand in the world. Disney is movies (Pixar, Marvel, Lucasfilm), music (Hollywood Records, Disney Music Group, RMI Recordings), television (cartoons), streaming (Disney+), theme parks and hotels (Disney World), and, of course, merchandise. If you want to get a sense of scale, just go visit a Disney theme park.

The Disney experience is not cheap, especially at their theme parks. Guests book online to cut queues, choosing their rides and where they want to have lunch. Disney then delivers the 'magic band' by mail. The band cuts queues and within 30 seconds you are in for your favourite experience.

Disney trains their employees to see things through the eyes of their customers. The focus is always on detail. So, while customers are experiencing the 'Cinderella magic', employees are ensuring that the magic does not get disrupted. People can 'feel' that perfection. Whether its architecture design, landscaping, lighting, colour, signages, music, smell, taste, and even floor surfaces and carpets, everything gets the same attention to detail. What's more, the Disney Institute also provides custom advisory solutions around CX to other businesses.

But the company's success came from failure. Walt Disney, the man himself, turned failure into lessons he could imbibe to improve. As he said at one point in time,

'I failed . . . I think it's important to have a good hard failure when you're young . . . I learned a lot out of that.'

Disney offers a number of innovative CX solutions to ensure customer satisfaction. Disney theme parks attracts a lot of children who stand in queues for rides and are often ineligible for those rides due to height restrictions. Disney employees are trained to recognize frustration and give these kids priority passes to skip the queue for their next ride.

Disney also recognizes that its customers speak many languages. Disney employees are language certified and wear pins for them. They are also given adequate training to imbibe the company's customer culture of courtesy and great communication skills.

Disney respects guests with special needs who are given DAS (disability access services) cards to reduce wait times.

The Disney magic extends into their hotel rooms that are embedded within their theme parks. Their FastPass+ service allows you to reserve rides, a customizable magic band allows you to unlock your resort hotel room, connect to Disney's photo-pass account, and check in at FastPass entrances. To add to all this, there are many other surprises waiting for you at every turn.

Why have they put in so much thought to detail? Disney regards their customers as ambassadors. Hence, they intensively train their employees for soft skills and with the values and cultures that they want to showcase to their customers.

Even for a market leader in CX like Disney, they have had to continuously transform to remain at the top and adapt to keep up with the times. Their customers moved to digital and they had to too. The effort put in by Michael Eisner till 2005, and Bob Iger afterwards, set the tone for their transformation. His impact was so important that Iger was requested to stay on till the end of 2018 to continue the transformation. Disney's board is no stranger to transformation as illustrious people like Jack Dorsey (Twitter), Steve Jobs (Apple), Sheryl Sandberg (Facebook), or Orin Smith (Starbucks) have been part of it at some point or the other.

Disney transparently puts out its R&D efforts on YouTube. Disney Research, for example, extended their technology to edit footage from their cameras into coherent videos. Other examples of their transformation efforts includes movies, remote controlled Internet of things (IoT) toys, 3D printed teddy bears, player-created Disney video games, a gaming community and more.

All of this goes on to prove that Disney's physical age and brand leadership of decades did not matter. The company and the brand were young at heart and continuously took initiatives to move forward. In every respect, they embraced the 'digital' future.

TURNING TABLES

'Losers quit when they fail. Winners fail until they succeed.'

—Robert T. Kiyosaki

My parents have often repeated a proverbial saying in Tamil, 'Even elephants slip and fall.' What this means is that past success is not a guarantee against future failure.

As an adviser, I have had the opportunity of looking at businesses that were highly successful, and others that practically had their backs to the wall.

Even big businesses have had their fair share of failures. But because their successes were more massive, they learnt great lessons from their failures and moved on. However, those companies that did not learn from their failures paid the price.

The reason for those businesses' failures can be due to many accounts—failure to innovate, failure to adapt to change, failure to leverage and integrate, failure to understand the market, failure to recognize risks, or failure to plan. Ultimately, they ran out of funds to support their failures, and were consigned to the history books.

Individual failures can be rectified quickly, whereas failures in the market place have a far-reaching impact on the company, product, or service, and even the nation, that becomes difficult to unentangle and reverse.

The biggest failures start to appear when you begin to over-leverage your balance sheet. Failure is extraordinarily expensive, but learning from it can be extremely sapient, fulfilling and rewarding. You don't necessarily need to fail to learn but being aware of shortcomings prevents you from repeating others' mistakes. In the following section, I have cherry picked some classic examples of failures to provide others a better chance at success.

STARBUCKS[9] IN AUSTRALIA

My trips to Australia provided me with the delightful opportunity to drink great coffee from local cafes. I noticed that there were very few Starbucks in comparison to other developed countries and I started digging into this by talking to colleagues and friends. I also did a bit of research and that led to this story.

Australians love to spend time at cafés and attach a great deal of importance to the quality of coffee that they drink. They acquired the coffee-drinking culture from Italian and Greek immigrants in the 1900s. The Australian market has matured over time and has developed its own version of specialty coffees. The per capita consumption of coffee is one of the highest in the world and most notable is the fact that Australians consume one cup of coffee out of home for every two consumed at home.

Starbucks, an American coffeehouse chain, prides itself on its high quality coffee. Its unique CX started at its first store in 1971.

Through aggressive expansion they went global in 1992 with 165 stores. Starbucks entered Australia in July 2000 by opening its first store in Sydney when Australia's coffee culture was already thriving. They were hugely successful with more than 87 per cent market share in the US and opening a store every day somewhere in the world.

Their competitor in the Australian market was Gloria Jeans Coffee, a Chicago-based coffeehouse chain which had entered Australia in 1996 and was already successful by following a franchisee model. For Starbucks, their entry into Australia seemed like it would be a walk in the park and the Gloria Jeans story validated this assumption.

Starbucks read into the Gloria Jeans Coffee example as criterion for their own success, and started opening multiple outlets to tap into this demand and by 2008, they had 87 stores. However, they landed up with $142 million in losses in the first seven years of operation and Starbucks Australia simply could not sustain itself. It announced shutting down of sixty-one of its stores in 2008, in the midst of the global financial crisis which added to the company's growing troubles.

The important question here is 'Why didn't Starbucks succeed in Australia, while boutique cafes did?' This, despite the fact that Australians travelled out of their way for a good cup of coffee?

Let's remember that everything starts with understanding your customer while we look into this case. Australians had developed a palate for straighter and stronger coffees without flavours and syrups that was one of the cornerstones of the global success of the US chain. Also, Starbucks stuck to their successful formula of coffee sales focusing on 'to-go' or takeaways. Such coffee was cheaper at local cafes across Australia.

The sector is customer-driven and the survival of coffee shops is driven by a strong understanding of their local customer. In Australia, the national average consumption of coffee per cafe was high at 11 kilograms a week, but coffee shops needed to sell more than 15 kilograms to make profit. Also, since good coffee needed good baristas who had deep knowledge of local flavour and culture, they were naturally in high demand.

Starbucks came into a mature market and stuck to its own range of coffees that had their own flavour profile, and asked customers to adapt to their products. Starbucks didn't really try to adjust to local flavours and culture and relied on a success strategy that was based on international presence and quick expansion. However, without localization and the lack of customer expansion, Starbucks Australia failed to create a unique brand personality and suffered by the 'sameness syndrome'.

So, my questions are, 'Was the market too crowded? Or, was there a downtrend that Starbucks rode through?' Research indicated a market consumption growth of 5 per cent between 2000 and 2007, with over 14,000 cafes and restaurants generating $9.7 billion in income.[10] Clearly, then, answers lie elsewhere.

LESSONS FROM BARNES & NOBLE

During my time in the US, looking for new books to read at the bookstore chain Barnes & Noble became my favourite weekend hangout. The chain had become a household name with a reputation to beat. There obviously wasn't anything similar in India at the time although Kinokuniya filled that gap for me in the UAE and South East Asia. Yet the story that played out in the Barnes & Noble case was a failure to recognize an emerging trend.

Barnes & Noble was first in a number of innovations; it was the first bookseller to advertise on national television (1974), the first bookseller to offer *New York Times* bestsellers at 40 per cent of their listed prices (1975), and others. The chain grew through acquisition of Marlboro Books to achieve a nationwide status (1979), of the shopping mall-based B. Dalton chain (1987) to expand into this retail space, and Fictionwise (2009) to become the leader in the growing e-book business. Innovation also came with experimenting with different store formats and sizes and Barnes & Noble combined physical stores, mail-order and online presence to reach Superstore status as early as 1992.

But Barnes & Noble made a serious mistake as they didn't think much of another formidable competitor Amazon's strategy. At the time, Amazon was just another book reseller that didn't make profits till 2001. But in 2007, the e-book reader, Kindle, came along giving Amazon a much-needed foothold in the publishing sector. Competition was fierce, but by 2007 Barnes & Noble[11] saw their profits sliding. Physical books weren't selling as much, and toys and games made their way into bookstores. Footfall in malls was going down too as a direct impact of Amazon's e-tailing strategy. By 2010, Amazon started selling more e-books than hardbacks and paperbacks. By 2011–12, things were out in the open—print sales were dropping 9 per cent annually and digital sales were on the rise. To make matters worse for physical bookstores, Borders, Barnes & Noble's chief competitor, was declared bankrupt in 2011, and established consumer players like Sony joined the bandwagon with their own e-book readers.

Amazon was hungry for survival and redefined innovation. In addition to its Kindle strategy, it got into audiobooks with its purchase of Audible, the digital comic bookstore Comixology and the go-to social network for readers, Goodreads.

In effect they got their CX strategy right. First, by understanding how book lovers like to consume books, and, secondly, by introducing the delivery model that, in effect, changed delivery times from a few days or weeks to an instant!

THE BIG VW FAIL—THE PROMISE
THAT NEVER WAS

'The difficulty of being good.'

—Gurcharan Das

'You simply can't play rugby in a soccer field.'

—Anonymous

As a youngster, I was schooled in Dusseldorf, Germany, thanks to my father who got posted there. In those days the Berlin Wall still existed, and we were in West Germany. My father's German friend drove a Volkswagen (VW) Beetle, and its quirky shape appealed to my youthful senses.

But as history folded out, the brand created an even more powerful lesson for me to digest with great difficulty. Here's that story.

It is well-established that people connect to a promise of value and fulfilment of that value creates the brand. Brands have to play within the ambit of strict regulations and benchmarks that customers also associate with. This, in turn, leads to innovation and the sunset of traditional technologies.

For VW, the case was no different. VW needed to provide fuel efficient cars with excellent emission standards adhering to benchmarks and regulatory guidelines. The reputation of VW is linked to marques like Audi, Bugatti, Porsche, Lamborghini and others in its group. The US has always been a competitive market and the likes of Toyota found answers with hybrids. With the Environment Protection Agency (EPA) pushing strict emission standards for diesel engines in 2004, it became a steeper engineering challenge for car makers. Standards continued to ratchet up between 2004 and 2007 and players like—Hyundai, Mazda, Honda and Nissan—backed off from the diesel vehicles market. VW saw an opportunity there as their market share was only 5 per cent and this segment was of strategic importance.

Over the period from 2010 leading up to the 'Dieselgate' scandal, their growth in the US market climbed steadily. From the initial low double digits growth to over 20 and 30 per cent in some years—a fantastic market share to boast of, for a European manufacturer. Its brand reputation also climbed steadily and with increased localization and positive sales of other products, VW's profits surged.

VW's engineers seemed to have pulled off the impossible by meeting those stringent emissions standards. But in 2015, the truth came to light. Their squeaky-clean image, built on top-notch engineering and innovation, with an outstanding reputation suffered a big dent. It was discovered that VW conducted tests with devices and software fitted to circumvent the emission requirements. So, in effect the engineers circumvented the problem and met EPA norms not by meeting standards, but by faking it during the tests and turning them off during normal driving. The details of the story emerged and the authorities realized it wasn't a rogue mission but calculated deception from VW. The intent here is not to go into the barebones of the scandal but to explain the impact that faking had on the company.[12]

The repercussions from VW's point of view was imprisonment for its leadership and US $32 billion in lawsuits, fines and penalties for starters. It also meant a serious dent to the image of the German car industry in the US, and its reputation across the globe. Within weeks nobody came in to buy VW vehicles anymore.

Unsurprisingly, VW's ratings tumbled more than 17 per cent in a single year in Temkin Experience Ratings,[13] representing the biggest decline of any company in any industry.

With time, however, the company did pick themselves up, clean their act and get back into the market. Even today, the numbers aren't quite the same and the impact has still not rubbed off with pending lawsuits and claims for damages.

As an unfortunate poster child, the lesson for VW was to carefully tread the difficult road to growth and success like competitors such as Mazda and Honda.

Had VW considered the consequences, the outcomes, the impact on CX and other deeper ramifications, it could have prevented this. Short-term success came at the cost of long-term failure. Their competitive strategy was inferior and the emissions technology did not exist at its parent company in Europe as well. VW would certainly have benefitted many multiples by just putting the money into research and development (R&D). The reputational damage to VW due to Dieselgate was global and will continue to impact the brand in the near future. This case is an important lesson in consequences to making false claims given that the event was controllable.

THE BIG AIRPORT FAILURE

I have always seen that when we engage with customers, they start discussing their issues with us. Often legacy issues play a significant role in driving businesses out of competition. The answers often lie in transformation. Transformation invariably involves technology upgrade and large software platform shifts. This presents one of the most difficult experiences for organizations that fail to adapt. Adaptation is often difficult and it doesn't matter if it's a new line of businesses or an existing one. The challenges are very similar.

We do educate clients on things that could go wrong on Day One. But no two projects are the same.

The common denominators to success are rigorous preparation and to start slow. Soft staff launches are preferred with a few known customers to manage the glitches associated with a full launch. With extensive trials in the first month, and ironing out issues, you can keep adding customers and expand thereafter.

That is easier said than done when a country is trying to launch a new airport. As an interim strategy, some new airports in India start with a few airlines, test the robustness of their operating model before going full steam with all major airlines.

That wasn't the case with London Heathrow's Terminal 5. Heathrow's T5[14] was a spectacular feat of engineering and promised flyers a big boost in service. Opened in 2008 with self-service kiosks, fast drop bag services, two security zones, massive baggage handling capacity, shops, dining areas and hotels to support every need, it offered the best to travellers. With an overall budget of over US $8 billion, it was one expensive airport to boot.

T5 launched as a massive airport with a full-blown systems failure and caused a bit of a national embarrassment. Before the opening, the baggage handling system was tested and re-tested to get the final nod. On Day One, however, it was bugged by real life scenarios like manual baggage removals, computer software glitches that erroneously told passengers that their flights had taken off, amongst other issues. The result was mayhem. With over 500 flight cancellations, ten days of disruptions and 42,000 bags that failed to travel with passengers, it affected operations of Lufthansa, British Airways and American Airlines, amongst others.

The advisory from the airport was a clear one, 'Please pack essentials in hand baggage. We are sorry for the mistake, and we are investigating the issue'.

While it's the right thing to accept and fix the problem as soon as possible, the problem itself possibly could have been avoided in the first place.

While I look back with my notes on handling large transformations, I notice many similarities in what I have personally witnessed with the Heathrow Terminal 5 case:

- Lack of sufficient training for staff;
- Overproviding staff on opening day wasn't really done;
- The absence of a crisis management team on that day at the terminal;
- A 'software filter' to prevent the generation of specimen messages by the baggage system was forgotten. Hence, the baggage system did not seem to recognize some bags and they were sent for manual sorting;
- Server capacity was not stress tested adequately enough;
- British Airways turned a deaf ear to staff concerns, leading to more chaos;
- When things go into Plan B, baggage handlers were required to bail out. There simply weren't enough baggage handlers to manage the situation;
- The Big Bang approach to move everything in Day One;
- Staff complaints about not understanding the system went unheard;

- The airport was under pressure to meet the deadline, despite knowing those risks.

THE BIG JUICY FAILURE

'Life's too short to build something nobody wants.'

—Ash Maurya

Every time I help a client build a new product, the question invariably starts with, 'What does the customer want?' The next 3 sentences that follow indicates whether we know or we don't know. But what about if that answer cost you a whopping $118.5 million? That's what this story is all about.

In 2013, Juicero,[15] a Silicon Valley start-up introduced a $699 Wi-Fi connected luxury juicer, and the company's founder Doug Evans labelled it the 'Keurig for Juice'. This was based on the founder's idea to build a solution. However, the problem was that 'nobody saw this as a problem that required solving in the first place'.

The company found out quickly that the price was too high. So the price was cut to $399 after negative press about the product. But if you add to this facts like the product was not adequately user tested and the company tried to expand too quickly, the unexpected starts to become expected—the founder simply ran out of money.

The product did not have enough 'common sense' built into it. It required proprietary juice packs, which were diced fruits and vegetables, that were juiced. There was a joke going around that it would have been easier for a user to squeeze the fruits with their hands than use the expensive contraption.

This start-up lesson is no different from other failures—90 per cent of all start-ups fail, 70 per cent as they scale up too fast and 42 per cent because they didn't serve a market need. Juicero failed on both counts. If they had launched this on Kickstarter and done consumer research they could have avoided an expensive blunder. Juicero cost investors US $118.5 million.

There are larger companies that bury such failures as unsuccessful R&D; the story is different for start-ups. Take the case of the Bose Sleepbuds. They were officially retired on 31 December 2019 after their batteries failed to function leading to dissatisfied customers even though they had a successful campaign on Indiegogo.

IN SUMMARY—FOUR

The easiest thing we love to do is to envy others' success and laugh at our neighbours' failures. Under both circumstances, what we need to do is to pay attention. For each of these success and failure stories, there were dozens others that couldn't make it into the book. As I continue to learn from experience, I have noticed that mistakes don't really happen in isolation and are often repeated time and time again.

Five

Why Do It?

If you look at the once great organizations that have lost their share of customers, which, in turn, led to a rapid decline in their top and bottom lines, that would immediately tell you that CX is the only way to grow.

Over the years, I have unravelled the simple secrets to CX success. The Great Wall of China between me and my customers has to disappear. The more invisible it is, the better is the CX.

'70 per cent of buying experiences are based on how the customer feels they are being treated.'

—McKinsey & Company

Too many marketeers don't understand how they and their consumers' minds interact. As a customer, I recognize that I am emotionally connected to my favourite brands. Forrester, the American market research company, puts the mark at consumers being '4.5 times more likely to pay the premium' for an excellent CX. The expectations of consumers from their preferred brands keeps going higher, and they truly expect these brands to know them. If the brand cannot adapt, they move on.

CX is not established in a single step. It's a 3-step process: 1) active customers for longer periods of time, 2) becoming loyal to you, and 3) driving advocacy. Loyalty and advocacy drives revenue growth while bringing down costs of acquisition and the cost to serve. In addition, advocates also reduce stress. All of these drive long-term success.

The confidence in taking steps towards CX comes from results, which in turn comes from measurements. If I can't measure it, I don't pursue it. My clients always talk about mileage in terms of '*Kitna deti hai?*' or 'What do I get in return?' in English. A CX programme is built around 3 pillars: measure your CX, measure your return on investment (ROI), and measure your composite results.

Measurements start with leading indicators. Leading indicators always link back to a financial metric—revenue, churn, customer penetration or customer life-time value.

Again, to establish measurement, you start with a hypothesis using a simple formula. The hypothesis is based on the number of customers you think you will gain by putting out value. You charge customers for the perceived value, deduct incidental costs and arrive at profits. Customers hear and fully comprehend the firm's offerings, which merits the purchase. By listening to this constant dynamic between customer perception and your strategy, you drive your CX.

This is why I love the crowdfunding method. It starts really small and doesn't cause a dent to profit and loss (P&L) of the idea. In crowdfunding, investments follow the route of customer perception and this leads us to acquiring active customers.

That long period for active customers to turn loyal takes nine months or more. My clients always want to get 'fast food' results. This means they are after quick wins, execution and monitoring. However, client excitement in quick wins and low hanging fruits have pitfalls. These early gains need to expand into full blown maturity across customers for a CX strategy to be successful.

Let me give you an example. Bose, the American audio equipment manufacturer, managed to acquire active customers with its Sleepbuds through a crowdfunding campaign. Yet, the product was undermined with battery quality issues leading to its ultimate withdrawal from the market. Negative word of mouth spreads quickly, so Bose had to get to the root of this soon enough. They broke down the problem into its constituent elements.

For moving from active customers to loyal customers, the biggest underlying factor is consistency.

Let's take another example. My Hyundai dealership has been giving me consistent service for the last fifteen years. Every time they take a car in for service, they call the day before and confirm the appointment. Their service adviser calls when the car has been inspected and confirms the servicing tasks that need to be performed, followed by confirmation that the service has been completed. After this, a customer experience executive calls to confirm whether a 10/10 service level has been achieved and offers to fix anything that may have gone wrong. The service engineer is rated on each and every individual interaction for his performance. Hyundai's improvements over the last fifteen years have turned me into an advocate for the brand. More the advocates, stronger the brand.

> Did you know that 'Your loyal top 10 per cent spend 3 times more per order than the lower 90 per cent and your top 1 per cent of customers spend 5 times more than the lower 90 per cent.'

> —RJ Metrics Study

There are multiple ways to test your customers' advocacy. A great example these days is the introduction of customer schemes, where a customer gets enrolled into a customer programme. These programmes are a little different to a referral programme we have been undertaking over the years. In these programmes, advocates recommend the product to friends and followers with a 10 per cent discount code. That discount would then be honoured by the company and the advocate, in turn, gets additional benefits. The more the referrals, the stronger the influencer.

'After 10 purchases, you refer 50 per cent more people than a one-time purchaser.'

—Bain & Company

In this journey of turning an active customer into an advocate, you will find many opportunities to upsell. In fact, I keep re-enforcing my belief in the fact that it's five times more expensive to acquire a new customer than to retain an existing one.

Many of my clients have a strong belief in chasing new customers. I see 80 per cent of marketing budgets going towards acquiring customers. Yet, even a 1 per cent increase in the number of good and repeatable customers improves revenue by as much as 10 per cent. Over time, many of my clients discover that you have a much higher probability of selling a product to an existing customer (60–70 per cent) versus a new prospect (5–20 per cent).

When an established organization has such a disproportionate marketing spend towards new customers, it's generally a direct reflection of a poor 'Say:Do' ratio. In these cases, the general approach taken by marketing professionals is to conduct focus groups which throw up raving results only to be followed by disappointment in market acceptance. This is because they didn't focus on all of the elements of CX.

Over the years, in my travels to other countries, I see organizations trying to establish a forced means of stickiness by putting customer contracts into place to prevent defection. I can't think of a poorer way to try and gain customer loyalty.

These kinds of strong-arm tactics lead to a stronger attrition rate of customers. With adequate corrections, we have been able to establish that a 2 per cent increase in customer retention has the same effect as a 10 per cent reduction in operating costs.

But what happens when you do just the reverse. You have a strong 'Say:Do' ratio and you start looking at your CX parameters and getting down to executing it? The result is clear. You definitely retain more customers.

'A 5 per cent increase in customer retention can increase a company's profitability by 75 per cent.'

—Bain & Company

THE ROI FOR GOOD CUSTOMER EXPERIENCE

I love the Indian mindset of jugaad and asking for mileage. It's a simple way of asking for a good ROI. It's often the basis for business sponsorship for new products and services. Yet not everyone goes back to check on the actual ROI after the hypothesis has been laid bare. Eventually, the products are relegated to the history books but not before the damage to the organization has been done.

Now that we have established the 'Why' we need to do it, we can lay foundation to the next section of the book and talk about the three important steps in this direction for creating the ROI that our business desperately needs:

1. What do we need to do?
2. How should I go about executing it?
3. Measurement frameworks and counterbalances to correct.

Remember that by sticking to indifference, we will continue to dig our own graves.

'In the last year, 67 per cent of customers have hung up the phone out of frustration that they could not talk to a real person, or get an answer quickly.'

—American Express Survey

As I was helping one of the banks 'humanize financial services',[1] I recognized that strong intentions need to be backed by strong commitments. And these strong commitments were always established by investments in the right direction. From two other experiences, that I will discuss in the next section, I also recognized that if the vision and direction is not clear, the whole exercise becomes a money burning exercise.

The commitment in all of these cases was on a multi-year transformation.

The next section of the book is designed to be a little more prescriptive. In it, I have penned down clear lessons from my experiences to help you put them into practice in whatever stage of your CX journey you may be in.

IN SUMMARY - FIVE

While benchmarks are good to acknowledge, it is important to test these with your own data to tailor them for your industry. Your investments into CX data sciences will pay off and you will take informed decisions on your next CX programme. But by postponing those decisions to invest, you are inviting a larger problem to solve in the coming months.

Lastly, but more importantly, you need to recognize and embrace the fact that you exist because of your customers. By focusing on your customers, and by being prudent, you will get good ROI.

In Section II, chapter ten talks about standards and measurements that deal extensively on key performance indicators (KPI's) and how to measure your returns. If you are curious, please feel free to go there directly or come back here to continue your CX journey.

SECTION II

EXECUTING FOR RESULTS

Six

The Commitment

'Excellence is not a destination; it is a continuous journey that never ends.'

—Brian Tracy

My experiences have defined my thinking. I work with clients globally to improve their organizations. Yet, more powerful lessons are out there that are unbelievable and beyond our imagination. When you want to expand organizational level achievements to a country, you can imagine the daunting task. Yet, one country that I have continuously been awed by is Singapore which I frequently visit to meet family as well as conduct business.

Singapore[1] is an island, country and city in South East Asia with less than 6 million people living across 721.5 square km. Although it does not have any significant natural resources, it boasts of one of the highest per capita incomes in the world with zero foreign debt. Singapore's progress can be assessed from photographs over the past 60 years. One of Singapore's jewels is its airport, Changi, which contributes over 6 per cent of its gross domestic product (GDP) and employs over 1,60,000 people.

Changi has been rated as the best airport for several years running. It connects over 100 airlines to 400 cities in 100 countries, with over 65 million passengers passing through their airports each year. Changi is committed to doubling passenger traffic and employment over the next twenty years. Though it will remain a small market for passengers actually visiting Singapore, it is making strides to improve that as well.

It remains one of the easiest airports to pass through, with cameras and monitoring technology to help planes, laser-guided technologies for disembarkation, friendly self-check-ins even for eighty-year-olds, and an automatic robot vacuum 'Buddy' to help keep the airport terminals clean. There is enough to do to recharge and relax on a transit. There are multiple gardens, massage chairs, movie theatres, a roof top swimming pool, shopping, gaming, or even a visit to its latest attraction, the Changi Jewel.

This success is built on the foundation of commitment.

BUILD YOUR CUSTOMER EXPERIENCE BRAND

Changi chose CX for its success and then turned to *kaizen*. The Japanese word 'kaizen' refers to the art of continuous improvement from factory workers to CEOs and across all its functions. This is a daily process and each small idea makes a one-degree difference to the organization. Imagine how small changes implemented everyday can make a massive change by the end of the year.

I started to dive deeper into the one-degree difference principle after I spoke to pilots during my long waits.

Assume you need to take a flight from New York to Chicago with an average flying time of two hours and thirty-three minutes. It needs a flight plan and involves a fuel calculation to ensure that the aircraft can safely reach its destination. It combats against headwinds, tailwinds, air temperature differences and caters for diversions due to unforeseen circumstances. This requires millions of calculations and calibrations to make sure you reach your destination safely at the scheduled time. It is one of US's busiest sectors catering to over 3 million customers boarding over 30,000 aircrafts over the course of a year. The minimum expectation from a customer flying this route is that they will arrive at their destination on time. While the schedule does not change every day and the commitment to punctuality remains uniform, the weather and other conditions like airport traffic, holiday season, competitor flight cancellations, etc. do not.

I figured that my client's commitment towards CX is no different. It involves millions of interventions every day of every year to make that experience exponentially better. So, every person involved directly or indirectly with the customer (in short, everybody), has to think about CX. Ideas, however big or small, can make a difference towards calibrating that experience.

As an apprentice, I had the privilege of visiting various factory floors. Many years later, I figured out the connection of the kaizen (5S) principles to the smooth working of the factory floor.

1. Sort—reduce the number of moving parts in a process, eliminate obstacles and create useful space;
2. Set in order—create a smooth workflow;
3. Shine—regular maintenance, operability, safety and inspection (somebody walking within 50 feet can detect the problem within 5 seconds);
4. Standardize—establish principles, procedures and schedules; and
5. Self-discipline—do without being told.

In the flight path, automation assists the pilot on keeping course and continuously calibrates to provide for the 5s. When the pilot chooses a manual mode, they override it. For example, for take offs or landings, abnormal circumstances, or when something, say an animal or debris, shows up on the runway, the pilot has to factor in time to switch from automatic to manual and be ready for the unexpected. Similarly, your organization has to continuously keep its hands on the controls to ensure you can quickly switch from automatic to manual mode.

When I look back on why I shop at Amazon, the simple answer is 'convenience'.

The entire Amazon business model is built around 'convenience'. In 1994, the closest thing to convenience was the convenience store. Yet, Amazon managed to turn that into a completely different industry. Back then, customers had to go to the bookstore to browse and then buy books. Jeff Bezos started out of his garage without even an inventory of books and no fancy equipment or software. All he had was a brand promise to be the world's most customer centric company.

It wasn't until a year later in July 1995 that it sold its first book. A computer scientist named John Wainwright became the company's first customer when he bought a book on artificial intelligence. Books were difficult to damage during transit and easy to ship. It took Amazon more than two years to grow to more than a dozen employees and move out from the garage into a small warehouse.

Like the 5S in kaizen, Amazon realized the pain of people having to pay 'shipping and handling charges' and then wait for weeks for the delivery. By 1999, One Click was born (now known as Amazon Prime aka, fast fulfilment). Customers found ways of doing business with Amazon easier as they could return what they didn't want or if the product failed the promise given by sellers. During their initial days, Amazon introduced the 'Customers who bought this also bought' feature. This was an early data analytic tool that enabled Amazon to understand its customer. However, their big data analytics continuously evolved to what it is today. They mastered the ability to ship in anticipation using predictive analytics for which they have a patent. This is quite risky as, after all, returns would destroy their business model completely if they got this wrong. Today, their data model includes what customers have bought, information of other similar customers, virtual shopping carts, browsing experiences, ratings and reviews and wish list information. Traditional organizations have not taken advantage of many of these aspects towards creating their own data models. Amazon took analytics to a personal level to determine what you need or want. This involves 'embracing agile' and doing extensive regression testing before allowing these analytical engines to go mainstream.

To get back to their history, Amazon quickly realized that it needed capital and sourced public funds in 1997 to expand. In August 1998 it announced its intentions of moving beyond books but it wasn't until the year 2000 that they allowed third party merchants onto their site. Significantly, it wasn't till 2001 that Amazon turned its first profit. This was also the year when users were finally able to see previews of books but it wasn't till another few years that one could search for key terms inside books. Kindle was launched in 2007 and e-books provided Amazon the technological leap and in 2008 shareholders noticed an exponential growth in stock prices. By 2011, they had partnered with Bank of America in providing business loans for small establishments. It was only in 2012 that India with almost one-sixth of the global population became a market for Amazon.

The above shows that it took Amazon a great deal of time to decode customers bit by bit. But in all of this the promise that they had always reiterated is the big lesson—to 'commit for the long haul'.

MAKING MISTAKES

'The man who makes no mistakes does not usually make anything.'

—E.J. Phelps

One of the biggest challenges I see with my clients is their fear of failure. It drives them to take safe bets that eventually puts them out of business. I am not talking about a brash spirit to destroy what you have built, but the inability to take controlled risks to leapfrog business. Betting on things that ultimately don't work happens all the time. Trends evolve, change and become something else. Somebody else's success does not guarantee yours, even if you copy the same model. My advice is to 'choose your own identity'. Be honest to yourself and to your customer.

Even the giants have made their share of mistakes. Take Amazon for example. Was their journey all hunky dory? No, they have had their fair share of failures[2] with the Fire Phone (2015); Amazon Local—similar to Groupon (2011–2018); Amazon WebPay—similar to Paypal (2007–2014); and many more.

Amazon found ways of reducing their fixed costs to create 'lowest possible prices' for customers.

They learnt that abandonment is one of the warmest leads to a potential sale. The opportunity to convert abandonment into a WOW can generate significant revenue. Amazon has embraced kaizen for CX using 'agile'. Agile methodology promotes continuous iterations and development, while allowing the customer to look at the product much earlier in the life cycle so that small projects can be implemented much faster. By breaking down a large project into a series of small ones, you can get things into execution within a period of 4–6 weeks. By doing this, you derive results much faster than the waiting period of six to nine months in a traditional model. Of course, in this model, the energy required is higher and software developers need to be ready to cater to this massive shift in ideology.

'There are no big problems—there are just a lot of little problems.'

—Henry Ford

You may ask, 'What are the typical challenges that I will face on this journey?' The challenge actually starts with you. Too many organizations are still focused on 'making money first', and they put the customer a distant second. You can see from the Amazon example above, the challenges that organizations need to face in order to succeed. You need to remember that profit is an evolution but CX is a revolution. For this, you need to get obsessed about your customers and you do need to follow some of the personal examples set by leaders.

So, in this journey of mine I have put down my four core pillars of commitment:

- Build trust with personalization;
- Build convenience;
- Build a strong foundation of honesty and transparency; and
- Commit to excellence.

My engagements also led me to another confusing question that I deal with all the time, 'When do you use people and when do you use technology to create powerful customer experiences?' People create unique experiences, while technology standardizes. Replacing people with technology is not an answer for higher CX. Balance is what creates tranquillity.

COMMITMENT TO EXCELLENCE

When I talk about becoming one with my customer, the first thing that comes to mind is 'emotion'. When I think about how to conquer the emotional realm of my customer, I invariably go back to my hobby that stands out as an significant example, photography. After all, photographers are in the business of evoking emotions.

Let's take a specific example. David Yarrow,[3] a renowned wildlife photographer who is guided by Robert Kapa's view that 'If your pictures aren't good enough, you are not close enough'. After spending eight years as a stockbroker in UK equities, working in London and New York, he went on to found his London-based hedge fund, Clareville Capital. Throughout his career, he had a second interest in photography and kept up with his double life and took some amazing photographs. His award-winning snap of Diego Maradona in Mexico in the 1986 FIFA World Cup holding the trophy was internationally acclaimed. These days, with digital single lens reflex (SLR's) and mirrorless cameras one can quite easily get over 600 photographs a day. Yet, when David was asked to comment on his exceptional snaps, he said that he gets just a handful of 'sharp' snaps that pass muster in a year. No doubt that his standards are set very high, and that gets translated into his reputation for amazing photographs. His photographs like 'Mankind' sold at Sotheby's annual photography auction for £60,000, 'The Wolfe of Main Street' fetched $1,00,000 at the New York auction, while '78 Degrees North' fetched £81,250 at a London auction, creating a new record.

Let's reword Robert Kapa's quote to fit into the CX paradigm, 'If you are not committed to building superior products for your customers, you are not close enough.' My clients are likely to have a handful of opportunities to shift perspectives and get closer to customers. That puts the enormity of that responsibility on me as well in my capacity as a consultant and adviser.

I have found that this pressure creates a 'strong behaviour'. Or, in other words, 'It's okay to be evolutionary rather than revolutionary.' Yet, while I worked at Citibank, I found that their stronger performance came to bear fruit when they were 'revolutionary' rather than evolutionary. You can see similar traits at Apple—after Steve Jobs's era of the iPhone and iPad, they have had to reinvent themselves with revolutionary design changes with the iPhone X, Apple AirPods, and a strong services business to support such massive appeal to the hardware they had distributed. Their pursuit of agile changes, and taking cut offs to put the best possible products into their customers' hands is what is driving that company forward.

FROM GREAT TO GREATNESS

A real question that I have often pondered over is, 'How do you make a great product even greater?'

As a kid, I had the good fortune of living and studying in Dusseldorf, Germany, where the automobile major, Mercedes-Benz, ruled the roost. To me, the answer to the question above came from them.

Mercedes-Benz paid homage to its founding father with its first TV commercial—'The best or nothing'.[4] Its tradition has been to provide its customers with 'technological leadership' and the core values that the brand reflects are of perfection, fascination and responsibility. These traditions and values are also interwoven into their corporate culture.

Their loyalty programme, 'Mercedes-Benz Circle of Excellence' provides owners with unforgettable experiences. It's not a programme, but a way of life. Their employees truly love cars and it is in their DNA. Employees put their effort in social media to promote the Mercedes-Benz brand. The company's focus on quality, design, customers' driving experience, attention to detail, and orienting themselves to a customer's ease of use has been part of the Mercedes-Benz promise.

Let's move on to another example. During my Citibank days in Mumbai my lunch was delivered by dabbawallas. *Dabba* in Hindi refers to lunch box, and *wala* is a synonym for person dealing with a trade. Their core job has been to deliver people their lunch boxes in downtown Mumbai. This 125-year-old tradition inspired me with their unparalleled story of perfect execution.

There are around 5,000 dabbawallas delivering over 2,00,000 meals a day. They have been studied by Harvard academics and royals around the world have met them. Two of them even attended Prince Charles and Camilla Parker-Bowles' wedding.

The core process is very simple; a person collects the freshly cooked lunch, the lunch reaches a drop-off point, sees its way on a local train, and reaches a central hub, and, after being sorted, it reaches an office block to be delivered by mid-day.

There are no computers involved, only codes in containers into which the lunch box goes. The magic lies in the codes and their ability to sort the codes. A dabbawala takes over three months to master the codes. Each letter, symbol and number indicates a pick-up and a drop-off point.

Why is this business successful you ask? It takes an hour or more to reach your office from your home and younger employees tend to stay further away for affordability's sake. Spouses attend to other pressing needs like sending their children off to school before lunch is prepared. Cramming everything within the early morning slot is tough and food invariably gets cold. That is where the dabbawalla comes in.

Only one in six million meals misses its destination, despite the mode of transport being the local train where more than 7.5 million people travel every day, and the peak hours are extremely crowded with literally no space to stand.

What does it cost? Less than a dollar a day.

The system is more like a social co-op. Each man finds his own customers, and collects his money and makes around ten dollars a day. It becomes his source for a stable job.

The dabbawalla is one committed individual. He has to reach the home right on time, then reach the drop-off point at an appointed hour, has to ensure that the codes are rightly affixed, and the delivery needs to take place by lunch time. Anything going amiss will mean unsatisfied customers and a threat to their livelihoods.

It's by no means easy, and visitors who come to study the model are still in awe of it.

IN SUMMARY - SIX

You cannot be on a journey to excellent CX until you start. But you need to have the commitment for a long-term haul. It has to be built on the foundation of trust, honesty, convenience, transparency and excellence. I know it sounds cliché, but I ask you one question, 'If it's so well known, why isn't everybody there yet?' After all, it's the best or nothing.

Seven

Build Your Strategy

BUILD YOUR CUSTOMER EXPERIENCE VISION

'First, think. Second, dream. Third, believe. Finally, dare.'

—Walt Disney

When I started my consulting career, I had great difficulty putting domain knowledge into a concise capsule to get people to understand my point of view. After all, you get only minutes, or at best an hour, with a client and you cannot let that pass. One of my mentors was kind enough to show me the path.

While I was working on the first vision statement for a client, I went up to the said mentor for advice. He defined his strategy to me in this manner,

$$V2 = A + P + V1$$

And quickly added,

$$P = C1 + C2$$

I asked him what it meant. He said that V2 stands for vision, V1 for values, A for aspiration and P for plan. Then I asked him what

C1 and C2 were, to which he replied, creativity and clarity. So, you could say vision is a plan for the future with imagination or wisdom.

Walt Disney once said, 'Whatever you do, do it well. Do it so well that when people see you do it, they will want to come back and see you do it again, and they will want to bring others and show them how well you do what you do.'

Using the simple analogy above, I got to a point when I could relate that same equation to CX,

$$CX = V2 + P + RE$$

Here, CX is customer experience, V2 is our vision statement, P is the passion to follow through and RE is the relentless execution of that vision. CX will be incomplete without each of these components.

Disney (the man himself) had an extreme passion to create the happiest place on earth. He got knocked down 302 times by banks before that one funding moment that made all of this possible. Your CX vision has to be fortified with strength and drive in order to create an environment like that of Disney.

Pixar, a subsidiary of Disney, is a very creative company where success or failure is recognized at the end of a very long journey of creating movies. In order to be successful, it needs to create an emotional connection using imagination and creativity. Pixar recognized the impact of aspirations rather than relying only on the moment of sale. You may disagree but look at other CX champions like Amazon who have turned a simple business of buying and selling of books and other products into a creative one. At the core, Pixar believes that 'everybody deserves quality'. So, customer delight naturally follows.

Another good example is Uber, which positions itself as 'everyone's private drive'. They create an experience of upgrading from a taxi to your own car. Uber is predominantly a software and logistics company which enables convenience and consistency using technology to manage its taxi ecosystem. Grab (South East Asia) and

Careem (Middle East and North Africa [MENA] and Turkey) have replicated the Uber model.

Many organizations focus on a single plan and stop when they have fulfilled the human and local market needs according to that plan. Obviously, competition will copy your approach if you are successful. So, by becoming complacent you stagnate. I have seen that only when my clients include agility and innovation in their plan, do they stay ahead of the competition.

When you try and remove the boundaries between the organization and their customers, values and ways of thinking would invariably come in between. For example, the customer wants convenience, and you want profit. In his book *The Convenience Revolution*, Shep Hyken shows how deeply convenience is linked to higher sales and helps you stand out. The international chain of convenience stores, 7-Eleven created a revolution in the small format, easy to get in and out neighbourhood stores. So, the key question is, how do you recognize convenience? The obvious answer is that your customers will force you to act on it. In his book, however, Hyken explains how shops force customers to keep discount coupons with them to benefit them instead of recognizing loyal customers automatically. You would have seen this at your local convenience store or at your café.

Another aspect that customers look for in products are sensual experiences that evoke all five senses; in effect, the complete package. For instance, a great looking, underpowered car is an embarrassment and fails to woo customers because it does not offer the complete experience. One such example is Daewoo's Cielo sedan, which was their flagship in India in the mid 1990s but had multiple functional inconsistencies. Daewoo also failed in product positioning against their competition. Initially positioned as a luxury car, but quickly re-aligned into the value-for-money segment, Daewoo's strategy created confusion in the customers' mind. It over estimated demand to start with and steeply cut prices to desperately stay afloat. This shows the clash between the functional and the sensual dimensions of a product.

Another example would be that of the durian fruit. Although it has a very pungent smell, it is very tasty and enjoys a wide fan following across South East Asia. Functionally, it's a tropical fruit that tastes great, but deters many sensually due to its foul smell because of which many airlines and hotels have banned the fruit.

Functional and sensual dimensions create novelty. The more the novelty, the greater the attraction. Novelty wears off quickly as a better product comes along, especially if it is aesthetically pleasing as well. The glue from the customer's perspective is the emotional connect that creates memorable and unforgettable experiences.

When Apple created the first iPod it evoked the functional (carry all your music in one box) and sensual (easy to navigate) dimensions. Many competing MP3 players were clunky and failed on either or both counts. With the iPhone and iPod touch, they expanded the sensual to include multitouch and gestures and its uniqueness and reliability evoked positive emotions. Multiple successful Apple products reinforced positive emotions in their customers and this created the loyalty that is synonymous with the brand. In delivering this emotional appeal, Apple relied heavily on design and each product was conceived in four steps: think, dream, believe and, finally, dare.

Uber is another good example where we see a combination of the functional dimension (click to ride with our partners) of the taxi ecosystem operating within local regulations with the sensual (global positioning system [GPS] tracking, assured fares, transparency). It added the emotional dimension through innovation (Uber Pool, 5 seconds emergency tab), cleanliness, reasonable price, and driver and passenger evaluation. Uber, however, failed in China both functionally (no great partnerships, regulatory gaps) and emotionally (gap in understanding the local culture). Uber has faced similar challenges in some other countries as well.

These lessons are universal, causing many to pull out of markets. Its nature differs from market to market; for example, Japan has a set of unique yet popular car models that have failed at the global as well as Asian stage. Misjudging the emotional aspect can have wider ramifications that include Uber's inability to manage unreceptive taxi drivers' unions or McDonald's being forced to bring in Indian flavoured burgers to please customers in India and the UAE.

High performance brands like Amazon, Airbnb or Disney use customer centricity principles while looking into the functional, sensual and emotional dimensions in order to set themselves apart from their competition. Products, processes, technology and human capital decisions are all built around this.

The market research firm, Forrester, confirms that nearly three-quarter of all companies list CX as one of their top priorities. According to the market consultancy company, Bain, more than 70 per cent of companies fail to provide superior CX the way customers perceive it. Going back to Viktor Frankl's quote, the space (gap) really is in extreme execution.

Based on my experience and lessons in CX from CX leaders, I have been able to narrow down a set of guiding principles for superior CX. They are:

- Make a difference to customers' lives with customer insight;
- Align it to the corporate vision and brand promise;
- Drive competitive advantage with ownership, collaboration and buy-ins;
- Ownership is a company-wide culture and includes the chief executive officer (CEO), the chief customer officer (CCO) and the chief human resources officer (CHRO); and
- Create lessons out of failures.

So, how do I go about building out my CX strategy? I use these nine dimensions to create that difference:

1. Ownership—executive and employee;
2. Market expectations;
3. Focus—vision and mission, define standards and benchmarks (real, believable and constantly improved);

4. Commit—publish expectations, communicate the differentiated value, purpose and impact;
5. Change—fundamentally changing behaviour and building momentum by getting champions and role models who will walk-the-talk;
6. Collaboration—inspire and align teams, guide frontline employees, create active communities;
7. Create standout experiences—Innovate and inspire;
8. Be human; and
9. Agility (covered in Section II, Chapter 10).

All these dimensions need to fire in tandem as part of this strategy.

The final outcome of the CX strategy is the blueprint which includes customer journey maps on the basis of in-depth, qualitative discussions with customers. The organization needs to feel connected to the cause which is the basis for the guiding principles.

YOUR BRAND PURPOSE

'It was so important for me to lose everything, for me to find out what the most important thing is.'

—Ellen DeGeneres

'Take a chance on being who you really are, or you are going to kill who you really are, and fall into your grave grasping to your character who you never were.'

—Jim Carrey

As I start to peel the onion of my clients' vision, I quickly bump into purpose. Purpose is the fundamental reason why we exist. It's a vital, soul-searching question and we can struggle for months and years to get an answer. The answer to this provides the brand its purpose. Simply put, purpose is a statement of commitment that you put out to the world, for your customers to choose you over your competition.

An example will probably make it clearer. Dove's brand purpose is 'To achieve real beauty, build your self-esteem'. The purpose and the product directly resonate with their audiences. But, how did it connect so well? Dove brand purpose appealed to customers with low self-esteem who felt better about the way they look using their products.

Let's take another example. The Japanese home store, Muji's brand purpose is 'Promoting simplicity, moderation, humility, self-restraint, serenity and the natural environment'. Muji, which in Japanese means 'no-brand quality goods', created an identity through rational manufacturing processes and designs that are simplistic, aesthetic, minimalistic and modern.

As your brand becomes more successful, the brand ownership actually transfers to your customers. They talk about it, they share videos and they live with it. They either participate or boycott it. Nintendo's 'Activities for Active Families' brand purpose stands out in this regard. When you say video games, the first thing that come to mind is the image of a person on a couch, gazing at the TV, without ever wanting to get off it even to go to the toilet. With the launch of the Wii, Nintendo, put active, physical participation of the customer bang into the centre of the game.

If you take Dove, Muji, or Nintendo's examples, their efforts to connect to customers with the brand purpose is directly visible and the brand is being both human and authentic at the same time.

So, in effect, your purpose has to reflect back to your end customers through relentless execution.

BUILD YOUR CULTURE

Once, we were in deep discussion about the vision and purpose of a brand with one of my clients. The discussion turned around to culture and what we need to build. An agreement on vision and purpose can be met with the CEOs, CXOs and the board, but the larger community needs to buy into 'what they truly believe in', which then translates into collective purpose.

So, why is there a challenge you may ask. We know that each individual has a purpose and the ability to align individual purpose with corporate purpose creates your organization's culture.

It's only then that you can lay down policies, decisions and actions that support your vision, purpose, values and culture.

To take the Walt Disney example. Disney's vision is 'To be one of the world's leading producers and providers of entertainment and information'. Its purpose is 'Using our portfolio of brands to differentiate our content, services and consumer products, we seek to develop the most creative, innovative and profitable entertainment experiences and related products in the world'.

If we break that down to Disney theme parks' purpose, 'We create happiness by providing the best in entertainment for people of all ages everywhere', we can see an immediate connect with the parent organization's vision and purpose.

Disney's values also include their commitment to creativity, technology and innovation, quality, community, storytelling, optimism and decency to generate 'unparalleled experiences'.

As you can see, the dots indeed connect. Let's return to our formula from the beginning of the chapter to look at the Disney example:

$$CX = V2 + P + RE$$

We can see that Disney's actions are supported by their sense of purpose that gives their customers a unique experience every time they visit.

As you grow, you often start to question your values, but it usually comes down to problems in the organization's culture. This, in effect, boils down to differences between individual goals and corporate values, and is true even in the case of CEOs. Remember that solid values are the bedrock of 'leaving a legacy' and creating a culture for the next generation.

Disney instils the brand's values in their employees through their hiring practices and training. Culture gets created over time and the onus is on senior leaders to understand and then emulate the vision, mission and values of the company. This way of working provides an opportunity for employees to appreciate their environment. It is important to note that consistency helps attach meaning to events or issues, and work in general.

Employees are motivated when their organization is consistent with its values. Prospective employees should be encouraged to have discussions with organizations to embed themselves into the corporate culture based on such values.

In retrospect, it is interesting to see that we have had failed transformations. The reasons for this are primarily attributable to businesses driving short-term gains by changing their culture, and not connecting it back to its values. A strong indicator of this is a lack of employee motivation and starting to look elsewhere for inspiration.

FROM CULTURE TO CX CULTURE

'By putting employees first, the customer effectively comes first by default, and in the end, the shareholder comes first by default as well.'

—Richard Branson

Going back to my mentor, he once explained to me that 'Business leaders globally recognize the competitive advantage of excellent customer experience, and it can't get far into the organization unless endorsed fully by the CEO and the Board'.

I also realized by studying firms that seemed to have a strong vision or mission statement, issued a big, pompous press release to customers and shareholders of its commitments, followed with near zero execution towards that goal, made the easiest sitting ducks for competition.

'A good leader doesn't get stuck behind a desk.'

— Richard Branson

So, having arrived full circle, we go back to the question 'What does the customer really want?'

In Disney's case, it was happiness through the best entertainment. By connecting the dots between Disney's purpose and the customer purpose, it has created unparalleled CX.

To make sure that this connection was consistent, a set of standards and principles (embedded into the fabric) had to emerge. Embedding this includes putting this out into your logo, letterheads and all communications. These standards become non-negotiable and success is based on tangible outcomes. In time, activities, processes and customer journeys will be mapped out or re-defined based on these standards and principles.

My mentor also advised me once, 'Don't mistake the forest for the trees.' He said this to remind me to always keep the bigger picture in mind when I drafted out the vision, purpose or culture documents for my clients for discussions.

For a customer, their interest is never in the process or individual actions, but around their individual experience and outcome. If you take the cue from Adidas's customer journey, you realize that it was not short term but took a sustained period of time to embed it into the organization's culture.

We are talking about individuals here, and their need to embrace a work culture. Complicate this by including corporates with multiple business lines, departments, cities or countries, etc. I think you get the picture.

Motivation comes from success, and success comes from an initial set of highly motivated employees who connect with the customer and the brand promise. They are the champions and success especially comes from early wins.

When I was working with a global bank on humanizing financial services, I noticed the power of storytelling within the organization for positive impact. With a lot of discipline and patience, they saw results coming through.

The other lesson that came out of this experience is not to be impacted by failures in parts, but to move onto things that work. Transformations are never 100 per cent successful and have their fair share of experiments and failures.

When I engage with a client as a consultant, I am respectful of the privilege of full permission and access. Yet, I have often found difficulty when leaders fail to recognize the difference between their responsibility and that of a catalyst who is aiding in this transformation. Every failure can be attributed to one fact, indifference. This can be indifference to purpose, passion, vision or relentless execution.

At the global bank that humanized financial services, all communication and team sessions were held with groups of employees. There was a continuous broadcast of changes that were taking place from the leadership. Top-line CX metrics were re-aligned to specific business outcomes. To put it another way, this was nothing different from adopting a new way of life if you had to lose 50 pounds.

As we progressed through the journey, standards were created or evolved. A continuous feedback loop improved customer effectiveness and competitive edge. During the transformation programme a competitor got hot on the heels and launched their own version of a transformation. So, we weren't the only ones transforming and this meant that we had to set our own benchmark, very similar to Amazon that set standards of CX for online shopping.

Since we had to visualize an interaction model, we created customer journey maps to drive relationships. Since there were many types of interactions, there were multiple journey maps. As we progressed through this, we also had to train employees to understand

and imbibe these journey maps to be able to see through the eyes of their customers. We recognized that while each employee was doing their part, the benefits were far greater than the sum of parts.

Asking people to do more, in their already busy schedule would come with its own challenges. To cut back manual labour, the only way to turn was to go digital and automating boring processes. None of this was possible without the catalysts—the top management providing adequate sponsorship. But execution was still in the hands of employees, and that is where the magic really begins to happen.

If you look elsewhere for examples, you will find that products like Gmail got created from empowering employees (Paul Buchheit) to spend 20 per cent of their time on a side project. Richard Branson regards himself as the 'Chief Enabling Officer', to nurture 'intrapreneurs' who would go on to become tomorrow's entrepreneurs. Dr Spencer Silvers' (the intrapreneur) accidental discovery of an adhesive that stuck lightly onto surfaces but did not bond firmly, allowed for the creation of 3M's Post-it Notes. The product spread like a virus within the organization and became a ground breaking discovery that nobody thought they needed until they really did.

You need to understand that the best way to recognize excellent CX is my being in the customers' shoes. As my mentor said, 'Experience what the customer experiences; if you believe that you are being treated great, then you are fine, but not as a senior executive, a board member or as a CEO.' I also found another secret to understanding CX better through the mystery shopping approach. By disguising external people as customers, a few thousand samples can quickly identify bottlenecks that need to be fixed. Since the mystery shoppers are external to the organization, the operations staff does not recognize them and the evaluation completed by these shoppers records the actual CX. This delivers unbiased results that are very useful for organizations to identify areas for improvement.

BUILD YOUR PLAN

An agreed outcome between me and my client is always a blueprint. It defines actions and steps for execution with timelines and priorities. The plan also embeds a business model.

We always start zero base with customers, and identify their personas, values and price sensitivities. It is also important to identify industry nuances like freebies at this stage. Also, the culture should incorporate all of these factors.

Remember that a customer selects us for the value we provide, and we need to validate customers' interests based on the proposition. Value comes from convenience, price, design aesthetics, past brand value, ability to reduce their risk or costs and the differentiation that we can provide.

Then we look at the strategy. We need to outline our key success criteria and key measurements for our success at this stage. Keeping in mind that our budgets are limited, the brand will automatically rally around those values. Great CX demands great customer relationships, combined with innovation and agility. In order for us to do that, our channels, technology and processes must lend support. The number of key resources is based on our strategy and our execution model built around technology and processes. Our attention to detail will make all the difference here. By looking at partnerships, we can figure out a way to create wonderful things with a fraction of the resources and with acceleration. These partners bring in expertise that we may not have, or cost us more to build. This is how we arrive at our ballpark costs, to which we need to add other incidentals like taxes, add a healthy margin and finally arrive at our target revenue.

Once we have our costs and revenues penned down, it makes it easier to estimate the number of customers and arrive at pricing and service fees. Since all other assumptions would affect the price and fees, we visit and re-visit our assumptions, with a margin to spare to provide for shocks based on customer reactions.

Since this whole process is very delicate, and based on our ability to arrive at correct assumptions, my advice is to always start small.

Having seen many start-ups and scaled enterprises use crowdfunding before mass production, I am completely bought into that idea, and would strongly recommend this for any test. You may do a spin off with a similar strategy but the way the outcome presents itself is very useful. Surprises in the form of licensing, brokerages, taxes, marketing and other fixed and variable costs can also be quickly avoided.

Since our information technology (IT) costs were quite significant, it may be worthwhile to look at a transaction-based pricing model initially with an option to convert to a buyout at a specified time period.

If you are looking at riding an Uber versus owning a car, it may be better to do a rental model like Uber, or a subscription-based model like magazines, or credit card fees, rather than an outright purchase. Many companies have stretched their revenue while improving their CX by changing the revenue model (for example, Adobe, Microsoft, Apple, Edelkrone, to name a few).

All of this gets built into the blueprint ready for extreme execution. The final layer on this is the timeline with commitments, deadlines and regulations based on the limitation on resources, funding options or competitive pressures.

MANAGING COMPETITION

'Power comes from the head first. You need conviction that you can compete.'

—Justine Henin, seven-time tennis Grand Slam champion

In the initial days of my working life, I saw everybody feeling quite insecure when they saw the competition launching an attractive product. I have become much wiser since.

There will always be a new kid around the block who wants to be the next hero. If you look back into the history of sports, it's not the strongest who wins all the time. It's the person with the maximum conviction. Look at the number of underdogs who go on to win major tournaments. A fierce competitor will always say the game is won even before the game starts. It's all about the visualization.

Business competition is no different. Our competition is not interested in our business. They are interested in our customers and our best response is to provide our customers positive experiences that they cannot forget.

When newer digital companies were launched, most of my clients started thinking about responding to competition. Over time, some of those started rethinking their business model and plan. Slowly but surely, they found ways to co-operate and partner with competition to create products with unique features and benefits.

Belief in something sometimes comes when you look outside the window and often one realizes that co-operation is beneficial. Sony and Canon are monopolies in the production of camera sensors. Fujifilm uses Sony sensors[1] in their cameras like the X-T3 and Nikon in its Z6. Amazon marketplace brought in third party sellers into its online store which exponentially expanded their profitability. Samsung made the OLED displays, NAND flash and DRAM chips for the iPhone.

Sometimes, it is important to partner with competition in order to enter into new markets or market segments, like in the case of Ford and Toyota collaborating to create the Atlas Ford F-150 hybrid pick-up truck.

My trips to the Middle East provided me with other insights. The Middle East market consists of many financial services companies, but most of them can't afford to buy IT infrastructure that have better features and benefits. Competitors have, therefore, come together using a hosted services model to provide common infrastructure. So, this is a case of partnering to create economies of scale.

At IBM, we worked on large transformation engagements where CISCO provided networking services. This is an example of complementary services.

Today's competition may not come from traditional rivals but from asymmetric competitors. Take the case of Apple and the way it disrupted the way music is subscribed to and consumed through devices like iPod and iPhones and platforms such as Apple Music and iTunes.

Partnerships built at the right time creates value. If ignored, and our competitor finds a way around it, our business model itself may be under threat. BlackBerry's messenger service BBM was one of its brightest assets, a significant differentiator for them even when their handsets business was rapidly declining. Yet BlackBerry refused to partner with Apple to keep the BBM service alive.[2] Apple, in turn, built its iMessage service that replaced the need for BlackBerry's service for many users. WhatsApp, the messaging service owned by Facebook, on the other hand, stayed platform agnostic to reach an even wider audience.

Apple needed Google Maps for differentiation in 2007. In 2012, however, the partnership fell through but Apple's offering, Apple Maps, failed to make a dent for most users. Even in 2020 it is still playing catch-up. What you have to give to Apple is their conviction to compete.

I think Apple has learnt a lot from this experience. These days they partner with chip manufacturers for their Macs, while creating new chip designs for their other products since everybody was moving out into an unchartered territory. Rumour has it that they will replace the Mac third-party chips with their own quite soon.[3]

Our best bet here is to use 'leverage' and facilitate partnerships with firms having different business models.

Today, the arrowhead is new innovation. I can't think of examples better than Banco Bilbao Vizcaya Argentaria (BBVA), DBS Bank or ICICI Bank in India who leverage start-ups to accelerate better CX.

While I worked in the Middle East, I saw how global organizations have increasingly taken onboard the 'value train' concept to use its resources and abilities to create a competitive advantage. Focusing on 'core competencies' and 'differentiation' is a better bet than relying on cost advantages. Increasingly, organizations have understood this and used supply chain efficiency and outsourcing for cost advantages with adequate quality measures, while retaining differentiation elements within the organization.

In *Blue Ocean Strategy*,[4] W. Chan Kim and Renee Mauborgne, describe how value innovation has become the cornerstone for creating 'blue oceans', which involves recreating the definition of the marketplace to make it uncontested and the competition irrelevant.

An old but apt example of this is how the iPad launched in 2010 went on to create a new category of personal devices, the tablet, but in its initial days it was hotly debated whether it was a laptop replacement or cannibalization of a smartphone. The full-fledged launch of foldable smartphones in the market will start this debate once again. In the language of the blue ocean strategy, this is a revisioning of market boundaries.

Other examples would include Uber's and Airbnb's business models, which are based on the digital fulfilment of demand. They don't really own cars or real estate, but use technology to bridge the gap between demand and supply.

Competition also takes cognizance of 'value curves'. At the right value, they will sell their business to you. Take the example of the service provider Waze, which was once competing with the map services offered by Google and Apple. Waze customers provided information around traffic congestions, accidents and road closures that allowed it to identify the fastest travel routes rather than the shortest. Ultimately the Israeli start-up was acquired by Google[5] for around US$1 billion, in the face of fierce competition from Apple and Facebook. Facebook itself fended off several buyers along its journey, including the likes of Google, Yahoo and Microsoft, and went on to create a very different market value.

When we launched our first co-branded credit card with an airline at Citi, others quickly followed. In the case of Pepsi and Coke, both companies were forced to switch their focus from carbonated drinks to healthier alternatives to avoid customers defecting to the competition.

Other examples which strike me are those that create new markets with the help of a blue ocean strategy. Biotique, an Indian venture by entrepreneur Vinita Jain, which relies on a 5,000-year-old science called Ayurveda, collaborated with a Swiss company to use its modern biotechnology.[6] Twenty years ago biotechnology was not a common buzzword and the market for natural products was also nascent. In 2006, when Baba Ramdev launched the Patanjali venture and penetrated into the food and personal care segment, one of India's largest retailers, Future Group, partnered with it to resell some of its products. As a first-generation entrepreneur behind Future Group, Kishore Biyani saw the opportunity to pioneer through a partnership rather than oppose its competition.[7]

So, my conclusion based on all of this is that our business model can be made collaboratively with a positive medium- or long-term outlook. If we manage to get our CX right, the rest will follow.

RECOVERING FROM FAILURE OR SETBACKS

'Everything you want is on the other side of fear.'

—Jack Canfield, author of the Chicken Soup for the Soul series

'Success does not consist in never making mistakes but in never making the same one a second time.'

—George Bernard Shaw

As a kid, I was taught that when you fall down, you need to get up and start again. I find that lesson very apt for businesses as well.

Things can and will occasionally go wrong. That's a fact of business. The question always is how do you quickly rebound?

Many years ago, when I was at Citi, we had great difficulty lending to the self-employed. We found our NPAs (non-performing assets) pretty steep with that group. Yet, when I moved to HDFC Bank, I found out how they had actually figured out how to minimize risk with that segment of customers. So, I learnt the hard way how Citi had got into a conundrum of 'learned helplessness'. Though mature, they had lost their conviction to fight and find answers. They had forgotten how to understand, document or acknowledge failures, or even to work on them with a contingency plan to get through the woods.

I am reminded of an example of putting customers first even in the case of a setback. Cathay Pacific, the Hong Kong–based airline, made a serious ticketing error by announcing business and first-class fares from Vietnam to New York at US$ 675, instead of the standard US$16,000 during a New Year's Eve sale.[8] Cathay became aware of their mistake, owned up to it, and confirmed that they would honour the fare. Singapore Airlines made a similar error in 2014,[9] and honoured it as well. United Airlines made this kind of a mistake in 2015, but didn't honour it. I don't need to describe whose customers are more likely to remain loyal, but it goes to show that owning up to commitments is a far richer way to save your customers for the long term than trying to hide your tracks.

In one of the banks I worked with, we faced what they called a 'mass error'. It involved them being proactive in acknowledging it, communicating the issue to the affected departments, having people available down the line to tackle the problem and reporting on it every few hours for two days after the problem has been closed. Putting in the effort to manage such contingencies, and fixing them before they caused further damage really helped.

In the previous chapters, we have discussed how you can plug that into the customer journey maps, and how that could get embedded into processes and touch points.

Zappos is a great example for CX. A rare mistake from Zappos's delivery partner,[10] happened when the shoes that were ordered reached the wrong place. To compensate, Zappos sent a new pair to the right customer, upgraded him to VIP status and even refunded him on his original order. They recognized their responsibilities and wanted the customer to feel good at the end of the experience. They have a 75 per cent plus repeat customer base. Any guesses why?

That leads us to the question, 'Can we avoid all mistakes?' Possibly not, but there are ways to catch these before they blow up if we have the correct measurement systems in place.

In CX, the net promoter score (NPS) says the same thing. Am I good enough? Your NPS would tell you whether you are good or not. Then the deep dive can happen and you can look at matrices that drill down from it. These are the next set of topics that we will touch upon as we get into the subject of measurements.

IN SUMMARY—SEVEN

The CX strategy is built through vision, passion and relentless execution. My success was always in our ability to build out a strategy blueprint that clearly outlined the journey we needed to take by putting with customers at the centre of everything we did.

By working together, recognizing mistakes and embracing competition we got better at CX. At the end, we measured and course corrected our journey along the way for sweet success. Failure, if encountered, was yet another stepping stone for success.

Eight

The FIRST Building Block for Execution—Your Team

CREATE TEAMS TO LEAD, INNOVATE AND SUCCEED

'Teamwork makes the dream work, but a vision becomes a nightmare when the leader has a big dream and a bad team.'

—John Maxwell, American clergyman

Over time, while I worked with successful leaders, the number one challenge in a leader's mind is how to redesign the team structure to meet business demands as well as the business climate of today.

The greatest business demand in today's business climate is CX. So, what better way than to marry the two. While organization structure remained distinctive, the responsibility and responsiveness matrix were often collective.

There are four layers of responsibility: the board and the CEO, the CXO, cross functional teams (or X-teams) and followers. Responsibility flows down from the CEO to the followers. Interestingly, when it comes to CX, responsiveness works in the exact opposite direction.

Teams need to be made up of multiple components. Leaders who are 'the torchbearer and sponsors' and a coach, who is 'the lighthouse' and acts as the mentor, philosopher and guide to get them to their goal post. It also needs 'the entrepreneur' who works with the torchbearer and the lighthouse to embed values and culture within their teams. In addition, an 'X-team', which act as change agents working closely with the coach, is also crucial. And, finally, 'the followers' who embed the values and transform them into the 'culture' or the living-breathing organism that the team then becomes.

In our experiments, when we tried losing one element, we found that the team was incomplete. Team sizes and mix are critical for success. Also, team spirit between groups creates conviction, a culture of innovation and helps leap-frog the competition.

When I introspect on large transformation failures, I find that some of the biggest failures lie at the torchbearers' and sponsors' end. I also found that there is enough inspiration within the organization and outside to recover ground. Another aspect of critical failure is losing track of values, losing track of culture and that's when resistance sets in.

WHY DO GOOD TEAMS FAIL?

Let's take an example to illustrate this.

We put together a team of six highly competent and motivated individuals to work on a project. The team was composed of members from various departments and to deliver the results with this team size, there was little room for a slip-up. The goals were well thought through and the team was carefully chosen to suit these goals. Three weeks into the eight-week project, the other departments took back three team members from that team and replaced them with others. The team started to lose momentum and slipped. Does this sound familiar?

I have always noticed that any change of direction for the team from its goals, or changes in products or vision, or, even, a change in the mix of team members can create serious derailment to programmes.

The reasons for these kinds of changes are many. There is a redundancy in the department, something new has come up that warrants a particular team members' attention, the team member had an imminent holiday planned and the X-team was not informed about it, and the list goes on.

What I found most useful is to lay down the boundaries clearly on Day One, so that there are minimal surprises to work with and things move according to plan. You need to remember that the more important the challenge is to the company, the more careful the planning needs to be.

ROLE OF THE TORCHBEARER AND SPONSORS

'A BOSS has the TITLE; a LEADER has the PEOPLE.'

—Simon Sinek

Having seen leaders push CX to embed these values into the organization, I can say that leaders are respected but bosses are not (automatically). The torchbearer (CEO) and sponsors (Board) have the responsibility to become leaders. They need to translate the vision, mission and instil values for CX.

It's interesting to see how the understanding of leadership changes when you have a founder instead of a CEO at the helm. The founder truly understands the vision and mission of the company. They are passionately involved in the business and their deepest desire is to leave a legacy behind. They instil values and drive the culture for a significant future advantage.

When family businesses grow too big, the founders often hire a CEO who has big shoes to fill when they take over. Support from the founder will help embed the values and the culture deeper into the organization. Take the case of Narayana Murthy or Nandan Nilekani, of Infosys, who came back as mentors in order to do just this. When I speak to staff inside the organization, I quickly realize whether the CEO is the 'chief role model'. CEOs who are role models are people who have gone to extraordinary lengths for causes they believe in, and they keep their commitments towards them. I see the CEO's mindset towards commitment and ownership also changes when they acquire the role model's status. The transition to CX requires commitment towards a continuous transformation combined with extreme execution.

Reflecting back twenty-five years, my then CEO at a large global bank took it upon himself to ensure that the bank met unparalleled customer service standards for any phone call, query or complaint. He communicated those standards to his teams, who endorsed the same and transmitted them on the followers. This broad agreement on standards kept the culture of the organization at a high pedestal. When customers responded positively, it motivated the employees, who rose to higher standards still, and in turn the bank's profitability improved rapidly.

When I see a chief role model, I see automatic commitment. The role model's subsequent actions come down to communication and re-enforcement. Their involvement automatically re-enforces the commitment in the team to go through the pain. I have repeatedly seen in large transformations that people have questions, doubts and need clarity repeatedly. This chief role model is all about that.

When the chief role model is hungry for success, he goes for the low hanging fruits to drive motivation and confidence. He pushes teams to share these successes to make them believable. These teams in turn share valuable lessons from their own successes and failures. The motivation shown by the chief role model is the catalyst for replication.

I often see teams trying to emulate the chief role model. This then goes from being professional to being personal. When I attended an offsite hosted by one of India's respected central bank governors, I saw a chief role model. He shared the successes of his colleagues with their family members and invited them to company workshops.

This joy gave families hope that their spouses were engaged in doing something pathbreaking. During the workshop he laid down the foundation to the next three years for the bank, asked for the commitment of his colleague and re-iterated the values and culture that set them apart.

You can also feel success when you see similarly charged Boards. The clarity, guidance and measurements while assessing risks helps them stand apart from the crowd. That's what creates great CX.

I can never cease to learn, especially from things that make a huge difference. Every Amazon meeting has an empty chair. That chair is for the customer. Jeff Bezos is obsessed with CX and he always says, 'Start with the customer and work backward.' Amazon makes it impossible to forget the customer!

At the bank that was on the path to humanizing financial services I saw how they treated CX as an organization-wide engagement. You are either directly involved in delivering CX or supporting it. In those situations, one cannot fail to notice that while sales and product divisions create CX, human resources (HR) supports it by either hiring the right employees or training them.

Sometimes a catalyst or accelerator is required and this is where the consultant to help the cause comes in. A consultant is not an 'us versus them scenario', but is merely there to help get your organization from one point to another. Without the CEO's support, he will not be able to do that.

THE ENTREPRENEURS

'If you choose somebody who genuinely loves people and looks for the best in people, that's critical and if you bring someone in who isn't good with people then you can destroy the company very quickly.'

—Richard Branson

Whenever I see success in organizations, I notice that it is always preceded by ownership. Ownership is driven by the chief role model, and quickly latches on to the other members of the C-Suite. These are the people who I call entrepreneurs.

The 'lighthouse' supports the entrepreneurs in their journey. We will talk about the lighthouse in the next section. The CXO then takes on the mantle to re-engineer the organization for the transformation through a series of tweaks.

The same characteristics drawn from the chief role model—conviction, empowerment and motivating teams—are passed down. The difference between success and failure at this level lies in relentless execution. With outside–the-box ideas, I see this group translate the vision into something more executable. Underperforming teams lack visibility to innovation and possible ideas. The CXO can combine skill sets with the vision, empower the teams to create an approach for execution with agility. Coaching, mentoring, guidelines and frameworks give them a helping hand. Staying hands-on keeps the team real.

One thing I often realize as a paradox is that teams are already stretched from their day-to-day assignments. That's where the motivation to stretch needs to come in. The ability to integrate teams based on the goal is the secret to that success.

I see every successful entrepreneur driven by value—value to customers and value to the organization. I see them assess ideas based on cost–benefit ratios. Yet, it's the teams that have provided successes. Putting together an X-team and chairing them drives objectives. I often encounter an inherent rivalry between two CXOs. X-teams drawn from multiple CXOs can help foster a sense of bonding in such cases.

The biggest set-back I have found with some CXOs is when they start to look at objectives department-by-department and consider their roles fulfilled when they have handed over the job to another team.

An entrepreneur looks at the end-to-end life cycle. So, it's not just a moment of truth but the entire customer journey.

THE LIGHTHOUSE

'Lighthouses are not just stone, brick, metal, and glass. There's a human story at every lighthouse; that's the story I want to tell.'

— Elinor DeWire

As a child, I was very fascinated by the lighthouse. I was told that the lighthouse shows the way and is strategically located—it emits light to navigate or to warn of dangers to approaching boats. Every lighthouse has a keeper and that is the human story that needs to be narrated.

If you regard CX as the lighthouse, the Chief Customer Officer (CCO) is its keeper. The lighthouse (CX) can't shut down a single night or during any storm. The lighthouse (CX) brand drives credibility to the boats (its customers). The light is customer insight. The keeper has to manage safety, reliability and manage customer expectations. There is a minimum performance level, similar to the minimum viable product (MVP) for the CCO to look after. Just as the government plays a significant role in the running of lighthouses, the CEO and his executives play a significant role as influencers to keep CX efficient. The keeper (the CCO) is the custodian.

Lighthouses have evolved over the centuries. Today beacons, buoys, lights, sounds, radio-navigation, traffic separation, bridges have been added to its functions. Look at them as products or brand extensions. This is pretty similar to the principles, methods, tools, technology and foresight to manage disruptions that have come to the aid of the organization for its keeper, the CCO.

Imagine, if the lighthouses were removed, what would happen? It's no different from organizations missing a CCO reacting to customer expectations post incident.

We spoke briefly about the collaborative relationship between the CXO and the CCO. Let's extend this further. The CCO is a guide, practitioner and coach who works with the CXO to embed the culture and the principles into the organization.

The keeper does not navigate the ships himself; he only aids in the navigation. When we ask the CCO to fix things, we are ignoring the responsibility of the CXOs. The keeper is responsible for providing necessary aid, which is to connect CX to business growth by providing insights to leadership for maximum impact (attract and deepen CX). The lighthouse enables ships to navigate dangerous waters through critical actions, rather than a series of random actions. The CCO has a similar role. Look at the role of the CCO as being the glue. He unites and enables the leadership to drive customer behaviour and growth through metrics decided by the leadership. He provides the data and information to drive these business decisions. Even where there is a CCO appointed for the role, there is a significant tussle between the CCO and the leadership as the CCO is expected to pitch metrics and then be responsible for the outcome solely. The prominent question that needs to be answered by the CCO is, 'Why did they leave, or why do they buy more or less?'

When I worked with large organizations to set up a CX culture, the role of the CCO became more evident. The CCO's role is a pro-active one. When metrics start to improve or slip, he needs to quickly alert the business units about the same, so that they can take recommended actions.

A part of the CCO's role is the ability to tell the right stories from their own organization and/or invite guest speakers from other organizations to share best practices. Engagement becomes stronger when customers share their real stories; roadshows or internal events can move people far more than just metrics. A few years back, while we were converting a microfinance organization into a bank, I was privileged to be invited to one of their annual events. They had invited all members of the institution and some customers as well. One of their customers started sharing her experience about how a small loan from the microfinance institution changed her life. As the evening progressed, more customers came up to share their stories of success based on loans that they took to boost their livelihoods. It was not surprising that many employees left the place teary eyed, full of gratitude and positive energy on how the organization had touched others' lives.

When I was working with a significantly large bank in India, the Customer Service Officer (CSO) shared customer insights to make our new products or campaigns better. That information allowed us to improve our connect with our customers.

At some of these institutions, I recognized how CCOs have helped in breaking organization silos. That was possible because of the strong value system directing them towards the customer. The CCO, after all, is responsible for gauging the reliability of the experience and providing avenues towards innovations, while actively working with the team to prevent potential threats disrupting the business.

'It's amazing what you can accomplish if you don't care who gets the credit.'

—Harry S. Truman, 33rd US President

THE X-TEAM

My mentor once told me that 'If you want to gain success within your department, involve the team members. If you want to get success across departments, choose ones across, that is the fastest way to get other people to see purpose in your vision.'

Over time, I also realized that the X-team needs to be given a very specific objective—like solving a complex supply chain issue, or getting a complex product to market by bundling different products from your stable.

My passion for reading taught me how leadership successes have actually been borrowed from the military. To get something specific done, create your own 'SEAL team' (US Navy Sea, Air and Land)— get in, get the job done and get out.

We have used similar techniques during my years in consulting. We developed a client pitch by getting together and delivering the engagement by drawing on the best resources. The results were significantly better than the sum of their parts.

In some of my failed engagements, I saw that when teams tried to solve the problem departmentally rather than through an X-team, a blame game quickly followed and leaders ended up fighting territorial battles rather than focusing on getting the job done.

At one point early in my career, I saw the sales teams getting frustrated with the operations teams because they were not approving loans. When we (I was in operations then) took it upon ourselves to educate sales on their mistakes and worked with them to correct it, a seemingly 'unsolvable' problem was quickly resolved.

Later on in my career, as we put together X-teams, we picked the best in the business. Team members started to feel it a privilege to be part of the team. By putting together several X-teams we were able to solve multiple such challenges. To be part of an X-team meant accelerated learning, recognition in public and rewards. The key here though was our ability to link our 'key' strategic challenges or initiatives to these programmes.

A follow-on effect of creating X-teams was that it also provided a credible means of succession planning. Through the process, teams got to know each other, natural leaders emerged and team spirit was fostered. It's important though to pair up the right individuals in order to find success though building X-teams.

The X-team itself is broken down into pairs so that they come up with alternate solutions to certain parts of the problem. The pair spends time with market trends, realities, competition, customer needs and wants, and their responses to stimuli within a pre-agreed timeline. By creating such alternate choices, the best course(s) of action are established before being presented for wider approval.

The action that is presented has to be comprehensive and include the full lifecycle, high impact areas, quality, cost and revenue implications as well as a full-fledged SWOT (strengths, weaknesses, opportunities and threats) analysis with course correction, where necessary, based on feedback. When we put together such programmes, we also consider it important to involve a project management team member to ensure timelines are strictly adhered to overall.

In addition, a definite set of rules of critique are also established in order to propose alternatives. During this stage, employees who are not part of that X-team are invited to provide feedback. These employees, based on their participation, could then become potential members of the next X-team engagement.

Conflicts are resolved by the chair. To enable a competitive spirit, different X-teams often compete with each other to bring about the maximum impact in their projects, and are rewarded amply at the end of the programme. Periodic checks and sessions with the leader are arranged so that the X-teams get closer to their overall goal of solving the challenge.

The other thing to recognize is the final outcome. Acceptance of the solution or the shelving it should be taken in consideration of the organizations' best interests, and both the leader and the X-team need to fully appreciate and endorse it. It is a good idea to set expectations clear right at the beginning of the programme as this will make things easier.

Based on my experiences, I have devised six steps to create the maximum impact:

1. Set ground rules;
2. Project manage;
3. Empower teams with tools;
4. Allocate roles for each team member and pair;
5. Document lessons learnt and don't hesitate to share them to become better;
6. Recognize and reward based on outcomes jointly agreed with the CEO's office.

THE FOLLOWERS

Through these exercises in CX, I found a surprising link between employee engagement and CX. I noticed that CX leaders have significantly higher employee engagement.

What's engagement, you ask? Engagement is about feeling good. It's about employees identifying themselves with their jobs. When employees feel good, there is a release of 'happy hormones' such as dopamine, serotonin, endorphins and oxytocin that enhances engagement (this is for the doctors out there!). So you see, HR is intricately connected as the owner of employee engagement programmes. So how does HR do that? Some of the ways to ensure this is through employee communication, training, new hire onboarding programmes, getting people embedded into the organization, awards, incentives, celebrations, employee listening programmes and others.

During the course of my visits overseas, I found two useful cases that I thought were extremely relevant in today's circumstances.

The first was around keeping a 7-Eleven type convenience store that is open 24/7 in your office building where any employee could pick up their groceries on the way home without losing focus on their work. The second was a restaurant run by a client that served free meals to employees beyond working hours so that they didn't have to hunt for a place to eat before heading home.

Consistently, I have been reminded that the power of an organization is driven by its employees. While decision-making mostly rests at the top, employees continue to stay engaged the most with the customer and it is they who drive the organization on a daily basis.

I also saw the tricks used by organizations to score well on employee satisfaction surveys that are usually carried out at the end of the year. Many of these surveys are preceded by an offsite event just to soften the impact of negative feedback from employees without a genuine effort to set things right.

Employees can be happier by understanding their roles better, serving their customers better, helping new joiners better and teaming up to create better results as well as by staying focused towards delivering results. Employees who go flat out to get the best results are recognized by their organizations and by the industry as well. It is important to remember that sharing, teaming and encouraging does not decrease your competitive strength.

As part of active engagement programmes, we got followers to work closely with X-teams, share their insights and observations, suggest ways things could be done better, and also work with their customers in a more engaged manner. The summary of the observations captured by the X-team often put forth a great solution that alleviated a lot of disquiet within the organization. The followers also get the opportunity to review the solution put forward by the X-team to validate it, and potentially this knowledge will help them become X-team members for solving another problem in the future. Followers also carry the mantle of tweaking the solution based on customer feedback from time to time with executive buy-in. No road to excellence ever stands still.

CX is possibly one of the few skills that will stand the test of time. No college degree or education in a specific technology will last that long a period of time. Organizations will significantly change their operating models, but customers are here to stay. CX involves critical thinking and problem solving that has to be shaped in the right manner for organizations to become more successful.

REWARDING RESULTS

Too many of us are guilty of not appreciating success even in small measure. Employee engagement drives that success. We forget the human element in the employee when they put in the extra time, effort and energy to drive success. This lack of appreciation ultimately leads to de-focus and, eventually, employees leaving the organizations.

Research shows that more than 70 per cent of employees are actually not engaged. Just like customers, employees too need a human connection. Recognition can come in many forms and shapes—recognition from management, peer recognition, enabling means of self-expression, creating a sense of belonging to a community, providing an opportunity for personal growth, being part of a motivated X-team, belief in the employee by the leader, optimism in their efforts to succeed, and others.

Interestingly, organizations see rewards as 'cash'. Yes, cash rewards create an element of excitement but not a sense of belonging. If that were true, the highest paid organizations would have the strongest sense of belonging, and the best CX metrics. Yet, metrics show that organizations with the best CX are at the 70th percentile of the industry when it comes to 'compensation and rewards'.

Some organizations see offsites as a mode to develop engagement. But more successful ones look at rewarding the top quartiles by inviting them to leadership offsites or training sessions. The world renowned Jack Welch's training centre is a good illustration of the point.

The biggest mistake that organizations make is by not encouraging new recruits (at any level in the organization), and putting in enough effort to make their transition into the new organization successful. By merely leaving this to their supervisor, organizations risk creating an unengaged employee. Asking new recruits for their views is a positive form of engagement. Successful organizations, that have created engaged employees, have also created better CX results for themselves. After all, your employee is your internal customer.

As a youngster, I was taught that it's not the doing but the how you do it that makes all the difference. After all, there are many good cars, but there are fewer great cars out there.

Again, this goes back to the discussion about the emotional right side of the brain in Chapter Two. It's always easier getting customers than keeping them. Likewise, it's easier hiring employees than keeping them. Humans have natural animal-like instincts and if they feel threatened, they will naturally close up. Encourage them and they will open up and become more engaged.

> 'What makes Virgin particularly wonderful is the wonderful group of people who believe in what they're trying to do.'
>
> —Richard Branson

So the real question is, 'How human are you?'

Remember that an employee can also make the first move when the organization has not stepped up to it. When the employee understands the goal, they can play a higher role. Your manager is very likely to reciprocate.

IN SUMMARY—EIGHT

Finally, results boil down to how you put your team together. Getting your team to believe in the values of CX and create a corresponding culture, emphasizing how human you are and recognizing that your employees' success is your customer success, is the way everybody sees the magic.

Nine

The Second Building Block for Execution—Your Process, Methods and Tools

'To me, ideas are worth nothing unless executed. They are just a multiplier. Execution is worth millions.'

—Steve Jobs

As I worked with organizations around CX, I discovered the importance of discussing customer-focused strategies in regular meetings and communications to employees. While we can always discuss details about creating the vision and mission of the firm, extreme execution is ultimately what will actually get us from point A to Point B, and also help differentiate ourselves better. In recent years, my clients have started focusing on digital-first strategies and research indicates that they are 64 per cent more likely to succeed than their peers. My more successful digital-first clients focus on 1 per cent improvements at a time.

Over the years, I have tested several tools and methods, which are outlined in this chapter. My clients have gone back to the same tools to recalibrate them to achieve even bigger gains. By stacking several of these tools, they also achieve a CX multiplier effect.

I discovered that the journey to great CX pushes the team to visualize better, and once they do, they will have a bigger buy-in.

THE BIG PICTURE—THE ELEVATOR PITCH

My typical meetings with CEOs are very short. They will give you a few hours of their time, but you need to take the maximum benefit out of it. If you aren't crisp enough, they get bored within the first few minutes. When a conversation revolves around higher profitability or market share, they are really interested. CEOs need to be shown the big picture. That's where I find an 'elevator pitch' really shines. The preparation time for such a pitch is sometimes pretty long, during which time, we try and come up with a solution that can solve complex problems with simplicity. You can compare the CEOs patience with that of a customer, so the pitch has to be precise and leave nothing to chance.

During my engagements over the last two decades, I have discovered that any transformation, including CX, can be carried out using an eight-step process, the first few of which I use for this pitch. A snippet is presented for the CEO for their endorsement of the idea which gives us the mandate to execute the plan.

It always starts with an idea, which is then elaborated during the design process, tested and finally documented into a blueprint for execution. As you start to deliver on the project, you take continuous feedback, on the basis of which you improve and innovate. All of these inputs are consolidated and this then goes back into the delivery cycle. Think of this as a continuous loop. If something is not working, you need to go back to the design stage. The more the number of cycles you make, the more successful you are.

BASELINING

In helping organizations build strategy and execute it over the years, I have discovered a strange truth. Organizations get into the habit of slowly starting to acknowledge something that may be far from the truth as the reality. In the process, the original strategy and direction is forgotten and many organizations don't even know where they stand. To our surprise, we find policies and process manuals not being updated in years. New employees are still asked to read these manuals but are quickly told by their mentors that many of these processes have changed. So, the actual processes vary significantly by branch, city, country or region.

A thirty to forty-five day reality check and a zero-based approach really helps in these situations. CX is one area where these interventions really work well. In CX design, interaction models and data visualization have made a significant difference in the last decade or so. The current customer journey maps capture empathy in order to understand the context of the problem, provide creativity for insights and solutions and solve problems through an iterative process. All of these processes involve baselining.

THE CUSTOMER LIFECYCLE MAP

My engagements as a consultant have proved that a customer lifecycle map is a good starting point to start correlating business outcomes. Since a customer has different perceptions at each stage of the customer lifecycle, the lifecycle map starts giving you a pulse of the business.

During the need, awareness and consideration stages, a customer compares his needs to the options that my client presents. If successful, he arrives at his purchase decision. Association with the product or service provides him with the necessary experience needed to make this decision, and positive experiences progressively take him towards loyalty and then advocacy. The customer, thus, goes through a metamorphosis to reach the point of becoming a 'raving fan'. If, along the way on this journey, the customer gets disappointed, or if the competition provides a better product, he drops off.

A great example to look at is that of my telecom service provider that sells fixed line telephone services, broadband Internet, direct-to-home (DTH) television and mobile telephony. I am currently in different stages for each of these service offerings with the service provider. I shut down my fixed line a while back, but have kept my mobile connection as I get better reception in my city with them. I have poor experiences with their DTH service, and am ambivalent about their broadband offering as well.

By translating each stage of the lifecycle into a score card, I found it easier to compare and benchmark them. It's also easier to improve the design and the interaction model and also convince the team about the changes required. The customer drop-off points become more apparent with such a scoring mechanism.

When I managed customer retention at banks, I discovered a new truth. You get three months after customer acquisition to manage loyalty. After that period is over, it's almost impossible to retain customers as they would have already firmed up their choice.

After all, interactions define CX. During these interactions, customers need to feel valued and the interaction needs to move in the direction of delivering on the promise. To take an example, I often compare my interactions with various relationship managers (RMs) for managing my assets. Where the RM keeps coming back with alternatives and options, and is responsive to my requests, I know they are engaged. I end up having higher relationship values with such RMs. With an RM who only ends up sending me birthday greetings once in a year, the value of the relationship is very poor. Similarly, if my broadband service provider keeps me updated about outages that I could face due to their maintenance requirements, I would look for work arounds and not mind the inconvenience. But when the company does not do so, I get taken in by surprise by the outage and this annoys me as I might have something important scheduled during that time.

Over time, these relationships have converted me into a raving fan of certain products and companies. When relationships changed with time, I have switched loyalties as I realized it was more the RM's effort rather than that of the organization.

If I take the case of Apple or Samsung, both companies stay engaged by providing free operating system (OS) upgrades, software upgrades, customer interlock sessions and news about new products and services to keep themselves close to their customers. Companies like Coke or Pepsi need to spend more time on advertising since their interactions are short, but in the case of car companies, they have the opportunity for natural touchpoints through servicing or workshops. The premium segment, for example, provides driving lessons to chauffeurs to help them handle the vehicle better, which demonstrates the care that manufacturers show to their customers.

Customer loyalty is a crucial element in the success of any company as over time, loyalty creates advocates. This happens when customers start telling more than ten people about their positive experiences. According to Harvard Business Review, 23 per cent of customers rank in this category.

I always go back to the example of Apple Stores and how they create raving fans. If you find a queue outside an Apple Store waiting to get their hands on the product, it is a direct reflection of loyalty. If lines become shorter, it means that the competition has caught up or the product does not carry the same appeal.

So, while Apple loyalists will continue to endorse Apple and pardon their mistakes, new-to-brand customers will react very differently. This is where visualization with interaction maps involving channels, departments and products become critical. These interaction maps are what translate the customer lifecycle map into a customer journey map.

The success of a CX programme is often translated as higher 'customer lifetime value (CLV)'. That's the value that a customer generates (generally net profit) over his lifetime. I have often found that organizations are hesitant to retire products if they have had high CLV's even though the last few years may have seen significant dips in such values. This is an unsound strategy as eventually these products are proven outdated and companies scramble to find new products to retain their customers.

SERVICE DESIGN

To get my clients to understand how to improve their service model, we used service design with many of them.

In service design, we move from the lifecycle of a customer to the lifecycle of a specific task. This lifecycle of a task involves both the front and back service experiences from a user-centred point of view, considering all relevant stakeholders and bearing in mind all touch points.

Service design involves four stages: design, envision, prototype and implement.

The first stage of the process, co-design, is all about idea sharing with the problem statement or the idea at hand. The process we followed involved sketching, using aids like Lego, Post-its, cards, and whiteboards. It's about getting into the characters, sharing their motivations and telling the story. Issue cards help bring out interpretations of the problem at hand. This helps define the problem in a deeper manner, so that all relevant ideas around it can be thought through. The mind map is a great visual tool to put the whole thing together. Tools like the affinity diagram helps in organizing large amounts of data or evidences while placing them in their correlations.

Envision, the next stage of service design, is the process of creating the service solution. We translated this outcome with visual translation using leading industry visual aids. These allowed us to communicate and execute this easily across the organization. Since service solutions differed depending on personas, we used persona and empathy maps to effectively classify different groups of customers. To do this, we mapped personas to actors and plotted actor maps using participating individuals (employees or vendors) who influence the solution. The map showed the actors who were in close proximity to the issue at hand and their relationships between themselves. In effect, it offered us the opportunity to identify the points where we could leverage the relationship and points that broke that chain.

We used this method for designing the business architecture and empower actors to create organizational wealth and decision-making powers. We also aligned a motivation matrix to explain the nature of the handshake between stakeholders, which clarified each of stakeholders' points of view. We recognized that speed was a key consideration to envision and the actor maps provided credible insights for the creation of the journey map.

The step in the process, creating the prototype, is extremely crucial to understanding customer sentiment if done in closed groups.

I am reminded about an instance which demonstrates the importance of prototypes. One of our friends is a very large biscuit manufacturer based in South East Asia, with distribution networks spanning multiple countries. During one of our gatherings, where we met over dinner with friends from all over the world, she carried a few packets of biscuits their organization had prototyped in order to understand what we thought about them. She distributed the biscuits at the restaurant as well to gauge consumer reception for the product. She quickly made a note of the constructive user feedback and asked for areas of improvement for the product to be successful.

Having a clear idea of the solution and having tested it out in the marketplace, gave her a clear perspective and prepared the platform to step into the implementation phase.

So, when we took all of our learning from co-designing, envisioning and prototyping, we could move to implementation using a set of agreed roles and responsibilities, plan and blueprint, and the necessary technical specifications. The blueprint itself included the maintenance aspects of the relationship and the product. The service blueprint linked the customer journey map to actors, processes, channels and touchpoints along with the user goals for the journey. We used different service blueprints depending on the nature of the transaction. If you are in telecom, for instance, your pre-paid customers and post-paid customers would have separate service designs. Likewise, if you are in the restaurant business, walk-in customers would have a different service design to take-out orders. Therefore, service design links customer actions, customer interactions and emotions, frontline service interactions and handoffs, back-office interactions and process steps, along with individual timelines all in one go.

In all of this, we always used the service blueprint as a companion to the customer journey map as this is a key component of good service design.

DESIGNING PROCESSES AROUND HUMAN EMOTIONS

As a youngster, I was brought up with strong cultural influences. Indian dance forms were part of the cultural education I was introduced to by my family. In Indian dance, emotions come together to form a complex interplay to convey stories. We call it *navarasa* or nine moods. These influence the way the viewer perceives the story being narrated through the dance recital.

As I got closer to understanding how moods affected CX, I began to appreciate how processes could also be linked to moods. In a recent study published in *The Proceedings of National Academy of Sciences*,[1] as many as twenty-seven moods that a human being echoes are discussed. I looked closer and found that it was nine main emotions with three varying degrees of intensity, making it a total of twenty-seven. In a 2010 piece published in the *MIT Sloan Management Review*, Sriram Dasu and Richard Chase[2] had established that emotions can influence memory and the goal of CX is to ensure positive feelings for customers in interactions. Since CX is all about encounters and making decisions based on memory, it becomes critical to pay attention to this.

While working with clients, we established that twenty-one of these twenty-seven emotions were directly correlated to CX. Of these, twelve were positive and nine negative. In the lists below, the left-hand side represents the extreme emotion and the right-hand the milder version of the same emotion, in the following format—Extreme – Moderate – Soft.

The 12 positive emotions are:
Ecstasy – Joy – Serene
Admire – Trust – Accept
Amaze – Surprise – Distracted
Vigilant – Anticipate – Interested

The 9 negative emotions are:
Rage – Angry – Annoyed
Terrified – Fear – Apprehensive
Grief – Sad – Pensive

We found that when a customer had extreme negative emotions, it was difficult to move to a positive emotion. However, when the emotion was mildly negative, it was easier to move the customer to a positive interaction. For example, it was difficult to convert rage to ecstasy, but easier to convert rage to annoyed, or annoyed to accept.

This formed the basis of our service design interactions. Increasingly, by using data design techniques like sentiment analysis, we can identify customer moods and work on improving service design. We could, for example, escalate the case to the right call centre executive using these tools, and that formed the basis of the operational actions that needed to be followed.

We also discovered that an organization's actions could bring about a change in mood. For example, innovation brings about amazement. As such, by repeating moods, we could potentially create advocates who would go on to build the brand.

In a new study, Finnish scientists[3] conducted a research on which part of the human body shows up emotions, and showcased this with the help of a heatmap. The subjects themselves were Finnish, Swedish and Taiwanese. While happiness had a positive glow across the entire body, emotions like pride, love and anxiety closely followed. Anger, fear, disgust and surprise were focused more on the upper half of the body.

As such, during a face-to-face customer interaction emotions can be sensed and interpreted quite easily, and your responses in such service environments can be actively programmed to suitably respond to them. We have used this philosophy and understanding of emotions to educate branch personnel for better CX efficiency.

The tone of voice carries similar information. The pitch, loudness, stress on syllables, speech rate, pauses and the actual words used define the emotion and the intensity of the emotion. Anger, sadness and happiness are easily perceived, but emotions like disgust lesser so. We used this technique to educate call centre executives to understand the customer's emotional state during the interaction.

Over time, I worked with my firm to use the science of sentiment analysis to benefit my clients. Since voice carried sentiment and was unstructured data, it provided critical insight regarding CX issues that were often overlooked. As the processing was being done by machines, the information could be translated within a fraction of a second, thus enabling organizations to take corrective action and also predict the outcome of the conversation. We were able to plot a series of these sentiments into a graph to reveal the state of the brand as well as changes in organization's reputation in the customers' minds. This allowed us to direct the necessary organization actions that needed to be implemented for services, products, campaigns and other areas.

By overlaying this information on the customer journey map, we were able to provide additional insight on the effectiveness of the customer journey. In addition, by using sentiment analysis tools on social media sites, we could track the success of the brand in the social media space as well.

When we work closely with our clients, our clients have often felt that such a sentiment analysis tool kit would be a powerful arsenal to their brand, product service or their end customers.

Why did this really click? On closer perusal, clients often found that more than 80 per cent of their data was unstructured and that data was not getting used at all. Traditional methods like call tracking were just inconsistent and un-comprehensive towards bridging that gap.

Another issue we found is that prioritization is based on methods like first come first serve, which fails to recognize already irate customers or repeated incidents of failure on the organization's part. The right form of escalation can attend to the customer mood with the right level of empathy and can go a long way towards retaining that customer and growing the relationship. Often, tools like chatbots are better off to test empathy to unaided customer centre executives for the same reasons.

THE SECRET CUSTOMER

In recent medical journals, there is a lot of conversation on nanotechnology inventions that monitor and diagnose patient health using nanoparticles. The same concept is being used by more traditional organizations by introducing a few particles (seeded/ artificial customers) within the larger base of customers to diagnose issues. These are the 'secret customers'.

Over the years, I have been using the same framework with great success and it has provided significant CX uplift.

These secret customers are mystery shoppers who pose as existing or potential customers. Their transactions are tracked through the arteries of the organization. Diagnosis reveals weaknesses, and actionable insights can then be implemented to turn weakness into advantages. It has become so popular that organizations have gone a step ahead to introduce mystery shoppers into their competitors' bloodstream in order to identify their strengths and weaknesses.

When we carry out these exercises, our seeded customers are carefully tagged and the process they go through within the organization is tracked till the end. The samples are chosen to be diverse, so that each branch of the process can be carefully tracked, and issues pertaining to each branch can be fixed quickly. The approach is not restricted to physical visits only; it could be calls or emails, or requests through websites or social media platforms.

Before mystery shopping techniques became mainstream, the only way we understood customer sentiment was to put out questionnaires or surveys. Customers hesitated to be brutally honest which made it difficult to collect facts as they are. In such surveys, processes did not necessarily link back to customer perceptions. Mystery shopping cuts that chase, and arguments and perception become redundant through data gathered by the secret shoppers. Mystery shoppers are not spies; rather, they are catalysts of change to bring about differentiation and avoid future embarrassments. Acceptance of this can drive broader organizational changes.

Banking, hospitality, airline, retail, telecom, real estate and hospitals are some sectors where we have put this to great use. I have often discovered that solutions to problems do not need to come from my client's industry. For instance, Amazon's excellent delivery model could provide great ideas to the banking sector.

We have often resorted to periodical repeats of mystery shopping to revalidate our improvements against competition. Once our goalpost changes, so does our customers, which creates the need for regular evaluations. The changes brought about through periodic mystery shopping visits warrants constant changes and improvements to our products and services, which in turn helps serve our customers better.

THE DIARY STUDY

Over the years, I did a bit of self-study to learn from some of my clients as to why their CX was stronger than their peers or competitors. I found out that the biggest reason was their engagement with their end customers. On digging further into that phenomenon, I discovered that their secrets in understanding key customer experiences were through their interactions with them.

The formal method I learnt later is what you could call 'diary study'. In the diary study method, you have a discussion with customers on the desired outcome within boundaries of expectations.

To do this, you need a meaningful customer sample size and ensure active participation. In order to have a meaningful conversation, you need to probe the right questions using the right guidelines. Also, insights gained from the conversation need to be captured within a definite timeline so that they stay meaningful. The next step is to follow up the interaction with clarifying questions, followed by monitoring their behaviour without your influence so as to understand root cause and effect.

A good way to review the engagement is to schedule another conversation post the experience to understand the overall outlook. You should also discuss your findings and areas of improvement that might make the customer's life simpler.

My successful clients also track behaviour across diary studies to review improvements over time. Since these studies deep-dive into problem statements, my clients took an average of forty-five days for such studies.

So what do my clients do with these studies? They pitch sharper and faster. They make sure that the results are fed back into new products or services, into campaigns, product enhancements or quickly swap the product for the customer into a more relevant product. This also helps identify attrition patterns that can be quickly fixed.

CULTURAL PROBES

In certain circumstances, my clients did not conduct a formal diary study. They used a concept that is formally known as 'cultural probes', a quick and dirty method that is especially useful in study designs to anticipate behaviour. A set of tools, artefacts or tasks are used to provoke the user to think about their environment in a new way in order to understand people's lives, values and thoughts better.

A simple example is where one of my client's (a bank) sends a set of marketing materials along with a credit card, and the end customer just bins them without even turning the pages. A cultural probe prior to launch would indicate to the bank that it may be wiser to get the customer connected to its website rather than send expensive material that would not be appreciated.

This reminds me of a question my mentor once asked me, 'How do you provide an experience to a customer who is miles away the same experience as if you are next to him explaining the product or service'.

If you have noticed, companies generally release beta versions of their software for customers to test and provide inputs. These are a form of cultural probes designed to help the company collect and compile observations to improve the end product. Along with the product, sometimes collages, photographic records, stickers, maps, and other tools are added to set guidelines that ensure users capture the kinds of thoughts that the company is looking for in their feedback. Once the task is finished, additional interactions are initiated in order to yield nuanced insights. These insights are also used for future requirements concerning similar customers.

THE MOMENT OF TRUTH

> 'An individual without information cannot take responsibility; an individual who is given information cannot help but take responsibility.'

—Jan Carlzon

Possibly the single most popular concept that is used by my clients who are keen on improving their CX is 'moment of truth' (MoT). Based on my extensive research, I found that some leading organizations, including SAS, Google, Disney and Amazon live by this concept.

In the 1980s, when Jan Carlzon took as President and CEO, Scandinavian Air Service (SAS) was a failing airline. He managed a spectacular financial turnaround and re-oriented SAS to become customer-driven. He documented his secrets in his book *The Moment of Truth*.[4] There, he describes how every opportunity to engage with the customer needs to be meaningful. The term itself was coined by Richard Normann, a Swedish management consultant, but he did not manage to popularize it as much as Jan.

Any time the customer comes into contact with an organization he forms an impression, referred to as MoT. Every successful moment drives higher customer satisfaction and repeat successes creates lasting impressions. In the MoT concept, manner, every small moment matters.

Disney has mastered that science. Their main customers at theme parks are children and the anticipation creates magic into their very hearts. As I mentioned earlier in Chapter Three, disappointments from height restrictions for rides and frustrating long lines in the sun are converted into magic with special passes which allows customers to stand at the front of the queue for their next ride—of course with height permitting. Every cast member, as Disney theme park employees are called, at that point could take the decision to hand out passes. Disney has further augmented every interaction into magic by adding castles, favourite characters, games, toy shops as well as friendly waves from a Disney cast member.

Over the years, MoT has further evolved into four distinct moments.

Google came up with the term 'Zero Moment of Truth' (ZMOT)[5] representing the first possible moment when the organization interacts with the customer. Customers do research online to solve their problems and identify a possible product or solution. This pre-interaction moment creates ZMOT. Google uses search engine optimization (SEO) to help such customers. Decisions like 'buy versus not to buy' or curiosity happens at this stage. If the right parameters are met, brands can use this as their first point of success. Customers using their mobile phones while waiting—for a doctor, in a bus or train, outside their kids' school, for the next meeting, in a café, etc.—presents a significant opportunity for brands to interact with potential customers. The substantial power of ZMOT can be gauged from the fact that over two-thirds of customers seem to be exercising these options.

Organizations respond by reaching shoppers at the right time, at the right place, with the right content. When decisions are made much faster, it enables a seamless experience. How would a slow website or network affect all of this?

The term, 'first moment of truth' (FMOT) was coined by Procter & Gamble (P&G)[6] to represent the first few seconds of encountering a product and the way it appeals to your senses and emotions. It presents itself as a candy bar when you step into a supermarket to pick up toothpaste. The lobby of a hotel or the greeter at a restaurant is another good example of FMOT. The attendant at a hospital, the meeter-greeter at a bank branch or cashier at the store all deliver FMOT. A digital signage at airport entries and exits or at boarding gates could be your customers' FMOT. FMOTs also trigger decision points and attract your products over your competitors.

After the purchase has been made, using the product is the 'second moment of truth' (SMOT),[7] also coined by P&G. A.G Lafley, the CEO of P&G from 2000–2010 and 2013–2016, emphasized the importance of using FMOT and ZMOT to win over a customer. Say–Do ratios, that we discussed in Chapter One, are a direct reflection of this.

Pete Blackshaw, a former P&G executive, coined another term called the 'third moment of truth' (TMOT)[8] to describe the moment when the customer falls in love with the product. The customer then advocates for the product through endorsements, word of mouth, ratings and reviews or feedback. Social media platforms and YouTube have become critically important for TMOT, with many brand advocates reaching out to several hundreds and thousands of their subscribers.

While there are other routine touchpoints, there are only three moments of truth. When my clients understand the need to transform a touchpoint into a MoT, they create actions centred around interactions to create meaningful relationships, and stop doing things that might break the relationship. They also aggregate multiple touchpoints into a single MoT, and look at moments of truth as critical loyalty drivers.

THE CUSTOMER JOURNEY

As my clients get more astute, they start seeing gaps in CX even though they had tackled many MoT scenarios already. A MoT represents a specific point in a customer's journey, which is made up of multiple touchpoints. So, while the customer may have had a great experience with a product browsing the web, another experience can offset that positiveness and make them consider that the overall experience wasn't so great.

While working with one of my clients on their credit card customer interaction process, we discovered that a customer who applied for a credit card based on research (ZMOT), had a great agent experience when they submitted their documents (FMOT), but somewhere in the middle the bank delayed the credit card approval process or lost the documents. This represented a clear gap between FMOT and SMOT and the overall experience in such cases is dissatisfaction. If my client had used the customer journey method at the outset, they could have eliminated some of these issues.

One of the best personal examples I could share is about my emotions when I visit a Starbucks outlet in South East Asia and India. Both these markets are challenging places for premium brands as customers are price sensitive and the marketplace offers many alternate choices with similar experience at more affordable prices. The premium Starbucks experience, therefore, begs other social and coffee experiences that can't be found at alternate locations. Starbucks coffee shops are often used by start-ups to either get work done or have an informal discussion regarding work and the Internet forms a critical component of such interactions. While looking for a place to have a coffee, the store location, appearance, ambience and the aroma of fresh coffee are factors that attract and delight customers. Factors like price, long queues, wait time for the coffee, getting a seat, poor Internet speeds and locating a washroom emerge as major deterrents. So, as a customer, while I have a choice between Starbucks and another coffee shop, I peek into a Starbucks outlet to do a relative comparison of all these deterrents before I make up my mind.

The other thing you would immediately notice is that there are multiple handoff points—the cashier, the person who prepares the food and drinks and the person who ultimately serves you the items you had ordered. Sometimes, the finer points are missed out— cutlery isn't provided, or it takes time to serve a glass of water that you wanted. All of these factors are MoTs in their own right and play equally important roles in ensuring the customer's overall experience.

The example of a coffee shop visit is no different when we work with clients to improve their CX. In most organizations, departments are often siloed, and their goals don't exactly map into that of a neighbouring department's goal. This results in poor customer satisfaction and escalations.

When we represent the customer journey as a visual story to clients we end up getting better participation from employees working in the organizations. The story is readily seen as an extension of emotions and frustrations with a number of parameters that employees can relate to. Since the representation is from a customer's point of view, employees tend to pay attention and they can relate to the story by imagining themselves in the customer's shoes.

While customer journeys start with a defining need, whether real or perceived, it covers handoffs between departments. This is where many of the issues start to crop up. Many senior executives don't realize that they are directly or indirectly involved with the customer in some way and a number of approvals get stuck at their desks beyond reasonable delay.

In our strategy, When the journeys become too long, it's split into multiple journey maps both for simplicity as well as to focus on each experience that is part of the journey. Sometimes, the interlinkages between the journey maps is the main culprit for delays, thus resulting is an unsatisfactory brand promise. As such, we need to recognize that journey maps are living documents, which require regular recalibration.

At a premier Indian private sector bank, we recognized that their products, however carefully crafted, often included uncompetitive features that warranted going back to design and eliminating discomfort. The bank fixed this by using the journey map for customer interactions from the call centre to the product team, and back to an outbound call centre for a call to the customer informing them of the fixes.

As a rule of thumb, when we capture customer journey maps, we capture the customer's expectations, their thinking process, insights and pain points as well as how the customer feels, and then combine them to define the guiding principles, defining values and target experience to mould these into the touchpoints.

Another important set of guidelines that is often missed is what we call 'recovery principles'. These define how to react at a specific touchpoint to an irate customer. It calls for escalation, or passing it on to another service staff member, who can intervene and turnaround any unhappiness.

My experience is that sometimes the gap arises from a lack of responsibility, which can be captured as part of the RACI (responsibility, accountability, consultation, information) chart.

Amongst best practices that I have picked up is that all long-term impacts on technology, brand and minimum viable experiences (that warrant product changes) need to be channelled for correction.

We have also made mistakes in assuming that customers take similar paths to acquire or transact. Nothing could be further from the truth. Real world experiences may differ by store or by geography, and this is an area where training becomes a key factor in CX.

Channel strategies become critical when a customer switches channels. For example, where customers use different operating systems—Windows or Mac, Android or iOS—consistency is the key challenge. Likewise, in areas concerning human to machine interface and vice versa also present bottlenecks. Therefore, the simple gospel truth here is attention to detail.

Most observations that we tend to capture are unstructured, and that can be lost in translation if they are oversimplified without giving due importance to insights and root causes.

VOICE OF THE CUSTOMER (VoC)

'If you are going to ask your customers for feedback, read it yourself and use it. Respect the time that your customers took to share.'

—Unknown

I have often encountered situations where customers just walk away without even giving feedback. So, when a customer does in fact give positive or negative feedback, it helps businesses hone their products or services significantly. Thus, the voice of the customer (VoC) is at the core of any successful CX.

Our customers interact with us in many ways—through an advertisement, by filling up a form or a document, interacting with a salesman, visiting a store or branch, through websites, mobile or social media, or by buying or using our products or services. With each interaction, our customers feel an emotion and form a perception.

While individual feedback is like a photograph, when strung together it creates a movie that comes to life and gives us in-depth evidence about what customers think and feel about our products and services.

So, the question is, how have we helped our clients use VoC to deliver successful CX?

VoC interactions have helped us increase the number of loyal customers, reduce churn, given us ideas, helped us acknowledge problems and avoid mass errors that are often overlooked, benchmark ourselves to competition and also given us opportunities to engage with customers. It has also resulted in lower cost to serve and pushed us toward innovation. Ultimately it has enhanced our brand value.

VoC interactions are best done throughout the year in order to provide us with consistent data. We should also take pains to publish this to relevant stakeholders on a monthly basis as an aid to decision-making. We have found significant value in integrating VoC into our KPI's like net promoter score (NPS), churn, revenue or cost.

When we build a VoC strategy, we first align objectives, understand possible issues and pen down the required success criteria by asking clear questions regarding products, services, channels, persona, customer touchpoints or journey maps. The VoC planning must cover all strategic and tactical elements. The idea is to collect enough data to make it statistically valid. One important thing I have observed is that it is best never to prejudge information but to arrive at findings that will be shared with the relevant stakeholders including the leadership and service teams.

Over the years, while we built VoC strategies, there were other places where feedback was coming back from, including blogs and social media, which gave us a lot of information about how the market was reacting to various products or services.

I have often noticed that service teams take negative feedback defensively. The feedback is not against individuals but against current situations benchmarked with competition. So, the first step is to encourage feedback and request people to take all feedback constructively. The second step in the process is to empower employees to 'act right' during customer interactions. Without leadership support and engagement these programmes would fail, so it's important that everybody takes responsibility.

ETHNOGRAPHIC RESEARCH

When we conduct quantitative and qualitative exercises, we have often found that customers don't give meaningful feedback if they are not in their natural environment. We have used ethnography as a method to observe customers in their natural environment in order to understand their perceptions and emotions. We back up research with evidence in the form of videos, photographs and traffic heat map beacons.

For instance, when we did an ethnographic research exercise at booths in shopping malls to review customer engagement and traffic, it helped us identify issues with regards to product placements or push offers. At stores, this can help you review your design considerations and improve customer traffic flow at branches.

There are some lovely case studies that further highlight the importance of ethnographic research. London's Heathrow airport derives commission from duty free shops on actual passenger purchases. Using information gathered from ethnographic research, Heathrow started placing duty free shops at passenger wait areas. By identifying the customers' needs it built successful outcomes into their terminal design. Another example is that of Meat Pack which devised the 'hijack campaign' for similar outcomes.

Planning shelf placements at supermarkets, branch kiosks and displays, studying customer browsing patterns and service interactions, and understanding customer behaviour in new stores, new markets or new geographies are all examples of ethnography. Studying competition in specific neighbourhoods along with their customers based on ethnography allows you to tailor your branch sizes to suit the location.

When I go back to present my case to clients, I often find leadership arguing about the findings. This is where photographic and video evidence comes handy to convince them about their incorrect assumptions. Hidden cameras are very useful in this regard as they allow customers to act in their natural environment without getting conscious about being observed.

Over time we found that different neighbourhoods required different strategies. For example, if you had an expatriate neighbourhood, you need to cater to that group. If the neighbourhood had small- and medium-businesses, you need to cater to that. To refer back the Starbucks Australia example from Chapter Three, it is crucial to note that if they had conducted ethnographic studies to avoid culture traps, they could have minimized their agony and losses.

Another really good example involving the consumer goods giant, Proctor & Gamble (P&G), narrated by A.G. Lafley and Ram Charan in *The Game-Changer*[9] comes to mind. P&G launched a reasonably priced detergent in Mexico for low income earners in small packages, with obvious expectations of it being a huge hit. However, it proved to be a big disappointment and the question that begs asking is, 'Why?' The authors argued that this was because the target segment—working-class individuals whose laundry is full of sweat and strong odours—associated detergent foam with confidence about the cleaning capabilities of washing powder, but the product produced very little foam. When P&G investigated the reasons, they found that the Mexican worker who did his laundry by hand, soaked his clothes manually in that detergent and lost confidence when it produced very little foam. The lesson here is, know your customers and their culture.

As a consultant, I made another observation on the importance of ethnographic research at my neighbourhood ICICI Bank branch. The branch was far bigger than customer requirements and was located in an area that was already overcrowded with other banks. Whenever I went into the branch, I noticed that the footfall was very low. It took the bank a year and a half to notice this issue. They consequently downscaled and moved a few blocks away, where it has been located ever since.

A great example where ethnography is used at customers' premises is food product packaging. If a homemaker finds it difficult to open a package, they would refrain from picking it up again at the store regardless of the quality and other positive characteristics of the food product. This wouldn't be highlighted automatically during either the design or the production stage till one observed such difficulties in its natural environment. A simple door-to-door exercise with a follow-up visit could avoid such mass-scale errors.

During one of my consulting assignments, I had the pleasure of visiting a Japanese restaurant that served us fresh fried items. But there was something special about the food there. The oil did not stick to our hands and we felt as if it was fried in water. We asked the chef who was preparing the meal right across from where we were seated, and he acknowledged that the sunflower oil was manufactured to cater to the preferences of the Japanese population. He also added that the product faced ethnographic challenges when it was introduced in neighbouring markets due to this very attribute.

Based on research, you will find that if you conduct ethnographic research, you won't be alone. Google, P&G, Intel, Xerox, Unilever, Lego, Wells Fargo, Ford, Heathrow Airport, Montblanc and Cartier are some examples of organizations across industries that use ethnography to understand their customers.

DESIGN PROVOCATION

I have often been moved by design because it provokes and demonstrates the art of the possible. Yet, not all designs will make it into the real world. You would have seen the different prototypes launched by car manufacturers that evoke a sense of emotion amongst its customers. Based on those initial reactions, whether positive or negative, these designs find their way into the real world.

Design thinking, pioneered by Tim Brown,[10] is a new way of leading an organization towards extraordinary improvements that has been proven to work really well. Design thinking has the potential to do for innovation what total quality management (TQM) did for manufacturing. With growth, organizations often fail to innovate and get wary of start-ups that could disrupt their very existence. As humans, we are driven by a fear of mistakes, and hence we are forever looking at the safety rails. With design thinking, organizations can effectively compete using a combination of structure and formatted tools. It is well recognized that the minds of creative people who make up the design teams of organizations are largely unstructured, messy and unpredictable. The need to synthesize and harmonize structure into the design process led to the genesis of design thinking.

Design thinking establishes three sets of activities:

1. Customer discovery;
2. Idea generation; and
3. The testing experience.

Customer discovery links back to framing the problem. With idea generation you are effectively oscillating between the problem and the solution. That's where we get into techniques like braindump, brainwrite and brainstorm. Another effective way of connecting the problem and the solution is through the use of mind maps.

Design provocation is an intermediate step in this process and challenges the status quo with the information being presented during idea generation. It's a lateral thinking technique that helps you to explore new realities. One of its guiding principle is that no idea is ridiculous till the end of the exercise.

In my experience, one of our biggest provocations was when we noticed that calls were not being picked up in time. Dr Edward De Bono coined the word 'PO'[11] as shorthand for provocation. Obviously, provocative solutions could include putting a pillow on top of the phone, to using vibrating and flashing modes in mobile phones. Yet, the simple solution was to build an organizational culture of 'three rings' within which each phone call needed to be answered.

A great example comes from Bank of America.[12] As part of their design thinking process, they started talking to people who were great at saving as well as those who struggled with it. One everyday habit that mothers who were great at saving followed was to round off their budget per item to the next higher number. For example, a US$22.6 spend would be rounded up to US$23. All this change added up and enabled mothers to save the pennies in an account. There was nothing like that in banking and the designers came up with an idea.

Bank of America launched the Keep the Change programme, prototyped it and got leadership approval. The programme was quite simple; in effect, the excess transaction amount got pushed into a savings account, with a 100 percent match (with a cap) from Bank of America during their launch period. It was launched in September 2005 and gathered more than 2 million customers in less than twelve months, and eventually garnered more than 12 million customers with savings in excess of US$2 billion. What's more, more than 99 per cent of customers stayed on with the programme. Not bad for loose change, eh?

While I was visiting some South African banks, I happened to visit one which had provided an innovative product to put pennies back into investments, such as a mutual fund, with high returns.

Digging deeper, I realized that banks are not the only ones that innovate in this manner. At Google, the design thinking philosophy is a deceptively simple three-step process to generate innovative ideas.[13]

1. **Know the user**—I feel you can always learn from people who are highly successful. If you look at management guru Ram Charan's approach to solving the problem, which often involves personally visiting the site where he uses his power of observations to look at areas of opportunity;

2. **Think 10X**—improve something 10 times, remembering that being able to describe the idea in six or less words, clarifies it;

3. **Prototype**—this is the step when it's time to take action.

Another example is that of Nike, which successfully transitioned from being just a sports performance brand to a fashion brand as well. It was all about pushing and stretching boundaries to create new market spaces. Nike's stand-out strategy comes from chasing down entertainers and appointing them as brand creative directors.

They also took advantage of a new crop of designers who grew up obsessing over Nikes—sneakers that already had a cult following—and now lovingly craft the shoes in their image of what the brand represents.

THE EVOLUTION OF FOCUS GROUPS TO SOCIAL MEDIA

Did you know that focus groups came from an unlikely place? When Austrian born psychologist Ernest Dichter carried out studies with small groups (or focus groups) of WWII veterans to understand the impact the war had on them, he managed to translate their experience to advertising.

Before Dichter pioneered this method, only quantitative measures were used as the basis for launching a product or a service. Focus groups are generally followed up with quantitative reasoning based on the ideas and perceptions thrown up by the focus group. Focus group participants are diverse enough to be representative of the larger social population and they are guided by 'props' to align their reactions to intent.

Mattel is a great example of a company that used focus groups to design their first Barbie in 1950 and then make a curvier one in 2014. Government agencies, too, use this technique to understand public concerns about policy changes, while political parties use it to sharpen their campaign messages.

Over the years, I have noticed that reliance on focus groups have declined. The reason for this is rather simple; a more direct and relevant approach using social media provides much faster consumer feedback.

Of late, the phenomenon of social media influencers has taken over this approach. Let's take the example of Samsung Galaxy Fold, the world's first folding smartphone phone, which commands a high end US$2,000 price tag and straddles the market category between a phone and a tablet. Samsung needed positive public reaction to the pre-launch to drive greater sales volumes but honest feedback highlighted a number of fragility issues requiring deeper fixes. Although many look at this as a poor publicity stunt, it was extremely useful to avoid further damage to their brand.

Amongst recent technological advances, analytics and artificial intelligence (AI), combined with robotic process automation, allows organizations to execute insights, including customer feedback, much faster. Amazon's 'more items to consider' or 'inspired by your Wishlist' tools are great examples of how technology can be used to deliver better CX.

SOCIAL MEDIA ANALYTICS

The importance of social media in business is growing at lightning speed. If you dig into numbers, 71 per cent of consumers are more likely to recommend a brand based on positive experience with it on social media. This trend is captured by the fact that social media advertising spend is growing at a compounded annual growth rate (CAGR) of 32 per cent according to many research firms.

With that kind of serious money being thrown in, how important do you think the insight derived from such spend is going to be?

Just to give you another quick statistic. The largest web search engine in the world is Google, which people visit to solve virtually every problem, and the second largest is YouTube, which is also owned by Google.

So how have organizations taken advantage of social media?

Let's take the case of Leo Burnett, which decided to explore the possibility of merging the virtual world with physical interactions by creating a united experience with their Nivea Second Skin campaign. The campaign focused on the hug, which was a simple act to convey emotion and feeling, by connecting people separated by long distances using virtual reality. This campaign was put up on social media as an advertisement and managed to connect people to the cause very successfully.

Other companies like Domino's (Domino's #EasyOrder) and PWC (#BallotBriefcase Snapchat campaign) have managed to create a similar impact. Given the immense amount of analytics being shared by YouTube, Google, Facebook, Brandwatch and others, social media and the Internet provide an extraordinary avenue to know about potential customers in a much easier fashion.

Another great case study is Coke. Coca-Cola consumers share their opinions on new products through social media, phone or email. In a social media campaign in 2018, Coke revamped its presence on Facebook, Twitter and Instagram, with custom-created content by well-known artists who also connect to the brands core values. The campaign put forward this connect by coming up with a 'World Kindness Day' to spread a little love.

Coke's brand campaigns on social media works on the understanding that social media is a two-way conversation, and without it spreading to other like-minded customers, the campaign would not be successful. Therefore, Coke uses uniform resource locators (URLs), commonly known as web addresses, to track all syndicated content, including those on other sites or social media, for impressions and engagement. That data is linked back to hard metrics in order to assess effectiveness. Those metrics, in turn, can be linked back to commercial metrics to assess the final impact of the campaign on the organization.

So, you may ask why all this fuss about analytics. India, for example, has one of the fastest Internet growth rankings in terms of absolute growth, yet social media analytics is still in its infancy in comparison to many other countries. While many organizations claim to have a social media presence, their penetration amongst their customer base is abysmal at best.

I would go back to the 'Sunday–Monday syndrome' that Francis D'Souza of Cognizant described a few years ago. He noted that when it comes to customers' personal lives, they are far more advanced (Sunday), while corporates (Monday), are still playing catch up.[14]

There are lessons we can learn from global leaders in the social media space. As one of the world's most recognizable brands, Nike, has built some of that success on social media as well. Their campaigns are focused on selling benefits and not products. Nike Football, for example, has over 43 million fans, Nike has over 32 million fans, while Nike Sportswear has over 15 million fans on Facebook alone. With consumers following the company's social media platforms for the latest news on Nike products like Mercurial and HyperVenom, celebrity endorsements and consumers using the Nike App to stay fit, the company provides direct avenues for customers to interact with the brand. Nike measures these engagements by creating multiple social media profiles on different targeted pages and uses metrics to process data gathered from posts, photographs, shares, views, likes, comments, conversations and criticisms. It also uses demographics like age and sex, and consumer profiles for deeper insights using social analytics tools.

Social media analytics has also evolved with the use of easy-to-read visual dashboards that simplify even the most complex data. To think that social media is only for fast moving consumer goods (FMCG) or retail is a misnomer. Other sectors also use social media to connect with their customers, including almost all US hospitals, and consumer and investment banks. Shell, a leading energy and petrochemical company, has a clear digital and social media strategy to create engagements.

However, one needs to keep in mind that social media can also break the brand, and it's critical to recognize that. When the song 'United Breaks Guitars'[15] by singer-songwriter Dave Carroll was posted on YouTube, it went viral and got over 10.5 million views. The song was written in protest to United Airlines's handling of Carroll's guitar and its refusal to pay compensation for damages. The airline didn't respond quickly enough, and by the time the song had got over 1,50,000 views, it was no longer about the compensation payment as the cause had become quite personal to Carrol. The whole point of this story is that the damages in question were just $1,200 for the broken guitar if United had handled it correctly. However, due to its initial mismanagement of the passenger's grievance and the power of social media, the airline took a hit on its reputation and was left with a clean-up act to handle.

THE CUSTOMER SERVICE TRIANGLE

As an avid hobbyist photographer, one of the basic skills I had to master was to understand the photographer's exposure triangle or the relationship between the three factors that one can control—shutter speed, ISO (exposure speed) and f-stop (aperture). The fourth factor that is outside the control of the photographer is light. If you think about the relationship between these four elements, they can be equated with the elements that impact customer service and CX.

In doing so, you can compare light to customers and personas. The ISO indicates the sensitivity of the film and the higher this is, the more light it captures. Therefore, more sensitive you are to your customers, the more they will come and transact with you. The f-stop (or aperture) refers to the opening of a camera lens, which allows light to come in. That can be compared to the number of channels that the business has—the more channels, the more customers you will attract.

Moreover, the combination of sensitivity and number of channels helps you build reliability and trust. Similarly, the more number of channels you have and the faster you respond to them (think about shutter speed), the more convenient your customers will feel. Balancing customer sensitivity and speed makes the customer sense whether you are responsive or not. What's interesting is that you can't fix this as standard because it differs according to lighting conditions, that is, the type of customer or persona.

Here, balance is important from a corporate's cost perspective as well. The thumb rule is that you need to be where your customers are but more channels also mean higher cost of maintenance. This is a fine balancing act that needs to be perfected given that if your customers use the Internet or the phone, you need to provide those channels of service in order to attract customers.

Further, sensitivity relates back to the time you provide the customer any service. So, if you have a high average customer handling time, the customers waiting in queue may lose their patience and leave. By using innovation, you could reduce that impact. For example, if you had a quick checkout for a few items, then customers will feel less upset. You could also give the customer an option to book an appointment and reserve his service window to minimize grievance.

Over time, as I have built multiple CX experiences for my clients, I am keener to emphasize on post processing and damage control issues to prevent them from taking wrong decisions.

ARE 'CUSTOMER SATISFACTION SURVEYS' (CSATs) STILL RELEVANT?

Many a time, while talking directly to customers, I have heard them saying, 'They have all the relevant information, so they need to get it right.' I can't help but agree, and that leaves the organization with little room to manoeuvre.

Customer satisfaction survey (CSAT) is a process of discovering whether your customer is happy or not. As a periodic exercise, it highlights changes to your product, service or business operations. While this can prove be a crucial element in measuring brand value and brand satisfaction, individual interactions with customers carry a lot more weight and create lasting relationships. As such, methods like social media analytics, NPS, VoC, focus groups, customer effort score and others have emerged as new direct probes into an already needle-ridden body.

When we ask a customer about an experience right after they had experienced it, they will let us know about the immediate outcome. But a post-service experience might not have gone right and that would not be captured till a CSAT survey is done. The worst fact is that the person would tell an average of fifteen people post a poor service experience according to American Express Customer Service Barometer 2017.

Moreover, CSAT also has a consistent set of questions being asked, which not only make it easy for the customer to comprehend, but also for the organization to monitor progress. This helps in making it a de-facto gold standard.

A case in point is BlackBerry, the erstwhile mobile phone manufacturer. In 2011, their sales peaked, but this was followed by a rapid drop. BlackBerry had four years to correct the slide, with at least four different CSATs being administered, and the definite possibility of countless other probes to understand the shift.

While CSAT is a great measure, it's not the Holy Grail. For instance, neither does it ask the question about advocacy which NPS does, nor does it address defection, which eventually caused BlackBerry's downfall.

I have also found other instances where a CSAT won't help solve the problem. When consumer drones became a trend, many companies including Parrot, Google, GoPro and 3D Robotics competed with DJI. In the face of competition, DJI's primary focus was on bringing down prices while managing quality to emerge as the market leader. CSAT's would not have been able to pin-point the problem of high prices for quality products that DJI identified and successfully responded to.

A startling fact made by Microsoft points to the fact that human attention spans have dropped from twelve seconds to only eight in the past eighteen years, which corroborates with my independent observations with regards to my own clients.

As I look back at lost customers, I can see the potential loss caused by customer defections after a negative customer experience. In fact, only recently I read a study which pointed out that US companies lost more than US$41 billion because of the same fact.

My biggest lesson in all of this is that customers are happy to respond to surveys where we have acknowledged our mistakes and devised measures to address them. Otherwise, they would simply defect to the competition.

THE MOBILE CONNECTION

Over the years, I have been following the changes that the ubiquitous mobile phone has played in use cases with amazement. Now the device is practically in everybody's pocket, and in a few years' time it will all be smartphones.

When I was deeply engaged with some of my overseas clients, I noticed four specific trends in the process of selling:

1. **Sales through mobile**—Organizations based abroad had embraced customer relationship management (CRM) systems like salesforce.com in a completely mobile fashion. The entire sales interaction was being carried out through the mobile phone and the tool helped the leadership monitor sales and sales teams' activities that enabled earlier closures. In addition, it was custom branded and helped the sales teams stay in touch with their customers. This was a 'win-win!' for CEOs as they could practically run their businesses from their mobile phones.

2. **Product bytes**—Continuing with the above example, the salesforce.com tool provided product updates practically on a day to day basis, with quizzes and ways by which they could show the customer the latest on their mobile devices including tablets. This allowed the company to showcase the product to the customer to facilitate a more meaningful conversation. These would include elements like return on investment (ROI), performance, add-ons, features and functionality and other product specifics.

3. **Product training and quizzes**—One of the biggest gaps that we found with sellers is the lack of comprehensive awareness regarding products and services, especially if they were selling more than a dozen products and were required to be

well-informed about the nuances of each of these products. The gap also came about because they were in the field most of the time and found it difficult to be up-to-date with upcoming product launches. Pushing periodic quizzes for sales teams, along with bite-sized information on products, helped accelerate their learning process as well as keeping their skills refreshed.

4. **Location-based tracking**—Even though many interactions have moved to the Internet, there are still physical interactions that can't be avoided. These are best served when the person is at the right place at the right time. To give you an example, if there is a service request that comes in and our service person happens to be in the area, the customer is pleasantly surprised by the short turnaround time that resulted from the ability of the organization to track service personnel based on their locations. The same principles can be applied to the taxi aggregator, Uber, which redirects the closest vehicle to your location for the quickest possible ride to reach your destination. We also use this when we want to track whether service personnel reached the customer premises or if they spent adequate time in resolving issues.

In India, we also use this to track cash collections so that we can measure fulfilments as well as lower frauds or cash defalcations in businesses such as banking and insurance.

Besides these mobility-based use cases, the proliferation of mobile phones has penetrated into other areas that are extremely interesting.

- **Mobility in factories**—Production downtime at factories result in a direct loss of revenue. Alerts for these events can be triggered at the right time to reach the right person or the right role and help minimize losses. According to Credencys, this has improved up to 10 per cent productivity for such employees, saving as much as 42 minutes of disruption per employee.

- **Busting queues**—At airports, I now see airline check-in processes getting accelerated with the use of tablets and kiosks to bust queues.
- **Guest experience**—When I visit Singapore, I now find local hotels offering mobile devices for customers who need a communication device that is affordable on their short stays. I also see automated check-in and check-out processes decreasing as much as 20 per cent pressure on the front desk. On digging deeper, I have found that these services are being provided by organizations like Openkey and Runtriz for hospitality chains such as Radisson, Best Western and the likes.
- **Chatbots**—When I lived in the UAE, I found the most unlikely use cases of chatbots. Pretty much every government business in the UAE uses chatbots—to identify the status of your visa, driving licence renewals, applying for electricity connections and many more. It just cuts out the clutter of waiting for answers from a call centre executive, or having to put up or log into an app and know the status.

In the past few years, a number of businesses have used new, technology-based customer service tools and methods to drive sales as well as deliver improved CX. I will highlight a few that, in my opinion, stand out.

- **BBDaily**—When I relocated to Bangalore a few years ago, I noticed that India had caught on to a unique business model where daily essentials like milk, bread, eggs and groceries come home through mobile ordering services provided by online stores like Milkbasket and BBDaily. With services available after office hours, and cancellations just a click away, these businesses provide for an increasingly fast paced delivery mechanism. I wonder why such services have not caught on to other industries yet?

- **Meat Pack/Hijack**—This was possibly the most interesting use case I have come across in years. A Guatemalan shoe retailer, Meat Pack, sold branded, limited-edition shoes from the likes of Adidas, Nike and Puma. They used an app called Hijack which enabled a brick-and-mortar store to interact digitally with its customers. The app used push notifications for promotions and to make things even more interesting, it also triggered a countdown timer of 99 seconds for the customer to get to the Meat Pack store. Their discount would be as high as the number of seconds left on their phones. Since the app was integrated into Facebook, it also enabled live posts. As a result of these promotions over only a few days, competitors lost over 600 customers.

- **John Lewis (visual product search)**—Sometimes, our customers come across products they are interested in but don't know the name or the manufacturer. The UK retailer, John Lewis, partnered with Cortexica, a UK based AI company, to test this hypothesis using an iPad app that allowed for visual search of similar products based on uploaded images. This was used to test the effectiveness of a sales strategy and they received over 90 per cent positive feedback from customers who used it.

- **Instore assistance**—Although there aren't any Apple or John Lewis stores in India yet, I was pleasantly surprised by the CX experience at many outlets where agents assisted customers using in-store apps to provide a significantly better shopping experience, including enquiries regarding products and stock levels. If the customer wanted to purchase a product, the assistant could initiate a purchase from the handheld device and have the product delivered right to the spot where the customer was.

- **Practo scheduler**—My Mumbai-based dentist uses a scheduling app called Practo. When I enquired about it, he told me that it helps doctors schedule appointments for their patients and even keeps patient records. This way, they have much better control over their day. In addition, the app also reminds patients of an upcoming appointment to visit the clinic and makes sure that the patient confirms their visit.

- **Fitness coach**—Over the years, I have found use cases that can be applied to a number of industries even though they started in one. For example, we have a number of fitness coaches on iOS and Android that help us lead a healthier life. Imagine if a bank launched a fitness coach for wealth management or an organization launched one for keeping employees more productive as well as taking the occasional short break for stretching to avoid injuries like carpal tunnel syndrome?

'BEACON'IFICATION

A beacon is a low energy, battery powered Bluetooth radio transmitter. These are small hardware devices and smartphones scan and display signals from these beacons. Why is there so much buzz about a device that emits Bluetooth signals and why should you take this trend seriously?

For starters, the beacon market size is expected to be around US$58.7 billion by 2025 according to Grand View Research Inc. With the proliferation of wearables and mobile phones, the number of use cases is exploding. The technology uses proximity for marketing and push notifications. To take a high-ticket example, real estate is a difficult sell and firms hold exhibitions and put up stalls at malls to push their products. Even a single sale can justify the stall. The beacon is used extensively overseas to push such sales. The Meat Pack example above is of a lower ticket that used beacons to translate into sales.

For the uninitiated, Bluetooth is migrating from just mobile phones and tablets to devices like cameras, lights, point of sale devices, digital signages and vending machines to name just a few. These are increasingly being deployed at retail stores, real estate properties, amusement parks, events and other public places. To marketeers, beacons have higher click through rates than technologies like

RFID, NFC, QR, WIFI or even social media sites like Facebook and Twitter. Beacons are now pretty inexpensive (less than $20) and their battery power lasts for a few years.

The push notifications allow organizations to look at offline analytics with data like click through rates by location, campaigns that perform well and details of visitors. Since these devices are inexpensive, it gives small retailers the ability to compete with larger ones on tech.

Beacons can be used in areas like advertisements, navigation, pushing information like services or business cards, or for areas like loyalty programmes and online payments. For example, at museums they can pass on information about the exhibit, whether it is a painting or the sculpture, to the visitor seamlessly.

IN SUMMARY—NINE

There are no shortages of ideas or innovative thoughts that come to our minds. The biggest differentiator amongst the successful from the failures is the courage to execute and follow through. Motivation, proven methods and confidence are factors that are often missing in journeys that don't result in success. I hope this chapter has provided you with enough examples of successes and failures to start you off on the path to understand the tools, methods and process of executing an idea. Remember that you don't really need a thousand ideas to make a difference; you just need to take one-billion-dollar idea and turn it into a venture that delivers a multi-million-dollar profit. Although many of the methods discussed in this chapter, such as MoT or customer journey maps have become par for the course, by executing them in a differentiated fashion using the examples given here as a guide, they can well get you ahead of others.

Ten

The THIRD Building Block for Execution—Surprise with Innovation and Outperforming with Technology

'When you change the way you see the world, you change the world you see.'

—Satya Nadella, CEO Microsoft at the MWC 2019

BEING FIRST

I remember the panic in the conference room, when a competitor launched a product that another company was preparing to launch. I could hear the moans and groans amongst senior executives because there was seemingly a loss of face in front of their bosses or a loss of market share that they had potentially started to think of.

The excuse was that competition had captured the position of 'innovating' and brought about a 'first mover advantage'. But history dictates otherwise.

Let me refresh your memory. How many of you remember Archie Query Form? Never heard of it? What?! That was the world's first search engine, launched in 1990. The ones that you remember are possibly Google, Yahoo, MSN and the likes.

Have you heard of the Simon Personal Computer that was brought out by IBM as the first smart phone in 1992?

So now you are getting the point. There is no disappointment in 'not being first'. Being innovative and different is what creates customer loyalty.

India was late in the mobile telephony business. So, we had significant global advantages in terms of service levels and service costs. Yet, even now we will push ourselves back if we don't keep pace.

We took advantage of being a 'late moving' organization for significant advantages—of proven technology, cost of operations, knowledge of failures from first movers, not paying the premium to make a pioneering breakthrough, and depletion of resources having spent it on experiments.

The truth however is somewhere in between. We will only reap the advantage for a brief period of time. It's up to us to continue that advantage by looking forward.

It's important here to distinguish between time advantage and pioneers. Coca-Cola was founded in the late nineteenth century by John Stith Pemberton, as a patent drug. It was Asa Griggs Candler who popularized the drink as we know it in the twentieth century. It is still one of the most valuable brands globally.[1]

Similarly, while the Germans had significant and innovative advantage in manufacturing gas-powered vehicles, a new breed of electric vehicle manufacturer like Tesla, has displaced them off their seat by looking at pioneering inventions. James Dyson, again, used his pioneering work to establish the world's first bagless vacuum cleaner.

I have been part of company journeys where a great idea didn't translate into value because we were simply too much ahead of our time. We tried launching virtual credit cards in 2006, when the market was just not ready for it.

Other market examples are: The first crude electric vehicle was developed by Robert Anderson in 1832. In 1901, Hubert Cecil

Booth and American inventor David T. Kenney, invented and coined the word 'vacuum cleaner'. And the world's first recognizable social media was Six Degrees created in 1997.

The lesson here is—you don't need to be first to get at something, but it definitely helps being a pioneer.

CONSEQUENCES OF 'THE FAILURE TO INNOVATE'

'Success is 99 per cent failure.'

—Sochiro Honda

The world is always full of innovators and creators. Earlier, the avenues for success were limited in comparison to what is available today. With crowdfunding, PE and VC businesses scouting for the next billion-dollar idea, the world is looking for innovation to disrupt the market place.

Some innovations come as surprises—Viagra and 3M's Post-it are a direct result of botched experiments.

As a country we rank fifty-second in the Global Innovative Index (2019), but are the seventh largest global economy in the world. So we have ample headroom to innovate and grow.

Our 98 per cent success in the 'Chandrayaan 2' mission is a testimony to our innovative prowess. The ability to launch such a complex mission at a fraction of the cost, got NASA to look forward to opportunities to explore partnerships.

At an organizational level, I found one truth—the real failure is in 'not trying'. Too many established organizations are putting effort into increasing revenue or sales, that would help them in the short term, but allocating near-zero effort into innovation and pioneering.

A simple example is how microfinance cracked open the unbanked sector in India, and they are now a soft target for acquisition from larger banks looking to import such know-how.

And innovators like Oyo, Ola, Swiggy and RupeeCoin are proving back to us that we have what it takes. These are real innovations perceived by customers who touch and feel and not in the research lab.

When Gillette reached out to Kickstarter for a hot blade campaign, it proved once more that established companies can also create a start-up mindset.

There is one truth for the future: We will be left on the sidelines watching if we don't get onto the innovation bandwagon.

TAKING ENOUGH RISK

When I was in my twenties, my bank's Indian business was audited by the bank's global internal audit team. That team had distinguished senior individuals, including CEOs of other countries. They could spot a problem from a mile away. We dreaded those guys, even more than the statutory auditors. A bad rating would cost many jobs, and would put us in a tight spot in front of our seniors. Hence the business of making sure we succeeded in our audit ratings was like a daily chore for three years till the guys actually landed up on our shores and still tried to find mistakes. Every document, every process manual, and every transaction was tested and scrutinized by backend operations and our own compliance teams to look at things with a hawk eye to avoid failure.

Funnily enough, the audit team couldn't find many issues when they left. We let out a sigh of relief but to our surprise we still just got an acceptable rating and not a progressive rating. Why? Because the audit team came back and said we didn't take enough risks.

That incident set me thinking and it became a lesson to succeed in any venture of life. Failure has equal status to success. If you aren't failing, you aren't taking many risks.

Over the later years, I found it wise to choose clients who would like to work with us on transformation agendas. By settling for weak companies with weak CEOs who just wanted to prove a point to their boards by showcasing a few unsuccessful attempts before burying a project for good into the ground, we were compromising our own standards of innovation.

When we have a willing client with a 'mutual fund' view, we harness success. What do I mean by that? In a mutual fund with individual stocks there are some that are likely to fail, some likely to do moderately well, while others will give you bumper returns. It's a reflection of industry, market sentiment, organization profitability, international buoyancy, currency, state of exports and imports, and the country's economic condition, and general trends in the international markets. However, when the performance of a fund is scrutinized over a five to ten year period, it is seen that an experienced hand provides healthy returns.

When these mutual fund type CEOs take on a transformation, they stick to the transformation beyond the lifespan of the programme and the specialized consultant, taking further lessons from it, and applying them to show more achievements.

WHEN NOT TO LISTEN TO CUSTOMERS

When I was first asked this question, I found it extraordinarily strange and difficult to reason as to why you may not listen to your customer.

But, on further pondering and trying to deepen my own understanding on the subject, I saw merit under many circumstances.

Customers look for things they are aware of, or want to experience in the immediate future. So they can't think further ahead about a problem statement that they can't connect to. The end result is always in favour of the customer.

Till Steve Jobs showed the world what a capacitive touch screen was, the world was using resistive touch screens with tiny sticks called styluses.

Artificial Intelligence had supporters, but it took more than half a century to find the compute power and its commercial application of neural networks to become mainstream in this decade.

So when a disruptive technology is at the brink of commercialization and shows enormous potential, the first few adopters or pioneers take the risk of getting customers to buy into the vision. At each of those points, a customer can't envisage the impact (examples of such transitions are film camera to digital camera, wireline phones to mobile phones, desktops to notebooks, notebooks to tablets).

Ultimately it finds a new set of customers (market making), and early technology adopters join that bandwagon. Others follow. That's when not listening to customers sometimes can impact innovation and make extraordinary gains.

In *The Innovator's Dilemma* author C.M. Christensen talks about SanDisk's 3.5mm floppy drive that didn't see enough acceptance within their company, let alone outside. It was launched, side-lined, and didn't see enough uptick till a newer 2.5 inch from Priarie Tek took the market.

In Apple's case there were several smart watches before the Apple watch, and it had significant resistance beyond being eye candy to many connoisseurs of wrist watches. When Apple realized purpose and focused on health and cellular, their third and fourth editions saw much higher acceptance.

Innovators have had serious struggle to get established manufacturers to buy their parts and services. If you take the case of James Dyson, innovator and founder of Dyson, famous for his cyclonic vacuums (and more), his journey to launch the bagless vacuum cleaners is quite revealing. After being frustrated by the inefficiency of the ones with bags, he decided to invent something different. His passion turned him to near bankruptcy and some companies like Conair and Black & Decker wouldn't licence his inventions. These trials and errors in partnerships led James to make the machine himself in the 1990s. The acceptance of this vacuum in the mid-nineties with British department store John Lewis marketing it saw tables turn. The rest of the expansion wasn't as painful, and now it's a global brand. The success saw James himself now being worth more than US$10 billion. His disruptive journey into electric cars is a story for another day.

THE INNOVATOR PERSONA

Over the last decade, I have come across countless headlines—that company X has launched an innovation lab. Within a few years, there would be a small article that explained that the same company found its grave in a consolidation effort.

After establishing that innovation is here to stay, while the rest will perish, a natural question is, so what is an innovator's persona?

At IBM, we had a research lab, innovators and a myriad patents we filed every year. So, do these make up innovation? What makes certain products tick? The answers I found were far more fundamental than this question.

Innovators simply think differently and are sparked by curiosity. They look at solving the problem in another way, different from what is already out there. For an organization it often comes out as a collective effort. A culture that you have to imbibe and breathe into your employees. You have to provide the team the tools and the resources to think differently and push the boundaries for growth.

It boils down to putting down 'a value' as one of the criteria, and relentlessly empowering and executing this through.

Empowering employees is a critical component of innovation, along with hiring smart, self-motivated, dedicated, value-driven people. Innovation happens as a result of collaboration amongst teams that spark creativity by dialogue, discussions and experimenting. Innovation requires freedom and breaking convention. Innovation could come from any part of the organization.

Innovation still needs accountability. A necessary framework within which ideas can thrive. Innovators need to be accountable for both successes and failures. They need to be accountable for delivering practical products and services without compromising on a culture of innovation.

It's with the application of these fundamentals that organizations like Google, Microsoft, Apple and Amazon have turned as the new line of innovators.

We think of innovators as the young brilliant kid who is developing a bright idea in his garage (Steve Jobs) or in a dorm room (Mark Zuckerberg). In the first half of the twentieth century, the average age of a Nobel laureate for physics, medicine, chemistry, or economics used to be forty-seven, but that privilege today seems to have gone up to the late sixties. The reasons for that is the queue and the validation timelines for the breakthrough.

So, when you put together a team that can innovate, you need to find the appropriate mix between young and old. Innovators become better with age.

THE DILEMMA OF SUCCESS

Having been on both the Nikon and Canon bandwagon earlier, I noticed a specific gap when it came to competing against Sony. That led me to the question: As you start to gain plenty of customers, and a new trend comes along, what do you do? Do you repurpose your products and services to redefine the new trend, or service your existing customers. With investments being hard to come by, it is a natural dilemma many organizations are facing.

The big camera companies like Nikon and Canon have been in the DSLR game for a long time—Nikon since 1959 and Canon since 1987. Sony was a relative newcomer, they started with the launch of their Alpha series from 2006. Sony's Alpha with their mirrorless cameras emerged as a disrupter to DSLRs. While mobile phone cameras captured the point-and-shoot arena, what was left is the serious photographer, hobbyist or professional. By 2012, it became quite clear that the mirrorless camera was here to stay. That forced a serious rethink for Nikon and Canon. Their first actual response came only by 2018 with a range of full frame mirrorless cameras, since this technology required years to adapt to and their matured organizations were naturally slow to change. In the meanwhile, Sony harnessed over 13 per cent of market share while Canon held 49.1 per cent market share and Nikon 24.9 per cent according to Nikkei estimates. The challenge for Canon and Nikon is that their captive customer base buys DSLR camera. What makes it even more difficult for them to launch into this market and makes them hold back investment in mirrorless cameras is that it's not the camera body but the accessories like lenses (with different mounts) which has traditionally been generating a lot of revenue for them. Their penetration in mirrorless is less than 1 per cent and every new lens that they put out from that stable fails DSLR customers. So it's an expensive investment with very little returns. For Sony, any migration is welcome as it is building its base with one type of customer—mirrorless.

This is a natural conundrum that many of my existing clients are facing. They have invested into technologies, and the disruption just ridicules their current business model as being significantly inefficient.

Two interesting strategies are emerging from these market lessons:

First, if you take the case of Android, they allowed for customisation and open source, resulting in a highly fragmented market. Apple kept the ecosystem tight, forging ahead with hardware and making its powerful App Store self-reliant.

In another strategy, Sony's camera division is encouraging third party vendors like Viltrox, Metabones and Sigma to join in to support existing Canon and Nikon glass on a Sony mirrorless system. They are thus pushing camera bodies initially, and Sony glass is slowly getting preferred as customers transition.

In all of this, I see one decision that my clients need to make. Take a step forward in the direction that will get them long-term benefits and create the transition plan that would take them there. Equip the customers with the opportunity to migrate and provide them with incentives.

The same dilemma exists when we migrate from 4G to 5G, the telecom companies need significantly higher ARPUs (Average Revenue per User) for the numbers to make sense. So the only way forward is to provide and communicate 'customer value'.

JUGAAD—THE INNOVATOR'S CHALLENGE

Jugaad, the Hindi word can be loosely translated to 'frugal solution'. As an Indian, I am embedded with this sense, and see this as a direct result of the deficit of infrastructure and abundance of people, leading to improvisation to solve the challenge. The Chandrayaan 2 mission or the Tata Nano, was a direct outcome of making the best out of a challenging situation.

When I trace its roots, it goes back to our ability to challenge status quo, and having to make do with one-tenth of the resources that the West is exposed to.

When I see the difficulties faced by an innovative business to hold on to margins for every subsequent year of business, I can immediately see the relevance of jugaad not only for India but for the world to embrace as well.

Don't mistake jugaad to be an Indian phenomenon alone. Jugaad as the Japanese use it is where a wash basin is mounted on top of a toilet flush to re-cycle water. Jugaad has been used long enough in China as well, just that it's called *chabuduo*, meaning 'close enough' in Mandarin. Chairman Mao encouraged the Chinese people to improvise. The result is that Chinese factories have become the common ground for manufacture, with a far larger supply of engineers, and other technical resources and are competing and innovating at the same time (take Huawei, or DJI for example).

So while we work in providing basic infrastructure to villages, jugaad innovation is working there as well. Mitticool is a refrigerator made out of clay. In this refrigerator, no electricity is used. The breathable properties of clay allow for storing refrigerated produce. The moisture improves the taste of the produce as well. Another example is how villages use motorcycle wheels to pump water into their farmland. While there is a lot of humour in some of the solutions, they work very effectively in villages at a fraction of the cost.

Whether we call it 'jugaad' in India, 'chabuduo' in China, or 'kaizen' in Japan, Asia's mindset to deal with resource paucity is the primary cause of such innovative thinking.

An interesting example is that of GE Healthcare, that has taken interesting steps in the diagnosis and treatment of cancer. India had been importing radioisotopes for imaging using CT and PET scans. Diagnosis of this kind is very expensive and unaffordable to the poverty-stricken masses. With the partnership of private diagnostic centres and airlines, GE Healthcare helped companies to produce these implements locally and distribute them to smaller town hospitals. It also uses a pay-per-use model to keep costs economical. After all, radioisotopes decay over time and such rotation allows for maximum use.

The way I see this getting integrated into the CX lifecycle is to challenge its participants to come back with a solution at a tenth of the overall costs, with some investment thrown into R&D, to make services more affordable to the masses. That's exactly what DJI did with drones, when it broke the price barrier—a case where innovation from the East pushes the West to respond or adapt.

THE VALUE NETWORK

As you are reading the book, you can sense that repeatedly we are talking about providing value to customers as the differentiating factor, and that value is closely intertwined with innovation.

As I read through the book *The Innovator's Dilemma* by C.M. Christensen, it connected to my personal understanding of how scholars and consultants attribute the problem of innovation to managerial, organizational or structural failures to respond to technology changes. That's where 'the value network' comes to play as another way to diagnose failure.

The value network is nothing but a way by which the firm can identify and respond to customer needs and solve problems, react to competitors and strive for profit. The book also attributes technology as a key enabler for solving problems, either incrementally by augmented changes of existing technologies or by being disruptive with a complete change of technology models. In *Jugaad 3.0* Simone Bhan Ahuja amplifies this by stating that these steps depend on the organization's appetite for risk and flexibility.

In my experience, I find large and successful organizations find it easier to adapt to incremental changes while finding it extremely difficult to adapt to disruptive changes.

Their existing value chains and rewards prevent them from realizing higher value. Since decision-making is pretty much an automated habit embedded into the subconscious, un-entangling is described as too risky an option. This rigidity helps start-ups to break the mould of incremental innovation, and move towards transformational innovation. There is a catch here though, sometimes the technology has not caught up, and we are stuck with transitional innovation. An example is Samsung's foldable phones, though the glass was not ready they took a risk and substituted it with a form of plastic polymer. If you look at the decision-making within organizations, management ends up taking bets on transitional innovation and transformational innovation all the time, since in the long term, all innovations are transitional.

As I spent time in Latin America, I heard about a leading Indian retailer who had reached its shores to negotiate for the purchase of a sunflower oil plant, to produce sunflower oil for their supermarkets. The current prices they were quoted from existing suppliers forced the Indian retailer to look for alternatives overseas. With a 20 per cent price advantage found overseas, it forced local manufacturers to review their decisions. Here, price was the pushing factor for a transitional innovation.

We are always at the brink of creating value networks to be competitive and stay ahead. An example is Intel, who realized that exiting from the mobile 5G market is the best strategy, based on a surprise settlement from Apple and Qualcomm.

THE RAGE OF INNOVATION LABS

In my interactions with clients, many hesitate to put up innovation labs, yet others invest into them without too much debate. That begs the question—is it worth putting investments into innovation labs?

As innovation is the single largest source of value creation, preceded only by media fanfare and buzz creation. It's separate and insulated from the rest of the world, with an ideology to create 'super minds' within the masses to create ideas that stretch possibilities. Yet a few years down the line, without much fanfare, many shut down.

The answer lies in examining the causes for failure of the innovation labs. When I dug deeper into the details, the results for failure became quite apparent.

For starters, I found that often there is a significant lack of ownership at the core of the company. Too many people on the side-lines have observations that detract the company from actually succeeding beyond the idea stage.

To add to this, a lot of effort goes into creating flashy offices and pricey staff, and a much lesser outlay is available for the actual projects. The objective of innovation labs seem to be towards showcasing this jewelled crown to attract customers or clients like magnets, based on the glitz and glamour rather than the results.

A number of times, I find that innovation labs are trying to build things that are far cheaper to procure from outside. We are trying to prove a point that we can develop innovation in-house rather than look at ways to best utilize resources. For example, a fintech can sometimes build a chatbot at a fraction of the cost for the bank.

Again, with meaningless hackathons, without the intention to integrate winning teams, solutions into an implementation, the result out of the experience is often zero-value.

Then again, the combination of a big plan, with no stepping stones and poor project management, results in predictable failure even before a project is started. Add to that limited patience, and diversion of resources for quicker and predictable benefits and we have killed the innovation lab's actual capability.

But probably one of the bigger reasons is also 'isolation' from business units who rarely co-operate to bring forth 'the range and width of client concerns' to deliver real results, making the exercise a tech project with a self-destructive behaviour to create a solution that nobody wanted in the first place. A part of the fault lies in the potential conflict for business unit employees trying to keep their jobs, versus labs that are trying to innovate, with the organization culture doing little to intervene to create new solutions, but just observing as a bystander and being victims of disruption.

In all of this, inflated expectations are meticulously crafted to create a flowing schedule for innovation labs to churn out innovative products like coffee from an expresso machine. Needless to say that in such cases the KPIs and metrices are misaligned.

So to sum it up, customers are looking for innovation and creativity. Too many organizations look for profitability without the creation of an underlying culture to breed innovation. Labs expect to be told, and business units refuse to participate. Nobody really owns the lab, and even if there is ownership, it is housed by people who are not best suited to run an innovation programme.

And as by-standers, nay-saying firms have the opportunity to say, 'See, I told you so!'

DOES TECHNOLOGY IMPACT CUSTOMER EXPERIENCE?

'The most profound technologies are those that disappear. They weave themselves into the fabric of everyday life until they are indistinguishable from it.'

—Mark Weiser

The best way I can answer this question is with a counterquestion, 'Does a better camera create better movies?' These days an emotive ad shot entirely on an iPhone can yield far better results than a poorly executed story shot with a fancy $10,000 machine. If you agree that the story is more powerful than the camera, you would also agree that customer experience comes before the technology.

So the first question I would ask is 'Do you know your target customer well enough?' If so what are their 'non-negotiable values'. Then you go about creating your part of the bargain—your story.

The follow-on question to this is 'What would bring your story to life?' To get to this stage, we are asking that your vision, culture, goals, business plans, operating model, organization structure, people policies and distribution channels be aligned towards that story.

Then we get to technology. Don't get me wrong. Customers are not lab rats waiting to be dissected for your science experiments. There is one exception though that's critically important. We often tend to create stories that are exorbitantly expensive without adequate returns or impractical to execute based on current technology (Artificial Intelligence took a good part of forty years to come through, yet we talk about it as if it is a 2019 invention).

The unfortunate part of the story is also that technology has a large lead time, and hence transformations which have pressure on delivering results bargain towards identifying the technology platform well in advance.

None of the top billionaires globally managed to create a 'sharp enough business' in their first years of doing business. If you ask them they will tell you that 'you will learn as you grow, and your investments will become more sharply focused'. Yet undeniably, not one would argue with you on the point that better customer experience will increase shareholder value.

Traditionally, we have been thinking in a linear fashion—for instance, one year to launch, one year to get your target segments right, etc. Businesses can change dramatically during that kind of time period.

My recommendation to get over this is my two-step advice:

1. Start simple, start small.
   Apple launched their first iPhone as a US only product through
   AT&T, cutting down the number of variables. Apple's focus
   was—the right product for the US market. Geographies
   would have added unnecessary complexity at that stage of their
   organization. Their sole focus was—get the product developed
   around customer needs.

2. Don't work on building your technology around a 'non-agile'
   model, which is built around rapid prototyping, allowing for the
   flight path to be continuously re-calibrated for efficiency.
   Inside Apple's notoriously secretive business, Adam Lashinsky,
   the author of *Inside Apple: How America's Most Admired and
   Secretive Company Really Works*, explains principles around the
   review day, iteration, packaging and launch plan, that closely
   align to agile methodologies.

If there is one takeaway from that book, that would be the focus on
resources concentrated to a handful of projects that are expected to
bear fruit. In all of this, the focus is on how technology weaves itself
into the fabric of customer experience.

GOING AGILE

Before you hesitate to embrace agile as your new culture, at the outset
let me open by saying, 'The giants worship agile techniques.'
    By going back to the Spotify story on squads and tribes, you
would infer correctly that small teams of people given responsibility
(directly responsible individual) can create miracles (Apple used only
two engineers to write code for the Safari Browser conversion for
the iPad.) That is Spotify's secret to be able to compete with Apple,
Amazon and Google.

If you saw the movie *The Social Network*, you would see the main character who plays Mark Zuckerberg, the CEO of Facebook, translating a brilliant idea into code within a short few hours. Though exaggerated in the movie, agile provides that same ability. Agile breaks boundaries and demands quick thinking.

Given that most businesses cannot afford wait times any longer, where competition can surprise us by the fifth month with a superior product, the method also helps you keep pace with the changing times.

To take some lessons from the giants implementing agile, at GE, their agile system relies on managers guiding and coaching employees to achieve their goals through regular performance conversations on a real time basis through an app. Accenture, Cargill, Adobe and CYBG Bank have similar frameworks.

At Adidas, their vision to deliver 'faster and better sportswear to customers' integrates agile into CX.

Adidas's journey starts with customer needs expressed quantitatively or qualitatively. Ideas and concepts are put through industrial design. Solutions involve customers and employees, process and technology in a rapid feedback loop to deliver results. Technologies like prototyping using 3D printing, Robotic Process Automation (RPA), Artificial Intelligence (AI) and Analytics make this possible.

Adidas recognizes that today's solutions won't stay relevant. Customer engagement and staying obsessed helps them innovate with teams and technology for their future existence. An agile culture and mindset helps them stay responsive, resilient and fresh in their customers' minds. Their ecosystem continually evolves. Their teams expand and are pushed to constantly innovate yet balance different things. Teams are encouraged to break hierarchy for innovation. This culture of innovation is supported adequately by tools and methodologies. Digital processes are integrated into the fabric of the organization to keep pace with a strong human connection.

The business orchestrated strategy and planning with pilots, insights and validations to scale and embed, change management with communication, culture with building and coaching teams, and processes with technologies. Alignment converts dreams to reality which becomes the new normal.

Actors differ in maturity, involvement will generate buy-in. Alignment demands push and pull—innovators to consumer wants and needs, execution to speed and sometimes slowing down, and actor relationships amongst themselves and with customers.

Adoption has its own bell curve, that differ by market and is price sensitive. Adidas had a modular offering allowing the market to choose. Capabilities take time to build that involves and takes people along the way, with patience and perseverance as virtues for critical success. Adidas saw improvements every month and much bigger impacts every year. But this journey of transformation requires between three to five years.

To ensure Adidas is clearly on that journey to CX using agile, it ties a part of all employee bonuses to the brand's Net Promoter Score relative to its competitors.

THE DIGITAL AGE

'In the digital age of "overnight" success stories such as Facebook, the hard slog is easily overlooked.'

—Sir James Dyson | Founder of Dyson

Increasingly my clients, their peers, partners and competition are being subjected to new expectations, threats and opportunities. My mentor's sound advice to me was, 'Look at the market expectation, and get your business to revolve around it.'

The ask has pushed my clients to connect more closely with customers and speed up the pace of innovation for higher human engagement.

Human engagement has been impacted by digital intervention to create that effect through—

1. online with social interactions,
2. devices like mobile, tablet, IOT devices, the smart watch, or
3. enablers like cloud, high speed wireless services, data driven products and services, predictive capabilities, automation, empowering workforces, fostering collaboration through improved workflows and personalization.

So what is digital really?

Digital is a new way of engaging with customers and doing business. What I find missing in some businesses trying to raise their digital quotient is their lack of understanding 'where the value lies for their businesses'. We have been talking about value all along in this book, about evolving customer experience through fostering ongoing product or service loyalty.

What digital has brought to the forefront is the ability to take faster decisions, create faster value, real-time automation and speed of innovation. If you notice this statement carefully, the crux is about serving your customer with 'SPEED and ACCURACY'. To fulfil this expectation, a user-friendly set of devices are emerging.

I got together with a group of friends and the discussion started revolving around digital and its importance for our clients and our current organization strategies. The discussion quickly turned into why this phenomenon has been prevalent.

The consensus that emerged was the most relevant target segment of customers for most businesses are the millennials (born between 1981 and 1996) and Gen Z (born between 1997 and 2012). The median age in India is 27.1 years and that of the world is 29.8 years in 2019, and these statistics substantiate our previous theory. With the average attention span for a millennial being 12 seconds, reducing to a disappointing 8 seconds for Gen Z, what solution could be more relevant to them than digital?

The new business models are centred around digital—Digital Banks, Digital Retail, Digital Healthcare and Hospitals, Digital Automobiles and more. The way we do business has changed—digital processes, digital marketing, digital sales, digital customer experience. Everyone wants in.

Digital can't be built without a foundation in place—core systems—a staple for generating invoices, calculating prices or keeping your product catalogue. The value from core systems has become par for the course. To break this entry barrier, many business models have emerged from co-working spaces to renting infrastructure on a monthly basis.

ARE WE MISSING THE MARK AROUND 'DIGITAL'?

While I help my clients build digital products, we drive our millennial and Gen Z model around immediacy, convenience, accuracy and relevance on a channel or device of their choosing.

All decisions are taken including automation and investments into technologies like AI, Blockchain or digital with the 12-second barrier in mind. If your business generates fulfilment in more than 12 seconds, you should be worried about your future.

A deeply connected perspective around digital is language. When it comes to language, the biggest common denominator is understood as English, which is a huge fallacy. There are only 360 million native English speaking people in the world (skewed towards US, Canada, UK and Australia), and 1.2 billion non-native English speakers. Overall that represents only 20 per cent of the global population. India is the second largest English speaking country in the world with 125 million people, but we speak over 125 languages (considering 10,000 or more people speak a language), and our overall population is 1.37 billion, growing 1.1 per cent annually.

By skewing our digital experiences in English, we are automatically excluding 80 per cent of the global population or 90 per cent of India's population. If we talk business language, native

English speaking countries account for only 20.28 per cent of global GDP.

Half the global population has access to the Internet, and only half of that to a self-service or assisted channel. The growth enablers for digital thus lie in breaking the digital language divide, even though English is today's global language.

START FROM SCRATCH OR LEARN FROM OTHERS?

Innovation is expensive, so it pays to build on others' successes. My mentor once told me, 'Good artists copy, great artists steal great ideas and join them together' referring to Picasso.

To get your innovative juices going, I have put together a great set of innovative digital ideas. Here goes:

One big advantage of digital lies in its ability to cut down turnaround time for a supply chain:

- My daily app of choice, BBDaily, is a cloud-based milk, grocery, eggs, bread supply connected to a wallet, that remembers your daily transactions with a built-in ledger. Cancel by 10 p.m. on a given day for the next day or the next few weeks, and the supply chain is automatically informed of your decision. The milkman handles only fulfilment. BBDaily does not own any milk supplier.
- Netflix removed physical mediums like DVDs and the entire supply chain to support it. Kindle removed physical books. Spotify removed CDs. Uber removed your own car. Apple Pay removed the physical credit card. Airbnb removed the hassle of holiday accommodation. Amazon removed the supermarket. WhatsApp removed the redundancies of physical letters. Takeaways like Swiggy and Deliveroo are part of a $120 billion industry. Telemedicine removes the visit to a doctor or the hospital, projected to become a $148 billion industry by 2025 growing at a 21 per cent CAGR. So what you can remove from

your supply chain could be part of a growing industry. Many of these business models don't have the burden to support a brick-and-mortar establishment. Uber does not own cars, Spotify does not own the music, WhatsApp does not own the messages, Swiggy does not own any restaurant and so on.

Digital has created convenience:

- Digital helped redefine customer value by simplifying transactions. Pilots had to carry aircraft flight manuals (AFM), pilot operating handbooks(POH), books and printouts which describe the aircraft systems and emergency procedures till about a decade back. That was almost 20 kg of weight. Now an iPad, weighing about half a kilo, that supports hundreds of aviation apps just replaced that. The added bonus was that old pages got replaced by new without error. It also allowed them to read aeronautical charts or notices (red, amber or green in order of importance). Now if you take the co-pilot's literature into account, that's just double the weight removed from the aircraft. It also has other side benefits like protecting the pilots back, or checking for any operational alerts or chatting with another colleague to find out some last-minute details.
- Amazon provides us with the convenience to shop in less than 10 seconds, with the ability to research and be prompted for the alternate products you are looking for. YouTube fills in the rest with reviews to ratify your choices.
- Amazon Go went a step further, eliminating queues all together at their stores. How this works is by using the Amazon Go app, which is linked to your credit card, as you shop for things, the app in tandem, with a sophisticated network of cameras and software, totals the items being taken in real time, and charges the customer as they exit the store.
- Zara and Ikea offered self-checkout at their stores to bust the queues. With clean interfaces, and provision of kiosks, they

allowed for scanning and payment for apparel, and even removal of security tags, and finally, of course, payment.

Interaction is another offshoot of the digital experience:

- Audi uses a VR showroom to showcase to potential buyers an interactive experience, much more immersive than a tablet or a TV. The VR showroom uses an Oculus Rift headset to recreate the experience of the Audi car at a 1:1 scale. One is even being able to look under the engine hood and into the car. The experience has an unprecedented amount of detail, allowing customers to experience the Audi in ways they could not do before.

- Ted Baker introduced the interactive store window campaign to attract shoppers at select UK and European stores. Customers are encouraged to place their hands on a palm print on the window, and with the help of a sensor, the customer's photograph can be taken immediately, and is composited back through a visual display. At their London store, the window has a speaker and sound effects are added to that interactive experience. Their goal was to maximize customer engagement with the brand, and bring about a fun experiences with Ted Baker. The technology also has the capability to track faces, and use composite images to be posted on TedBaker.com from where users can also share these on their social media posts.

- In real estate, the importance of drones, VR and BIM (building information management) has changed the customer and engineering aspects for the industry. Using drones, you can shoot views from a height at 360 degree angles, and showcase to customers what their view would be when they buy an apartment. VR allows for an immersive experience of walking around the apartment, the lobby and common areas like the club, to get a feel of what can be expected from their real estate purchase. BIM is being used by developers to put together different components of construction like plumbing, electricals, air conditioning, together. It helps in better collaboration, and communication, better cost estimation, visualising the construction even before a brick has been laid, identifying potential clashes, architectural issues, potential areas of risk and enabling productivity and pre-fabrication, safety, improved adherence to project deadlines, inventory management and ordering for supply chain at every stage of the project.

- With today's customers becoming extremely busy, online-only banks like Ally Bank, Capital One, Bank Simple, Digi Bank, ING Direct and others are offering complete online services. With that, customers are able to be onboard, keep up to date and transact on the platform, to carry out all day to day transactions.

Digital translates information into insights, and allows you to choose what you need:

- Hospitals have developed a greater focus for well-being and care, since our population is ageing upwards every year. As each doctor is looking at symptoms and capturing information, and simultaneously prescribing drugs to control or cure the problem, data is being collected for each case. Using records from the previous visits, doctors are able to continue or change the medication. This information, for example, can form the basis of predicting what helps patients under what circumstances. This use of predictive analytics is helping medical science in better diagnosis and enabling patients to lead a healthier life. Many companies working in the medical hardware business are also manufacturing affordable equipment like health trackers, CPAPs, blood sugar monitors, blood pressure monitors, digital thermometers, etc., which help patients self-manage their health. They are able to discuss symptoms with doctors, with far richer data which enables the doctor to pin-point to conditions that were not possible before, to get pro-active or preventive action where needed for patients to restore them to health.

Patient records are increasingly getting digitized and integrated with records at other places even in lesser developed countries. Patients can also find the best-suited doctors, with a referral management software, based on their patient record.

- In Education, skill-based education is becoming critical, and with the proliferation of sites like Masterclass, Skillshare and Udemy, it's becoming more common place, where you can learn at your own time and at your own pace. When you want to pick up a skill—say creative skills like photography, videography, painting, drama and storytelling or leadership skills, programming, software skills and language skills, appropriate courses are offered by the platform, by various professionals, and their courses are rated by past participants. The courses are available for download and can be accessed and revised whenever needed.

If you look at the business model for digital experience it's turned traditional businesses on their heads by providing superior client value at significantly better speed that brick and mortar establishment struggle to replicate.

A clear indication of that is the shutting down of malls in the US, which then are being converted into Amazon distribution centres and warehouses which have taken advantage of the strategic locations. In India, mills in Mumbai are being repurposed into restaurants and office spaces.

CUSTOMER EXPERIENCE MEETS DIGITAL

I am always amused by the trends of the consulting industry, of which I am a part, about the products that get sold to clients. The unfortunate thing about digital is that it is being sold as a technology product rather than something that solves customer experience challenges.

At its core, social engagement models are changing. Apps have been popularized by the proliferation of iOS and Android App

Stores. Apps have localized social engagement behaviours within the palm of your hand. So, the customer has already moved to the centre of the mobile experience, and the app is merely fulfilling a product or a service experience.

IMDB says that there are 2,577 new films produced in a year on an average, translating to around 6,000 hours of film length. New uploads on YouTube fulfils that in less than 12 hours currently proving that the customer is already at the centre of the mobile experience.

So we can assume that digital solutions need to cater to these binaries:

- One for interactions (like chats, websites, apps, social media forums, virtual assistants) or
- The other being change is the digital backbone of the organization (like STP, Cloud, IOT, RPA, Big Data, Platform as a service or software as a service), and the in-between (AI, VR, and AR).

The real answer lies in the challenge (in the field of CX) digital will provide regarding solution towards social engagement models for millennials and Gen Z.

Since CX is a transformative journey, it embodies all three levers—people (customers, leaders, employees and culture), process (simplification and innovation) and technology (innovation).

Some of the things that we already know and have imbibed into our way of working will not change. In the 2000s, as technology companies, we loved service-oriented architecture that was basically software broken down into standardized re-usable flexible services combined together to create a solution. It expanded into micro services that became cloud centric, which then became the units of execution.

I see CX and digital emerging into micro services that will combine together to solve a customer challenge.

If I were a doctor prescribing for digital's success, I would say that digital needs to release adequate doses of dopamine (curiosity, motivation and focus), oxytocin (connection, generosity, gratitude and trust) and endorphins (creativity, focus and relaxation) into the blood stream of our customers. What I mean by that is that humans are socially emotional, and a digital product that does not induce or stops inducing human emotion won't stand the test of time.

A question that I have often been asked is 'So how do you start a digital transformation programme?' My answer to that is 'Start by agreeing on an outcome.' I see organizations approaching outcomes like cost-to-income ratios, or profit or the launch of a product or a service quite easily since they have had years of practice. But when it comes to outcomes on CX or digital, it stops at Net Promoter Score (NPS) or pieces of technology.

I have seen banks in India debating on a mobile banking solution for months, and finally repurposing Internet banking into the mobile for no realistic benefit to customers or themselves.

So if you can't measure the CX, you don't achieve any benefits. Business and executions plans around digital transformations need to elaborate on self-funding opportunities with an adjusted cashflow. Project risks, mitigation steps and the escalation matrix need to be clearly understood.

The biggest risk that I see businesses running into is their inability to gauge their personal readiness to change or take the plunge. Without naming specific clients, I have seen millions, no sorry, billions of dollars wasted in futile half-hearted attempts to put out utterly useless corporate messages towards an ambition that very few actually believed in at the beginning, and even those few lost steam as time passed on.

Basic hygiene like programme management, work schedules and teams aside, a lot of emphasis has to be placed on the actual innovation from the teams, and its acceptability from customers.

A number of fantastic insights come from history—look at the VHS versus Betamax story. Betamax's standard was clearly superior. Yet from a feature perspective Betamax played only for an hour, was much heavier, had more complexity, added higher product and shipping costs, and positioned itself mainly as being first to market. VHS won the battle.

Again, the question is—which customers do you want to attract? While Apple and Samsung clearly attract the more affluent customers, the cheaper mobile phone manufacturers (Samsung included), like Huawei, Oppo, Vivo, Xiaomi and OnePlus, have clearly targeted another segment with some very competent innovations at an extremely affordable price.

So while I prescribe digital transformation-led innovation whole heartedly, I would say, put your intent on a document, and put your money where your mouth is. That document is what I would call your playbook for execution.

If you ask me what that document should contain, I would suggest the following:

- Vision—How does it benefit your customers, and how does it benefit you?
- Competitive Positioning—What sets you apart from the competition?
- Business Case—Why should it matter to your shareholders and company bottom line?
- Roadmap—How do you see the path to your success in this direction?
- Method—What is your step-by-step process and tool kit for success?
- Resources—What do you need?

DO WE KNOW EVERYTHING ABOUT DIGITAL?

The short answer—no we don't, since the future has better insight into its true potential than everything we know today.

I have often seen clients wait for that perfect vendor and the perfect solution that they can get to accomplish the maximum. That timing never comes. If you trade or follow investments, you would know or would have heard about the term 'candle sticks'. When the next set of candles are larger than the earlier set of candles in an upward direction, the stock is trending upwards.

If the height of the candle indicates a trend, and if we draw an analogy to the buzz on a trend in the market place, the more buzz there is regarding a trend, the more likely it is to become prevalent.

The winners in these areas are organizations that have correctly identified upward trends and break support on trend reversal quick enough.

As we mature in our innovation curve, we are continuously breaking down our units of measurements into smaller services while weaving them into customer journeys.

As an example we can cite how we have evolved from a trend like Search Engine Optimization (SEO) to ensure we are able to put our wares in front of customers who search for products or services on the Internet to, say, combining this with the BERT algorithm that Google developed in 2019, that moves from pure string matching to intent matching. Thus, keyword research tools will become less relevant in the future.

So our future involves digital miniaturization and segmentation that will require re-architecture of existing service models. But such change comes at a price. As I see, customer experience and digital transformations are invisibly interwoven, as we move from 9/9 to 24/7. Customers are responding positively to digital stimuli resulting in a significant shift of channel mix for organizations. So, employees require re-training, and newer learning methods.

If digital is miniaturizing, and customer experience is adapting, how can customer journey maps be the same over time? How can brick and mortar establishments and processes remain the same every year? When I look at leading organizations like DBS, and BBVA in the banking industry, they have realized that they need to embrace the change rather than resist it. Suddenly we find great demand for a new breed of 'Customer Experience Designers'. On the technology side, we need newer skills like Voice Biometric specialists, NLP engineers or RPA specialists.

While customer preferences shift over time, we still haven't completely rid ourselves of multiple channels. With more than one channel, we introduce CX inconsistency if we don't actively resolve it.

OMNI CHANNEL

'The journey of a thousand miles begins with a single step.'

—Lao Tzu, Chinese philosopher

As a concept milked to its last drop in several conferences, white papers and sales pitches by technology providers, the truth of what is really required has been lost in where it really matters.

My view is that we need to show the right things for the right customers, when and where it really matters, and to allow critical aspects of the customer journey to sing beautifully together. The idea is to eliminate friction points.

Technology service providers have expanded this scope to become omni, seamless or unified, which, to say the least, is a sixteen-year-old sales bid to corporates.

The problem, as I see it, is corporates freezing themselves into annual budgeting cycles, practising rigidity and thus failing to recognize the market realities around customer experience requirements.

As shoppers get introduced to new channels to experience ZMOT, digital is increasingly becoming a connective tissue. Though digital is one word, it is rapidly breaking down into multiple offerings as we continue to miniaturize. For example, instore experiences include QR Codes (Paytm), autonomous shopping carts (7Fresh), or mobile check-out without even speaking to anyone (Nike's Speed Shop and Amazon Go). Brick and mortar channels have integrated digital price tag technologies to include nutritional information (Kroger). ZMOT now encompasses AR experiences like the one found at IKEA, to visualize how a piece of furniture would look in your home, and facilitating instant purchase if you like it. Audi extended its own VR showroom experience at its brick and mortar dealership for a more personalized CX.

I see a traditional brick and mortar channel reinventing itself, and ZMOT is getting tightly integrated into it. For the neighbourhood furniture store that has not adapted, the puzzle on dwindling customer walk-ins will cause nightmares.

Over 91 per cent of customers are seeking more visual and interactive content, and existing channels need to adapt to this demand. So it's no longer about providing information across channels or seamlessness of experience, but the ability for the customer to interact and make visual choices.

I see transition by customers not only from physical to digital, but also from digital to physical. Several digital native brands like Bonobos, Warby Parker and Casper are moving to physical to accommodate this.

I am not trying to belie the fact that customers don't use multiple channels simultaneously (86 per cent of shoppers are regularly channel hopping across at least two channels according to CommerceHub), but to identify how our customers are adapting to ways of interaction.

The argument that my industry is not yet disrupted, will fall flat. Take banking, for example. A search company like Google has grown to reach 67 million users with $110 billion in transactions annually in India alone. If you take WeChat Pay and AliPay they have captured over 80 per cent of the Chinese market. And even if we consider Apple Pay to be a laggard in the US, they have over 9 per cent market share on payment methods. This indicates that traditional banks are losing market share to newer players and newer channels and ecosystems.

These trends in digital and e-commerce have driven organizations like DHL to increasingly move towards robotics and other supply chain innovations within logistics. Every last-mile delivery is being relooked at with the usage of robots and drones. But even these channels have to integrate seamlessly with the existing channels and information to provide the customer a seamless experience.

Every customer is now being fought for. I see Starbucks capturing on customer email addresses and eventually lead people into their Starbucks Rewards Programmes. Facebook Messenger channel is used for growth of its e-commerce base. Personalization is now a key aspect to transition potentials into loyalists.

So as we identify different micro services that sing beautifully together, we continue to sing for the customer. Virgin's customer service wraparound with Salesforce Automation to provide a great lead and prospect management engine is a great example of this. This integration into their cloud framework provides for sales and service interactions and personalization of customer interactions. This integration allows for smarter decision-making capabilities, and a view to see all of what was happening in-between.

I see the world getting into a phase of resets, and organizations that have had years of leadership may suddenly find the rug pulled from under their feet, if they fail to recognize and adapt to the trends.

Disney's business model integration across theme parks, hotels, restaurants, activities and events into one experience—My Disney Experience—is an exemplary instance of how one can continuously adapt to changing times.

YOUR DIGITAL WORKFORCE—ROBOTIC PROCESS AUTOMATION (RPA)

I see a big change in the way we are looking for solutions to real world problems. IT architecture and infrastructure does not justify implementation till a certain threshold is reached, yet the market is pushing us towards getting different atomized services to work in an integrated fashion.

The cost of services working 24/7 combined with three shifts for humans to work in, has reached maturity in several areas. We are not helping humans by asking them to do boring, repetitive, mundane tasks with the possibility of errors creeping in. With millennials not pursuing data entry jobs, some critical areas are also at the risk of labour shortage or turnover. The cost of risks also leads to audit and compliance failures combined with financial impact.

So what is the solution ? The emerging solution is RPA that works on the basis of creating software robots to act as synthetic users, and automating highly repeatable, structured tasks across business software. The whole concept is centred around software mimicking human actions based on a set of rules. With initial lower one-time costs, and repeated applicability and its productivity to replicate itself and create a workforce to do multiple shifts during the day or night, combined with the ability to make a three-hour process seem complete in three 3 minutes, made itself useful in areas like accounts payable, reconciliations, underwriting, pricing, claims and fraud detection, chatbots, checking on insurance eligibility in healthcare service providers, rendering reports, back-office activities, amongst others.

Since it requires very little coding, and thus very less IT skills, with a one-time license and our ability to create one-time automation for RPA to work, it's a win-win situation for corporates. Each time we create an RPA programme, we add to the skill library that can be used by other robots.

I see RPA as prime candidates to handle bookings and reservations, availabilities, check-outs, loyalty processes, managing employee rosters at hotels and restaurants, or reconciliation or commission calculations in the airline industries.

RPA is particularly helpful in lowering cost-to-income ratios at banks to decrease manual interferences and turnaround times, in insurance underwriting processes, or in cases like oil and gas where there may be fluctuating work-force requirements combined with widely fluctuating oil prices.

There is a ton of software and service providers out there—like Automation Anywhere, Verint, Blackline, Open Span, Blue Prism, NICE, UIpath, Datamatics, Kofax, EdgeVerve.

The bottom line is savings between 25 per cent to 60 per cent of overall costs, with other side benefits like accuracy, data quality, reduction in manual errors, higher processing speed and scalability.

What is changing however, is the ability to create a symbiotic operation of RPA with AI. The recent instance of AstraZeneca is an exemplary case. AstraZeneca receives more than 1,00,000 adverse event reports documenting ailments to serious illnesses. They also have devised an advanced RPA system to deal with these reports. But members of the AstraZeneca patient safety system spend millions of hours administering these tasks manually. By adding AI into the mix, it is able to bring down the total number of administering hours significantly.

A more prevalent use case that will make a significant difference over the next few years is the combination of AI and RPA using voice or chat. The ability to generally understand a typical human question using AI, and translate the voice or chat into a series of simpler signals for RPA to execute, and return the answer through a natural response to the customer will change the landscape immensely.

But don't fool yourself into thinking that this symbiotic operation is possible in only a few areas or industries. If you take outliers like legal, you can convert large manual, error-prone paper based processes requiring hours of research into quickly scanning every legal suit ever tried.

The way I see it, humans will focus increasingly on critical and creative thinking tasks. Taking a leaf out of David Epstein's book *Range*,[2] I would say that each of these technologies like RPA and AI are creating specialists. I see a role for generalists since they are more creative, can make connections between diverse fields that specialists cannot, ultimately making them more impactful.

As humans, we will need to question our pre-industrial work methods for creating skilled artisans based on hours and years of experience, only to be replaced by machines and software in the form of AI and RPA. AI and RPA will continue to gain on the basis of atomization of processes and tasks.

Employees can be great problem solvers and social animals if trained appropriately to take advantage of this situation, in a way similar to a number of firms across a range of industries like Toyota, or Southwest Airlines.

The story of a chess competition where a pair of amateur American chess players using three computers at the same time, emerged as winners against grandmasters and solo computers, effectively indicates a new line emerging between human and machine, to combine the human strategic guidance with the computer's tactical ability.

We can't fail to appreciate differences—machines react to tasks, and humans to knowledge. The knowledge of CX and social construct is the powerful differentiator to create tasks that can be used by machines to execute as AI and RPA.

There are however other ethical challenges. For example—if an employee with the ability to create and deploy the bot, uses it for his personal advantage to defraud a corporation, or uses it with malicious intent to send freeform emails to its customers to damage reputation.

These frameworks and rules will have to be created and regulated by humans with considerable critical thinking capabilities.

From an execution perspective, I see the need to button down requirements, business case and the total cost of ownership, and the ability to identify process impact and optimization opportunities as opposed to a rehash to satisfy leadership that we have put through a new technology, which is very attractive to speak about in the annual report to its shareholders.

THE AI REVOLUTION

The man-machine collaboration is here to stay. Not surprisingly, its already a part of our daily lives. In fact, too many of us are using it on a daily basis without even realizing it. I am referring to finger prints and facial recognition on your mobile phone.

So, what is artificial intelligence? AI simply refers to the ability for a software or a machine to think and learn. When we use a smart phone like Apple, the translation of 30,000 dots and the depth map on your face unlocks the phone. When we subscribe to Netflix, we look at recommendations based on our previous reactions, interests, choices and behavioural patterns.

The impact of AI lies in its capability to perform highly complex computations with high accuracy and speed, and thereby accelerate scientific discovery and learning amongst other things. At its simplest, AI can augment humans in their day-to-day tasks through virtual assistants, software or data analysis or completely automate using robots.

The boundaries expand into making sense of unstructured data, simulating different conditions, creating new data based on real-world data limitations lending to newer risk profiles, personalizing experiences and substituting humans for machines in areas where humans find it difficult to meet stiff deadlines.

During my many interactions, I find corporations seeking use cases to identify areas that may have been the guinea pig of another corporation's experiment, that they could use as a spin off. So I put together my own list of the ones that I find extremely helpful for practical application:

- At NatWest, customers open a bank account with a selfie. The selfie is compared to the photo ID such as a passport to verify who they are, all using AI.
- Visual AI can help in radically increase the speed of drug discoveries to monitor and detect cellular drug interactions on a mass scale.
- One of the biggest challenges in manufacturing is in quality control. AI solutions embedded within workflows can potentially reduce risks from dangerous tasks or other mundane tasks to free up worker time towards innovation and product development.

- AI augmented product development can put forth the best presented, most attractive offers to a rapidly evolving set of customer demands, like presenting a travel insurance and forex product for a student going overseas for higher education using a bank loan.
- AI could recommend changes to corporate relationships based on poor customer experience.
- AI's use in IT especially to look at detecting and deterring security intrusions or compliance issues or resolving user technology problems has become a significant use case.
- AI's use in supply chain towards demand forecasting, supply stock estimations (over or under stocking), combined with autonomous robots and vehicles for warehouse management or supply chain logistics has changed the accuracy and speed of supply chains.
- At retail stores, having stocked shelves, and fast and easy checkout helps keep traffic smooth. AI Deep Learning can help keep track of your in-store availability and out-of-stock replenishments, and recognizing the items in your shopping cart can reduce your check-out time by minutes. At Lowe's, an autonomous retail service robot helps customers navigate the store, and responds to simple questions.
- On the subject of security, signature verification has become smarter with AI, allowing for high volume of documents with increased validation. Using wet ink signature verification for documents and contracts, it provides an accurate authentication using special descriptive language, signature segmentation and neural networks. The AI algorithm can also predict its confidence levels for the match, and humans can take over for low confidence cases.
- At real estate firms, selling a large number of units, validating the signed-off sale deed with the original document, ensures the prevention of fraud using a combination of OCR, RPA and AI.
- At a global investment firm, Infrrd IDC, financial reports in various languages are translated into English using a hybrid AI and

OCR tool. Using a combination of Machine Learning (ML) and Computer Vision algorithms, the relevant sections are scanned with OCR and recognized using Deep Neural Network. Similar algorithms are being used to manage mortgage documents at banks.

- YouTube's AI algorithm is particularly noteworthy. Using embedded data from keywords, tags and voice, it recommends videos to users. Using sophisticated algorithms, it redefines the channel viewer base continuously. Given that over 500 hours of video is posted on YouTube every minute in 2019, an AI algorithm works to recommend videos just to you. It also uses sophisticated AI algorithms to take down fake news, harmful content, copyright issues as quickly as possible, while providing creators with a sophisticated analytics engine to look at their personalized performance on a real-time basis.

- Given that fraud is endemic with digital, AI is a powerful tool to fight cybersecurity issues, phishing attacks, or impersonation to name a few. AI can within seconds spot an attack, but humans can validate or pass it as a potential error. The ability of AI to adapt, and change, will make a criminal's efforts at fraud more time-consuming and expensive. With passage of time, it can make the effort meaningless.

- Amazon's built-in AI designer uses ML to spot and track fashion trends.

According to Tractica research, by 2025, the bigger investments for AI will end up going into algo-trading, image recognition and tagging, patient data management and predictive maintenance. Areas like contract analysis, object identification and tracking could get moderate investments.

THE CHATBOT REVOLUTION

As I left for the Middle East in 2017, the Indian industry was not quite disrupted by AI. We were starting to engage with clients in

RPA, but AI was too few to count. But on landing in the UAE, I could see the proliferation of AI based conversational AI assistants, called chatbots.

The Dubai Electricity and Water Authority, DEWA, uses Rammas, to respond to customers in Arabic and English, helping reduce visitor footfall in DEWA offices by more than 80 per cent. Given the shifting expat population in the UAE, there is a flourishing business around their residency (Emirates ID), and so enquiries are plenty. Their Ask Hamad service is quite useful here. I see a similar opportunity for the Indian government services, considering that Indian software programmers are quite in demand overseas for the same skills.

As we progress, I clearly see the shift from text-based to voice-based interfaces for speed, efficiency and convenience. This is also being accelerated by the introduction of a number of IoT devices including thermostats, appliances and speakers.

We have already spoken about the symbiotic relationship emerging between AI and RPA, and voice is just the tip of the iceberg.

With the ability to capture words and sentences in regular diction, the ability to search using natural language captions is also expanding exponentially.

Traditional technology has always been looked at as a cost centre, but what if I told you that chatbots can increase your revenue by attracting customers and holding their attention, offering products or services that are of intrinsic value to customers. Since chatbots are powered by AI, customers begin to trust the chatbot's recommendations based on interactions over time. Unlike the human counterparts who have to be individually trained for a specific skill, bots can replicate skills within seconds, and can assist customers immediately without any waiting period.

Today, without voice assistants like Alexa, Siri or Google Assistant, we would be stuck to an input device like a keyboard, that has limitations, when driving, for instance.

Here again, I see clients being confined to a limited number of use cases, largely defined by their peers in the industry. That has prompted me to put down a number of use cases that could provide cross industry advantage:

- The Whole Foods Facebook messenger bot is extending its effectiveness by providing recipes, products and cooking inspirations. Imagine what it would be like if we had a bot that could educate customers on phishing issues at banks!
- Baby Centre UK (part of the Johnson & Johnson family), interacts with customers through Facebook messenger, first enquiring about the age of the child and the challenge that they are facing and then coming up with personalized advice. Imagine, how hospitals could interact with potential customers to provide them with immediate guidance, while they are waiting for medical attention to arrive!
- Many customers stay at a specific hotel only once in their lifetime, but would have specific requirements like availability of rooms, tariffs, care for pets, time for breakfast, proximity to a tube station, places to visit, events of interest, etc. Beyond this chatbots can also provide for automated check-in and check-out, recommendations from the concierge, room service requests, etc. Chats provide for non-intrusive ways to get answers to customer questions. Imagine, how schools could help teachers reduce their workload, gain insights about students and generally innovate in the classroom!
- HDFC Bank, India, gets over 20,000 conversations[3] a day with their chatbot EVA, to answer over 50,000 variations in banking queries and can even connect over Google Assistant or Amazon Alexa. Imagine, if Government services started catering to queries using an intelligent BOT!
- Bank of America's Erica and Capital One's Eno allows customers to search for transactions, transfer, deposit funds and even pay bills. What if patients in India could search for their past medical records or the doctors treating such patients could quickly get access to medical records without a fuss!

- Hospitals have started using chatbots, to assist in booking appointments, to help evaluate symptoms, remind patients about medications and monitor chronic health conditions. They can also help patients answer questions regarding their inventory, or bills and claims. What if chatbots could evaluate and improve student knowledge during the holiday season, when schools are off!

- Even start-ups are getting into the game, increasingly cutting out costs required to go the traditional route. Nigerian students developed Simbibot to help students prepare better for exams, by using past exam questions and multiple quizzes to test their knowledge and highlight problem areas. Can commercial MBA and medical institutions follow suit?

- Polly works to improve workplace happiness, using surveys and feedback, to keep track of team effectiveness and provide feedback to managers before things escalate. What if each office had a Polly to provide discrete feedback, that could help team effectiveness.

- Niki, an Indian bot, helps book cabs, buses, hotels, movies, pay utilities, top up the prepaid balance of your mobile service provider, and even organize pick-up and delivery of laundry. I don't quite see this in some of the countries that I have travelled to.

- Fitness apps integrated with chatbots can send out personalized workout plans, while keeping track on your progress, and motivate you to keep on track. We could apply similar situations to education, for example.

- I see continuous evolution with platforms like Alexa and by using extensions like Skills. With time, in addition to robust speech recognition, accents and ability to cut through background noise, these assistants are moving beyond mundane tasks like reading and replying to emails, reminders, booking conference rooms, making a call or tracking packages.

  Virtual nurse platforms like Sense.ly use speech recognition with integrated sentiment analysis to engage with patients in conversations regarding their health. Depending on the symptom, the voice, the severity and duration of that experience, the assistant is able to quickly schedule an appointment or direct the patient to the emergency department.

As chatbots evolve we no longer use the 'wake' word, they converse naturally, and are integrating into consumer products like speakers and refrigerators. Given that voice assistants are being pushed by retail (Amazon) and search engines like Google, the way we search and information that is presented back to us using SEO techniques will change quite a bit. These voice assistants will also learn to differentiate between your identity, your spouse's, your child's or a guest's, and become a virtual human in and around the house. Today the assistant is tied down to the device, and personalization doesn't exactly travel with you in your new environment, but that could change as well.

Chatbots will thus find a way to weave itself into the fabric of human experience.

SELF-SERVICE

When I go back to the history of self-service, I see it as a tool to improve time and cost efficiency. So the CX that was built around it was towards saving time. The corporation derived value from cost efficiency, and hence it was a win-win.

The future as I see it lies in customer led automation. Digital, AI and RPA will drive customer engagement, and the new currency for the corporation is data. The king of the future will be the king of data.

So while the past has been about 'do it myself' and 'do it together', the future will be about 'let my bot do it' and 'let our bots do it'.

The new customer base is increasingly Gen Z, and they are most amenable to these technologies.

We can already see technology experiments at the airport in the form of kiosks and chatbots in various businesses. IT is building self-service tickets for IT service management, ATMs are spewing out transactions in addition to cash and supermarkets are starting to scan carts for a faster billing process on the likes of Amazon Go.

Generation Z are DIYers. As an Indian, we have the rare privilege of help all around—drivers, cooks, maids, gas station attendants, car cleaning guys and the list goes on. When we want to catch up with friends, we just go over without much thought or appointment. But times are changing, this rare privilege is vanishing, and along with it the fabric is changing from face-to-face relationships to interacting through social media. Gen Z's use of social media has evolved. They are better informed, looking to define their identity, and are also more impatient.

Gen Z, with an unimaginable 8 second attention span, believes in authenticity thus believing in seeing real people as digital influencers, people who use YouTube, Udemy and Skillshare as a learning platform. They favour brands that have a point of view and stand for something—being socially aware of global issues, they wear things that make them feel good.

All of these create characteristics for making individual and independent choices. These choices are great drivers for self-service.

With this comes business models that didn't exist previously—a takeaway service like Swiggy in addition to McDonald's and Burger King, or the now payments bank Paytm and Google Pay that started as an online mobile recharge and bill payment platform, where disruption from traditional channels are taken out and peer-to-peer payments are commonplace.

Transactions that can be clearly articulated and programmed are where self-service rules the roost. Where it fails miserably is in exceptions. The worst part about a failed communication is that even after I provide adequate data to the self-service channel, when I connect back to a human being, the whole experience has to be repeated, and it gets worse when I have to interact with a call centre channel, where repetition becomes the norm, and the solution comes as a distant call.

So while self-service is definitely a preferred channel, necessary CX safeguards have to be thought through.

I constantly ask myself about why these episodes occur. The answer, many a time, seems to be that customer journey maps are designed with a positive experience in mind, and less with the management of exceptions or escalations.

The evidence of self-service taking over can be seen in areas like banking where customer visits to branches are dropping by over 40 per cent over the last five years, and mobile transactions have become primary to customer interest.

With 80 per cent of customers regarding experience with a company as important as its products, and with a large part of that customer base being represented by millennials and Gen Z, their characteristics become important.

With over 92 per cent of millennials and 100 per cent of Gen Zs owning a smartphone, combined with a high proportion of them spending more than five hours on their devices, self-service models emanating through smart phones is a perfect choice especially when personal, visual and contextual communication is forming an important basis for decision making.

A NEW WORLD CENTRED AROUND THE INTERNET

I see the Internet changing our existence and our everyday life. From historically exchanging short messages between two points, to a world of the Internet of Things (IoT), our lives have become radically different.

The Internet has become a means to amalgamate hardware with software, but goes far beyond connected devices.

IoT is suddenly making inroads into our everyday lives with self-driving smart electric cars like Tesla, predictive maintenance to increase industrial safety and optimize resources, health protection and disease control, or smart homes.

The advent of faster 5G will enhance freight monitoring, air traffic monitoring, autonomous driving, traffic management systems, smart cities infrastructure, telemedicine, resource management and much more.

So why is IoT and 5G so important?

IoT provides us with an ability to monitor, and 5G provides speed.

Imagine a world where we could deploy medical personnel in real quick time, or prevent missing luggage altogether!

For a car rental agency, the biggest asset is their car. The ability to track the car as well as the car renter on a near real time basis provides the rental agency peace of mind.

Insurers can charge lower premiums for drivers with safe driving habits, and patients with a heart condition can be brought in for medical care much before an episode and reduce healthcare costs being borne by both the patient and the government in many cases.

For a corporation, industries like the wearable payments market exceed US$300 billion, with a 15 per cent CAGR, to exceed US$1,100 billion by 2026. So Apple Pay, Samsung Pay and other wearable payment modes are here to stay.[4]

The wearable health market is much smaller, but is likely to rake in excess of US$60 billion by 2023, according to market analysts.

Another interesting fact is what an increase in Internet speed does to our economy. A paper from Arthur D. Little and Ericsson in thirty-three OECD countries showed a 0.3 per cent growth each time the speed of the Internet doubled.

A reduction in data latency will also plough the case for new innovative IoT devices, and a better commercialization perspective for connected cars.

For education, search and research, it will mean availability of relevant information on demand without restriction, leading to a better use of time.

If indeed we believe that pictures say a thousand words, being able to communicate with ease on video on the go and without the hassle of a drop-out by itself should contribute to more meaningful interactions, leading to better results.

IoT itself is growing into different services—consumer IoT, enterprise IoT and industrial IoT with differentiated use cases. To add more granularity, there are applications emerging in medical IoT and military IoT.

Combining IoT, AI and RPA, we will be able to get use cases that were impossible to receive earlier.

Imagine the ability to predict the New Zealand volcanic eruption using IoT sensors or earthquake early warning systems using IoT preventing human catastrophes.

Full-blown implementations of IoT in Smart Cities and buildings, for example, are still in early stages, but are valuable for day-to-day life improvements for normal people and not a phenomena for early adopter 'geek'.

The age-old problem continues to haunt us—common communication protocols and standards in IoT. The reason I say it's an age-old problem is because I have seen multiple repeats—Sony Betamax vs VHS, Blu-ray vs HD, the rise of the EMV standard for cards and many more.

So how do we really make a difference using these new-age digital technologies? Provide the engineering teams with the knowledge upfront—what are the business outcomes you seek, the values that are desired for your enterprise, the benefit for your customers and what changes that you see as being required to commercialize the solution both internally and externally. In essence, this forms the basis of the business case for change. Without such clarity, this becomes the Internet of Nothing!

THE FUTURE OF CRM

I see the evolution of CRM from a combination of a static rolodex, rotary phone and notepad all rolled into one, into a precision engineered, predictive analytics driven tool carrying customer satisfaction and experience with decision-making insights. I can also see improvements in customer trust, repurchases loyalty and higher lifetime customer values based off the use of modern-day CRM.

With the evolution of CRM, customer data itself has become far richer, allowing for deep personalization, though its fragmentation has posed limitations. The combination of AI, big data, chatbots and RPA will allow for better interactions with customers. We have been successful in moving CRM from being a toolset focused on sales, to enterprise uses.

We are transitioning from older CRMs which have been in place for a long time, yet operate in silos where no individual owns the customer data and information is fragmented without a full view across businesses. Future needs are built on top of current needs as patchwork creating sub-optimal solutions. Measurements are individual—sales, marketing and customer service benchmarks are fragmented, and responsibilities don't quite carry across.

CRM is built as a technology solution, based on business clarity surrounding the value desired as perceived by businesses in sales or marketing or customer service. So the focus is driven around the moment of truth rather than the customer journey.

The CRM of the future needs to integrate social media channels, track interactions and engagements and provide that insight into various teams that need to keep pace with constantly evolving customer tastes.

Over the course of this chapter, we have spoken about individual technologies, and use cases, all of which work with the customer at the centre. Yet, in engineering terms, many of them are being developed in silos inside organizations, without communication, collaboration and cross functional roles, due to concentrated skillsets within the teams and departments.

Progress is being made with 20 per cent of organizations worldwide adopting AI approach to CRM, but a longer queue awaits for an overall improvement of CX.

Almost 80 per cent of the customer data today is dormant, and remains un-utilized for customer insights. In order for CRM to take the full power, that data has to make it back to the mainstream. Today a lot of effort is being put into digital end to end (the base plumbing), which in turn will help us embed ourselves deeper into actionable insights, and put new products into the customer's hands. To turn insights into action, in-time customer needs recognition will be the key differentiator.

IN SUMMARY—TEN

Being first is not the end all for decision-making, yet organizations that evaluate and take risk are the ones that are likely to succeed. Sitting on the fence because a technology is not mature or evolving is no longer a viable excuse. We are not in the first year of change when it comes to leading technologies like digital, AI, RPA, IoT, CRM or the likes. In all of this, we will miss the bus if we are unable to understand the demands of the modern day customer—millennials and Gen Z—many of whom are likely to be our early adopters and our early majority.

Eleven

Measuring Results

SETTING MEASURES AND VALUES

'The only true measure of success is the ratio between what we might have done and what we might have been on the one hand, and the thing we have made and the things we have made of ourselves on the other.'

—H.G. Wells

'The greater danger for most of us isn't that our aim is too high and miss it, but that it is too low and we reach it.'

—Michelangelo

'What gets measured, gets managed.'

—Peter Drucker

Of all the chapters you have read so far, this one is probably the most important. Imagine your business is running quite well, and you are happy with it. If you look at your profits more carefully, you will be surprised that there are some factors that are pulling down your results, and your attention towards them could increase your profit margins even further. Similarly, if you have had a difficult period in your business, closer inspection will reveal that there are a number of positives you could focus on to improve as well as a number of negatives that you could remove to turn the situation around.

At IBM I learnt a secret that artisans have known for centuries, which is, in order to make excellent products, you need to focus on the right tools. This means that using the right methods are essential tools in getting the right measurements. This, of course, involves asking the right questions and taking the right approach and measuring customer experience (CX) and customer satisfaction is no different. Here are my four observations with regards to measurements:

1. *What are you measuring?* The first aim is to understand how well your organization has achieved its key business objectives. That measure is defined as a 'key performance indicator' (KPI). The word 'key' refers to achieving the right objective that aligns with your business goals. For the purpose of this book, that key business objective rallies around CX. This translates into measuring how well your organization keeps customers engaged and happy, while at the same time not misaligning with its other corporate objectives.

2. Since the *measure is* numerical, it can be *calculated in many ways*—through enumeration, percentages, sums or totals, averages or ratios. For sake of simplicity, we shall call it a 'formula' (a method of calculation). The important thing to remember here is that the formula itself has to be an industry standard. Why? This is because you will want to compare this with other companies, with yourself down the road, and if the way you calculate it changes over time (which it will if you don't have a standard), then your past data will become meaningless. To take an example, say you are calculating something called 'turnaround time' for a loan application. If you calculate it from

the time you get completed documents, whereas the industry is calculating it from the time an initial document was received from the customer, then your measure (though better in some regards) will not be comparable. Moreover, the customer might still be annoyed even if you think you have great standards, and you will be left to fix a ratio that you never thought was wrong in the first place.

3.   The *outcome* of the formula (that is the value) has a *unit of measure*. A wrong understanding of a unit of measure can sometimes be catastrophic. In 1983, an Air Canada Boeing 767 ran out of fuel mid-flight after metric conversion errors.[1] Thankfully, due to pilot alertness, they made the first successful 'dead stick' landing of the commercial airliner.

4.   The last part of the measure is the *'benchmark'*, or the standard value against which your results will be compared. For example, the benchmark for a non-diabetic person is blood sugar levels of 4.0 to 5.5 mmol/L under fasting conditions, and under 7.8 mmol/L 90 minutes after a meal. Anything over this up to 6.9 mmol/L fasting, and 11 mmol/L after food, is considered pre-diabetic, while blood sugar levels higher than that means one is clinically diabetic.

Some measures could change depending on the industry, while others are the same across the board. Hospitality, for example, measures occupancy rates, which may not have much meaning to the retail sector. Measures relating to CX metrics, however, could stay the same across. It's also important to recognize that benchmarks change with innovation. For example, turnaround times have shrunk to minutes from days, which used to be the benchmark a decade ago. Additionally, depending on the situation, some measures require immediate attention. For instance, a patient who has very worrisome vital signs or a data centre with systems going down requires a separate set of measurements that are different from standard practices.

In my career as I helped organizations build their measurement frameworks and guidelines, I also saw how many of these earlier reports were lying on a shelf gathering dust like research papers. The employees never saw them or understood them and were not trained to read, calculate or interpret their results.

A really interesting, high pressure example where KPI frameworks are applicable, but an average person does not pay attention to, is in Formula One or F1. The instrument cluster in F1 cars are a great example of measures and indicators. It's not just a single indicator but an array that provides a summary of how well the car is performing. Further details are available by getting critical data from the onboard computer through the onboard diagnostics (OBD) port in the car.

A typical race lasts two hours with around 305 kilometres of driving and includes one or two short pit stops that are measured in seconds. The car itself goes through extreme stress with engines performing at 18,000 rmps. The car boasts of more than 80,000 ultra-lightweight parts and costs about US$10 million, of which 70 per cent is accounted for by the engine that is replaced after every race. The outcome that every team desires is a spot on the podium and the car generates copious amounts of data that is continuously analysed both during the race and after it in order to ensure fine-tuning for race performance, track conditions and weather. But, how many of us know that the real race is fought outside the car?

The race car generates 100s of gigabytes (GBs) of information about the car and its driver's health that is transmitted through a wireless data connection and sliced and diced by engineers in real time. The car itself has the equivalent of a black box, an 'accident data recorder', that stores information regarding the car's sensors and accelerators, and quickly cautions the race marshals about the severity of the accident. Even during the race, engineers stationed at the side are reviewing sensor data including tyre pressure, engine temperature and oil pressure, amongst others. Since you can't keep up with everything during the race, the indicators that make or break a race are the ones that are looked at. Those are what we call KPIs.

The data analysis exercise doesn't just stop when the race ends as a number of data points are analysed in greater detail post-race in order to be more competitive in the next one.

In essence, in the F1 race, there are four ways of looking at performance. i. Did you win the race?; ii. What was your relative performance versus the other cars (behind you, in front of you or the race leader)?; iii. How much better was your performance versus your last race or the last year?; and iv. How was the performance of your current car versus your other car(s) that had different settings to alter performance?

Our businesses are no different. With unrelenting focus and speed we need our frontline to focus on the immediate response, while the analysis is left to another 'engineering' team. We often call this team the 'business intelligence unit'.

For Formula One, you would define a KPI as 'a factor by which you can measure the performance or position of the car in the race or in the competition'. In this definition, the car represents your organization or business.

As I help my clients build their CX measures, I tend to ensure completeness across attract (customer acquisition), engage (customer contact) and retain or regain (keeping customers or winning them back). These, I have found over time, are built across 5 impact areas:

1. Speed and accuracy—first response time (FRT), problem resolution time);
2. Transparency—customer awareness;
3. Accessibility and empowerment—customer effort score (CES);
4. Friendliness—net promoter score (NPS), customer satisfaction score (CSAT), net customer additions, customers retained and cross-sell ratios; and
5. Efficiency—first-time resolution (FTR), customer lifetime value (CLTV), campaign return on investment (ROI), conversion rates, churn rates, cost of retention and abandonment rates.

YOUR KEY PERFORMANCE INDICATORS—
DRIVING CUSTOMER HEALTH

During my career, I have had to keep a close watch on customers as a practitioner when I worked in the business, as an IT consultant where I had to design systems to visibly indicate measures to my clients, and when I became a strategic consultant to advise clients on parameters that they need to look at and observe.

The biggest gap I saw during those assignments was the lack of clear linkages to close the gap between results and root cause, leading to organizations trying to identify this first hand as soon as they ran into problems.

When I moved from being a practitioner to a consultant, I saw the importance that critical thinking played in shaping how the problem could be solved.

The KPI tree to me was one such revelation. When applied to CX, I found four main areas that CX impacted directly—profit, growth, cost and satisfaction. Again, you could also look at these dimensions from an attract, engage and retain perspective, yielding a 12 box matrix.

The reason I find this approach important is that many a time things go wrong, and that's when you are trying to trace the impact across the tree, and the tree would immediately tell you what's going wrong. You could call it similar to the instrument cluster in the cockpit of a plane, where you can see all vital parameters for a successful flight.

With technology, you can now measure this in real time. As a YouTuber, I also see this being applied by YouTube in YouTube Studio giving creators visibility into search engine optimization (SEO) effectiveness, customer satisfaction and revenue earned from AdSense.

As I peeled the layers around CX KPIs of these 12 boxes, I arrived at 18 relevant KPIs strung together (see Figure 1).

If you consider profit as the parameter for an organization's CX success, new revenue for every fresh customer and campaign

ROI ranks high. For existing customers where engagement is a key parameter along with CLTV, you are looking at new revenue from existing customers, and, if you are looking at the retain pillar, then you are looking at the revenue you generate from retained customers.

Similar to this you can also see growth KPI's in net customer additions, retained and cross-sell ratios. Likewise, under costs, you are looking at conversion, retention, abandonment costs and the net cost of losing customers. Finally, Satisfaction has 6 key measures that are now popular amongst corporations looking to measure CX as shown in Figure 1. By considering only these 6 and ignoring linkages with (and between) the others, we may be missing crucial links that indicate CX.

Probably the biggest gap I found that organizations tend to overlook, or take for granted, is how you actually calculate these measures. Sometimes, we just leave these to common sense. Then when we do measure them, we find that our measures are quite good but they are not translating into positive CX. Another mistake

Figure 1: The CX KPI Tree

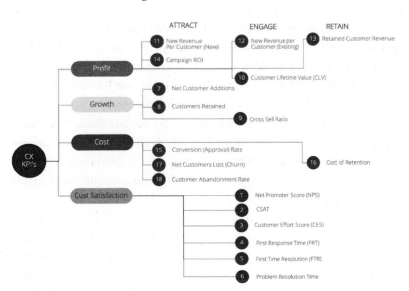

organizations make often is to compare CX measures between two different organizations. Many a time measures are calculated using different formulas and hence they end up comparing apples with oranges.

In order to understand the specifics let's deep dive into each one of these 18 measures, shall we?

CUSTOMER SATISFACTION MEASURES

1. NET PROMOTER SCORE (NPS)

This is probably the most commonly used measure to look at customer satisfaction. The main question in this measure is 'How likely are you to recommend to a colleague or friend?', followed by a scale of 1–10 representing least likely to extremely likely. This scale can be further broken down into three categories based on the score—promoters (9–10), passives (7–8) and detractors (0–6). NPS is calculated as the difference of percentage of promoters (9 and 10) minus percentage of detractors (0 through 6)

We spoke about raving fans earlier and NPS is a direct reflection of that. It's a good idea to check in with our customers once a quarter. The first survey could act as a baseline and we could go on from there. It's a good idea to send it to customers who have had enough time (7–30 days within their first contact) to interact with the company to form a basis to answer the question.

There are two ways in which we could administer an NPS survey. The first is a survey that is done to check the health of our relationship (relationship NPS) and the other is administered based on customer happiness after an immediate touchpoint interaction (transactional NPS).

We just need to make sure that you don't overdo the NPS. If the customer interacts with us once a month, a transactional NPS may be fine, but if they interact many times a day then we need to restrict the number of surveys that we conduct.

Transactional NPS is very useful in business-to-consumer (B2C) interactions where the recency really matters. Relationship NPS matters more in a business-to-business (B2B) scenario, where we have many ongoing transactions with the customer over a lifetime.

If our NPS is working, it would suggest the alignment of cultural, innovative and other inspirational elements that our company has got right.

Using NPS also works well when we are seeking feedback from our competitor's customers as it provides us with a competitive benchmark to compare against. I would call this the competitor benchmark NPS.

If we go back to the case study involving Blockbuster, which we elaborated on in the preface, there was a shift in consumer preference from Blockbuster to Netflix. If Blockbuster had administered a benchmark NPS survey on Netflix, they would have been able to catch the wave on time and would have been in a position to respond with conviction.

It's the same if you look at IBM who had bought the Lotus suite of productivity applications and did not take heed of detractors who essentially moved from Lotus to Microsoft over time. The general thinking at the time was that IBM was a more powerful brand (Microsoft was still a very young company) and people would stick to the brand that they were most comfortable with. However, Microsoft offered more to customers to transition and over time this resulted in Microsoft becoming the market leader in the sector. A competitor benchmark NPS would have told you the story long before it actually played out.

While it is easy to pick traditional competitors, it's difficult to pick non-traditional ones. Take for example the evolution of the electric car. Car manufacturers like Nissan (Leaf), Ford (Focus Electric), Mitsubishi (MiEV), BMW (ActiveE) and Toyota (Rav4 EV) would be traditional competitors to Tesla when it launched the Tesla Model S. While competitors would not be able to do a competitor benchmark NPS with Tesla Model S, the bigger surprise was when

Apple and Dyson got into the race without any background or history in car manufacturing.

When looking at NPS measures, the ability to subdivide and segment NPS data is pretty useful and it's a good way to deconstruct our statistical numbers. One set of customers may be very happy with us, while another may just be unhappy. By segmenting data by date of purchase, the type of product, the pricing plan, the customer persona, the location of the purchase, the size of the business making the purchase and the channel, gives us a good drill down on what is wrong. From a score perspective, it's good to look at bands 1–6 (detractors), 7–8 (passives) and 9–10 (promoters). While detractors are critical of the product or the service, passives are fence sitters, and it's important to understand the grades as well.

Additionally, to measure success of some of our actions, it would be useful to do A–B testing. This is done by measuring different versions of the product, location, channel and so on by varying one factor.

There are different tools available these days to automate our NPS segmentation, providing us with necessary insights to take adequate measures. These tools provide us a simple way to understand customer loyalties; they provide a common language that management would love. The challenge happens when we are trying to drill it down, it is not specific by itself, and gives you some level of deconstruction with segmentation. Which is why looking at other metrics starts to make sense in addition to NPS to understand our NPS better.

Temkin Group conducts annual NPS surveys to indicate good and bad bandings for NPS across twenty industries and more than 300 companies. The scores vary across sectors. For example, ranked highest in banking was a score of 65 out of 100, the best auto dealer scored 51, best supermarket came in with a high of 56, the best hotels recorded 49, best insurance company scored 64, and so on. Although the scores differed from sector to sector, on an average NPS leaders enjoyed a 21-point lead over NPS laggards across the board.

What I noticed immediately is that different industries have varied top quartile measures, and in order to piece that together, we need to be innovative and different.

But, why should we care? Numerous studies have established that a high NPS score can be directly linked to profitability. NPS is a journey that requires commitment, acceptance and investment but it is a rewarding one that keeps us up there above the competition.

2. CUSTOMER SATISFACTION SCORE (CSAT)

A very common measure to gauge happy customers is the CSAT score. The score itself is arrived at as a ratio of the number of satisfied customers to the number of survey responses expressed in percentage terms. It's an industry measure and can typically be used as a benchmark across organizations. The ratings are from 1 (very unsatisfied), 2 (somewhat unsatisfied), 3 (neutral), to 4 (somewhat satisfied) and 5 (very satisfied). This measure is a great tool to look at simple experiences such as product delivery, return, customer care call or a password change.

The typical question here is 'How would you rate your overall satisfaction with the good(s)/service(s)?' With automation which has become the norm these days, you can collate and quickly generate immediate reactions to an experience.

When I am helping my clients, I sometimes pair this with other short, qualitative questions. If a customer's rating is in the 1–3 band, the qualitative question that follows could be 'What could we do better?' for example. In these surveys, the mobile phone helps us collate quick responses. When scores are consistently poor, you can pass on feedback to teams to look into the issues quickly and regularize negative sentiment as soon as possible. When we inform teams regarding CSAT, it gets the teams involved and puts their skin in the game for business success.

Why is this important? According to *Forbes*, poor customer service costs US$338.5 billion globally each year. Research shows that existing customers spend 67 per cent more than new customers. So, if we can keep our customers satisfied, we get a share of the 67 per cent.

When I was running customer retention for a large bank, one statistic stuck out like a sore thumb—we found out that 91 per cent of unhappy customers would never buy from us again. The reality was that the first 120 days in the onboarding lifecycle determined the success of the product for us. Conducting a survey during that period, combined with a proper handholding programme, helps in converting a new customer into a loyal customer.

The charm of the CSAT measure comes from its directness and the fact that it is an excellent employee-to-customer engagement tool. While CSAT measures satisfaction, NPS measures loyalty and is a more powerful tool. However, when used together, they can be used towards improving your customer's overall satisfaction levels.

3. CUSTOMER EFFORT SCORE (CES)

Over the years, as a customer, I have had several instances of grievance and had to reach out to the company to fix the issue. It typically starts with a form or an email. After a day of unresponsiveness it becomes a phone call to the call centre, where I have had to repeat the story to explain the issue. After another day, you call again if the issue has not been resolved. By this time I am frustrated. Then I start looking at people I know in that organization who can help me solve the issue, and, sometimes, I end up writing a letter to the CEO for intervention, when the company is unresponsive for a prolonged period of time.

The instance above reflects the 'effort' I took to fix my issue. In 96 per cent of cases where customers had to make substantial effort, future loyalty suffered. The research and advisory firm Gartner surveyed this independently and concluded that 'Effort is the strongest driver to customer loyalty'. Monitoring effort, therefore, helps uncover high effort pain points. An article in the *Harvard*

Business Review titled 'Stop Trying to Delight Your Customers' highlighted that 'reducing customer effort does help build Customer Loyalty'. The article went on to explain that multiple interactions and channels created more customer frustration and disconnect from the brand.

So how can you measure your customer effort? The simple answer is, 'Ask your customer.' Why should we ask you may say? The reason for that is your understanding of effort is different from that of the customer. For example, many a time, we end up thinking it's perfectly normal to ask a customer to fill up a 20 page form.

The typical question I would ask the customer is simply this, 'To what extent do you agree or disagree with the following statement, "The company made it easy for me to handle my issue"?' The scale I follow here is 1 to 7 in the following order of progression, strongly agree–agree–somewhat agree–neither agree nor disagree–somewhat disagree–disagree and strongly disagree. In this scheme, frictionless experiences score either 1 or 2 and as we cross 4, I notice that we start to erode brand loyalty. When we want to know *why* customers feel that the effort is high, other data points like date of purchase, product type, customer persona, location of the purchase and the channel can help you narrow down potential causes.

The good thing about CES is that it can start you off in a particular direction, whereas the CSAT score just lets you know about satisfaction levels without offering any details unless additional questions to support it are also asked.

Increasingly companies are recognizing the value of relevance and the time to pop the question is becoming crucial. This simply means that if I asked the question right after my customer had the experience, I get a relevant answer. Otherwise, the experience may be forgotten and their answer will not help us fix things so that our next customer does not feel the same way about it in case there was a negative experience.

By stacking up NPS, CSAT and CES together, you can get powerful insights to analyse and get into specific zones.

In addition, I have often used an open question like 'Would you like to share anything else with us?' to get more qualitative answers to complicated cases.

4.   FIRST RESPONSE TIME (FRT)

Several years ago, I met with a motorbike accident. As soon as I fell, I knew my knee and my wrist were in trouble. Within 3 to 5 seconds, a crowd had gathered. They picked me up, put me on a stool, and asked me response questions. One of the Samaritans hailed a taxi, parked my bike on the corner of the road, gave me back the keys to the bike and helped me reach the hospital for a more thorough check-up. That day I really learnt the meaning of the term, FRT.

Even today, I am grateful to the crowd that took care of me when it mattered the most, and I can't thank them enough.

It was only many years later that I figured out that my gratitude to those who helped me when I met with my accident had many similarities with CX satisfaction as in both cases the key was 'speed'.

As I turned from practitioner to consultant, I realized the value of 'getting back' to customers with an incident ticket number. This needs to be backed up with customer communication, while simultaneously taking care of internal processes towards co-ordination and dispatch as well as getting back to the customer with shipping details. The final step is following through with feedback.

I realized that FRT made customers feel more comfortable and constant communication made them feel at home. My actions could in fact convert a potential customer into a loyal one, even before the product reached the customer's home.

The average of FRTs reflects our efficiency. The industry benchmark for online receipts is within 3 seconds, email responses are 24 hours or less, phone handling in less than 3 minutes, and social media in under 60 minutes. Similarly, benchmarks for websites for orders is less than 3 minutes, and response to queries, less than 48 hours.

So, the next time you want your customer to feel at home, try calling him back within the next 3 minutes of missing his call.

5. FIRST TIME RIGHT (FTR)

The other day, I had an issue with an electrical equipment. I felt I had to call for service, but took a chance to look up the FAQ section of their website. To my surprise I found the answer there, with an explanation on how to reset my equipment. That was an example of a great 'one touch resolution'.

I know that FTR is an old metric, in use since the Six Sigma days to measure quality and consistency. Yet, I cannot stress enough on how many current companies simply get this wrong. Getting things right on the first go, provides for less rework, consistency and proper planning in advance.

In my experience with advising clients, I have discovered some secrets to FTR success. These can be summed up as:

- FTR is made up of quality and consistency.
- Quality itself is composed of attitude and effort.
- Attitude is made up of commitment and engagement.
- Effort is made up of measure, knowledge, training and improvement.

Once you focus on all aspects of quality and consistency, FTR becomes automatic.

6. PROBLEM RESOLUTION TIME (PRT)

When we carry out customer experience surveys with clients and their customers, we have often encountered a gap in perception of problem resolution between a client and their customers. A company may feel that they have resolved the issue, while the customer clearly doesn't and continues to reach out to fix the issue.

Let me give you an example. I happened to buy a washing machine from a reputable company, which turned out defective. I reached out to their customer service centre and they sent a representative across to take a look. The representative tried to fix the issue over the next 48 hours and ended up replacing the machine. While I thought that was the end of the issue, it turned out that the product design turned out to be defective. Several conversations later, the company ended up downgrading me to the next lower end model and refunded me the balance.

This interaction provided me with several insights regarding PRT.

In principle, PRT starts from the time the customer makes you aware of the query or the issue and ends when the customer is satisfied that the issue has been resolved. The longer this takes, the less loyal they will be in the future. Therefore, it is crucial that before you attempt to solve the problem, attempt to understand and clarify it at the outset.

Many case studies have shown that problems like this can be fixed at much lesser costs *earlier than later*. Honda ended up recalling 5,088 vehicles in 2019 and 1,90,578 vehicles in 2016 with defective Takata airbags sold between 2003–2011, which could potentially result in safety risks to the vehicle's occupants.[2] Similarly, Mazda ended up recalling over 2,70,000 vehicles. While Mazda and Honda have a role to play in this, the question also arises about Takata's role in all of this.

Don't think that the problem is only with the automobile industry. Think about 4 years of Apple Macs that had keyboard issues which was finally fixed towards the end of 2019 that was done by reverting to an old keyboard design!

While some customers may make a compromise, many walk away without even complaining.

With every subsequent year, customer expectations are that things work the way they are advertised. Even if problems do crop up, they expect things to be fixed immediately.

Again, resolution time and unhappiness have a direct correlation with how critical the issue is. If you have a lost or stolen debit or credit card, you don't want to go through twenty-seven steps in the interactive voice response (IVR) call. Similarly, if you are trying to get an accident victim to the hospital, you want to be quick, or if an ATM didn't dispense cash due to some issue, you don't expect the bank to take seven days to rectify the error.

When thinking about PRT, I am reminded of something that my mentor once told me, 'The best way to resolve a problem is to deal with it even before others start to complain about it.'

Poor PRTs increases churn and according to American Express, more than half of the customers postpone or cancel a purchase or a transaction because of poor service.

GROWTH MEASURES

Over time, I recognized two fundamental truths about growth:

1. If you are not growing your business you may go out of business; and
2. If growing your business isn't growing your profits, you might want to stop and take stock.

Both the above factors drive very large consulting spends by organizations. The first type is centred around improving sales productivity and the second looks to reduce costs or improve the cost-to-income ratio.

7. NET CUSTOMER ADDITIONS

For some years in a row, we went through a phase where our credit cards business was not actually growing. There were zero net customer additions. We got in new customers, but lost existing customers to churn. You can envisage how stressful this situation is for the business and its viability.

The same principle is true across all 'mass market' segments where new customers are crucial for survival and existing customers and their loyalty gives a good boost to revenue. Yes, I am referring to banking, auto, real estate, insurance, hospitals, hospitality and others.

For these sectors, the equation looks like this:

Net Customer Additions = New Customers – Clients Lost (Churn)

In these industries, new profits come about when net customer additions are greater than zero. With additional costs the profitability of the portfolio will be eroded if the organization stays stagnant. Moreover, adding the right customers is also very important as every wrong customer you add makes you bleed.

The benchmark for net customer additions is usually provided by your industry peers.

8. CUSTOMERS RETAINED

The days when you acquire customers only one time may really be over. If you look at Apple, their endeavour is to get you into the ecosystem. This explains the diversification from products to services that will ensure that the customer stays in the family.

Churn occurs when the person actually leaves the family. It's like a hole at the bottom of your bucket. My experience working in the credit card sector taught me a lot regarding churn. The key point regarding churn is that when customers don't use my product, they will no longer be interested in the brand.

While working closely with corporates these days, I am seeing significant shifts in business models. Software is moving from the one-time payment purchase model to software as a service (SaaS), where we end up paying monthly usage fees. A similar trend is visible in other sectors as well: car dealerships are increasingly dependant on revenue from services; credit card businesses recover initial fixed costs over a number of years; real estate firms are looking to expand their revenue pool by levying maintenance charges to house owners. Even for soft drink manufacturers that have spent billions of dollars in bottling plants and distribution costs, their revenue model is increasingly targeted towards getting customers back to consume their products.

That leads us to the question of how we can correctly measure the number of customers retained. It can be expressed as,

Customers Retained = Customers Activated + Customers Saved from Churn

9. CROSS-SELL RATIO

When I was working in the credit card sector, while we were grappling to keep our growth up, we had a competitor that had a different strategy. They discovered that it made sense to focus on existing customers and cross-sell to them. The smartness of the move was as a result of them recognizing that it's five times cheaper to connect to existing customers and increase their lifetime value with such actions.

The way we would measure cross-sell ratio is:

Cross-Sell Ratio = Total Number of Products and Services Sold ÷ Total Number of Customers

The higher the ratio is, the more 'stickiness' you are likely to have with your customers and the higher your customer lifetime value would be. You could also call this the 'products per customer' ratio.

Globally, consumers hold more than 7.4 banking products per customer, according to research from RFi Group, with US banks topping the list at 8.5, Canada and UK at 7.1 and 6.5 respectively, and Australia at 4.9. Egypt is at 2.6, quite close to where India is at as well.

When Apple launched the iPhone, the mobile phone industry took notice. But while the industry was playing catch-up, Apple started working on other hardware products that might appeal to its customer base. Recognising that iPods would die in the wake of mobile phones, their strategy was to gradually graft customers from iPods to phones. That led them down the path of iPads, AirPods, Apple TV, HomePods and the like. This has been a successful move as an average US household now has 2.6 Apple products. In recent years, Apple has recognized that services is the glue for cross-sell.

Banks have long followed the cross-sell model, and telecom is following in its footsteps by increasing average revenue per user (ARPU) with TV, mobile and broadband offerings. We can also see similar trends with builders finding selling second homes lucrative, trust in hospitals driving patients to come back for other problems to the same hospital, auto manufacturers incentivizing customers to come back to them for a replacement car or a second car.

PROFIT MEASURES

As I said before, the second fundamental truth of growth is that 'If growing your business isn't growing your profits, you might want to stop and take stock.'

10. CUSTOMER LIFETIME VALUE (CLV)

My self-discovery around profitability came when I understood something rather simple, but less commonly realized, 'Making customers better makes better customers better.'

Traditionally, CLV (or CLTV) is the prediction of the net profit that the customer will generate over their entire lifetime. An increase in your CLV indicates advocacy, and a decrease indicates a negative impact that you need to look into. A comparison of this over time will determine whether you are making better customers.

Breaking down CLV into its bare bones, we can see that it is made up of three basic elements:

1. Annual profit contribution of the customer;
2. Average number of years the customer is likely to stay with you; and
3. Initial cost of acquisition of the customer.

Customers generate value at individual touch points and paying for goods and services in the form of sale, second sale, commission, licensing fees, processing fees, subscription fees, penalties, royalty, addon purchases like accessories, etc. The sum total of all these payments across the customer journey(s) allows you to calculate the average revenue you are likely to earn from each customer. The difference between this revenue and incidental cost of operations per customer, gives you the annual profit contribution of the customer.

If you are selling only one product, you could denote this using the following formula:

Average Purchase x Number of Purchases a Year x Average Profit Margin = Yearly Profit Contribution

However, if you can't really predict the number of years the customer is likely to stay with you, what do you do? If you look at your retention rate (the number of customers who are likely to remain with you at the end of a period, say a year), and you know the yearly fall in your attrition rate (your yearly discount rate), then you can calculate your CLV pretty easily as well.

Thus a generalized formula for CLV is,

CLV = Annual Profit Contribution per Customer x {Yearly Retention Rate/(1+Yearly Discount Rate-Yearly Retention Rate)} - Initial Acquisition Costs

As you get more analytical, looking into the reasons why customers leave you before the CLV date is good practice. If you get these reasons right, you will see your CLV improving naturally. By looking into your CLV data by customer segments, vintage, or say by actions taken towards customer retention, you could get deeper insights.

Also remember that sometimes, by just selling better and more relevant products to the customer, you can bump up the CLV for that customer. This metric is a sure shot C-suite winner.

11. NEW REVENUE PER CUSTOMER (NEW)

The addition of new customers may not signify an increase in revenue if they are not active and this is especially true for many industries outlined above. Additionally, if the customer buys a cheaper, rather than the premium product, from you, it indicates a fall in your new customer revenue. Tracking this along with its relevant segmentation can help you understand customer advocacy better.

The formula for this is,

New Revenue per Customer (New) = Incremental Revenue from New Customers ÷ Total Number of New Customers

If your net customer additions shows an increase from the last period, and if the above ratio is better, you are on the right path.

12. NEW REVENUE PER CUSTOMER (EXISTING)

This one is a no brainer. New revenue opportunities created by existing customers is measured using this metric. New revenue could come from new services or new products being cross sold.

This metric is critical to understand how your CLV is doing, and whether there is a chance that it may fall off a cliff. As I said at the beginning of the book, if your product is more than 3 years old, chances are you are exposed to your customers defecting to another brand. If you are losing customers who were not impacting your sales or profitability much, you probably have lost customers who did not associate with you in the first place. However, losing profitable customers is another deal altogether.

The formula for measuring this is,

New Revenue per Customer (Existing) = Incremental Revenue from Existing Customers ÷ Total Number of Existing Customers

The key thing to remember is that this metric needs to exclude new customer additions that you have accounted for in 'new customer revenue per customer'.

If your new revenue per customer is better than the figure for the previous period, you are on the right track.

13. RETAINED CUSTOMER REVENUE

I really love this metric. The reason is that this metric is solely the result of our actions. The revenue from a retained customer is a direct outcome of turning a disgusted customer into an advocate. Eventually, these customer give the organization far more love, revenue and it is highly likely that they become serious advocates for the brand or product.

This adds to your growth, advocacy, market share, revenue, and profits. Could you ask for more?

If you use analytics, you will find that retained customers require less marketing, and your returns on such customers can increase by up to 75 per cent according to retention studies by Bain and Company.

14. CAMPAIGN ROI

The real question is if you spend US$1, what do you expect in return? That is your benchmark and is what we call the expected ROI.

Your real ROI, is measured as,

Campaign ROI = Value of Gain (Value Won - Actual Cost) ÷
Actual Cost

This metric would also tell you if your customer actually thought much about your campaign or not. At a minimum, your margin should be 50 per cent, so if you spend US$100 on a campaign, you should get back at least US$200.

Gaining more customers and getting repeat customers is one of the outcomes from a higher campaign ROI. Again, this is one of the KPIs that has C-suite attention and will be a great basis for getting additional funding for future campaigns for your business.

COST MEASURES

While revenue and profit are always exciting features, costs are the real determinants in that journey. This section discusses this very important measurement component.

15. CONVERSION RATE (APPROVAL RATE)

This is a really common measure across sectors and we are constantly looking at our customer pipeline and measuring conversions.
The formula is:

Conversion Rate % = Total Number of Customers ÷ Total
Number of Visitors

The conversion rate reflects the power of your product or service as well as your ability to persuade visitors to take action. Amazon, for example, has a conversion rate of 74 per cent, which explains their immense stickiness once a customer visits their site.

I look at the conversion-to-customer rate in six layers: first, when they visit our website, we call them visitors. When they come back and show interest, they become repeat visitors. This is followed by the third layer when the customer indicates strong interest, downloads a specs sheet or a form, asks questions, reviews reviewer comments, or saves the product to his wish list. In this stage, they are clearly a lead. This is followed by a step when the customer clicks on the product and adds it to the cart, and in the meantime has reviewed more content, they are upgraded into qualified leads. When the cart translates into a purchase, and the prospect pays and requests for the product to be delivered, it becomes a sale. Note that they are not yet your customers and there are abandonments even after a sale—this is especially true in the era of online shopping. It is only once the customer receives the product, starts using it and the return period has expired do they successfully become your customers.

This journey to conversion has a direct impact on your cost of operations for each layer. A lower conversion rate means a higher cost of sales, thus reflecting wastage. There are some interesting situations in conversion rates: if you came off a holiday discount period, your conversion rate would go down steeply; or if you changed the look and feel of your website, you may want to keep a watch on conversion rates. A good example would be when Adobe increased their prices for the Adobe Creative Suite substantially in 2019, they would have had to re-examine their conversion rates very carefully. While an increase in selling price would be beneficial to the company's profit margin, a much higher abandonment rate would have definitely hurt them.

I spent over two years in my career fixing the conversion rate for credit card products at the bank I was working for. Interestingly, that was also time we were struggling with net customer additions. My biggest takeaways from that role was that it wasn't a single reason that made me spend two years to clean up the conversion rate, but rather a combination of issues that had to be un-entangled one by one. These issues were created through years of blind sightedness and dis-regard to many of the principles around CX that I am highlighting in this book.

16. COST OF RETENTION

The lesson learnt from churn is always a hard one. Normally a CEO is looking for an average number, yet the decline might have been created because of poor governance in many parts of the organization that have been overlooked. Avoiding churn requires time and effort, and retaining customers is an expensive affair. Therefore, costs incurred to avoid churn can be denoted as the cost of retention.

Churn adds to the costs incurred by the organization in the form of loss of revenue as well as costs associated with additional efforts to retain the customer.

Sometimes, the cost of retention is unavoidable. However, often, it's better to let the customer go. If there is a significant loss of future CLV, then you know you are going to lose significant revenue if the customer goes away. That way, if you look at the cost of retention and compare it to the retained customer's revenue, you understand whether your retention efforts were worth it or not.

The benchmark for cost of retention is actually marginal revenue versus marginal cost incurred. This metric helps us decide whether to retain the customer or not. In the past few years, using analytics to capture this information has helped us build a better predictive model to understand future retention efforts. The more you do your comparisons against CLV and retained customer revenue, the sharper your model gets. If our cost of retention goes up, it could indicate that our customers are not happy with the existing products and services, and we need to segment our data to understand it better.

17. NET CUSTOMERS LOST (CHURN)

Churn has many flavours depending on the kind of industry, customer type, relationship, etc. If we lose customers who have contracted with us for an indefinite period through cancellation of their subscription (Netflix for example), that would be voluntary contractual churn. If a customer goes away from us because he is moving country for example, that would be voluntary non-contractual churn. When the bank decides to discontinue a customer's loan for credit reasons, it would be termed involuntary contractual churn, and if a retailer cancels an order since it ran out of stock, that would be involuntary non-contractual churn.

It's not bad to have churn, and, in fact, healthy businesses have a churn of between 5–8 per cent. If you believe in the fact that 20 per cent of our customers end up giving 80 per cent of the revenue, then a loss from that 20 per cent bracket is the one that starts to concern you the most. It needs to be noted that these numbers are indicative and may vary depending on your line of business.

Net churn refers to total churn less the number of people who have been retained by the organization during the period in consideration.

A recent Harvard Business School (HBS) study, states that a 5 per cent increase in customer retention results in a 25–95 per cent increase in profits.

Actions for customer retention are not 'departmental action', but rather an organization-wide correction plan. This is where empowerment and encouragement play really critical roles.

Remember that churn hurts CLV, your brand, your reputation and your bottom line.

18. CUSTOMER ABANDONMENT RATE

In our earlier metrics, we have covered this measure to some extent. To repeat, the ability to persuade customers to act is the conversion rate. Its direct opposite is abandonment. One direct and really useful indicator of user experience (or CX) is abandonment. As the abandonment rate declines, you can infer that your user experience and CX are improving. Remember that lower customer abandonment rates have the potential for more visits from customers and repeat business.

According to Baymard Institute, the average 'cart' abandonment rate in e-commerce is 68.53 per cent. That's expensive cost of sale. Many industries like banking don't even bother measuring it as they only measure a qualified lead status. For B2B businesses like IT companies that cost is quite significant, hence they have to get a grip on it in order to be profitable.

IN SUMMARY—TEN

As we draw the curtains to the measurement tools that quantify performance and results, I would like to say that I have taken only the top 18 measures considered by my clients. There are more evolved measures like a KPI for innovation to measure the return on value created for our clients.

On the whole, though, the key principles to success remain the same. You need to rank top of the charts against your competitors and be able to trace CX issues back to your lead indicators for improvement. The leadership team also needs to be married to the outcome and all employees need to look at these measuring tools as a way of life.

Twelve

Conclusion

Thank you for the time and effort, and your investment in this book. Even after the book, I will always feel I have something more to say, since new ideas and new experiences will create new ways to approach the subject. I am humbled by your investment, and your aspiration to make your organization go to greater heights.

THE BRAND 'CUSTOMER'

'We see our customers as invited guests to a party, and we are the hosts.'

—Jeff Bezos

This section is dedicated to all of us who refer to ourselves as customers. Believe it or not, as a customer you have been a great influence to get organizations to completely re-orient themselves to focus on *you* or go out of existence.

You can connect with organizations emotionally. If you love their product, let them know about it vocally. Introduce them to your friends and family and make them feel good about the excellent job that they are doing. Talk about them on social media; they deserve it after all. A little goodwill will go a long way for them.

Join their community or forum; give them feedback; become their brand ambassador; participate in their contests and win some prizes; and, finally, be a part of their team, their focus groups to help them give you better things.

Your actions have made them what they are and where they stand, and the reward for doing so will give you better products.

If you have come back feeling less than satisfied, bored or even frustrated, you are not alone. But there is a role that you can play. Tell them what your expectation was, and how they fell short. If you are comparing the product you bought from their competitors, let them know what went wrong. Organizations won't have a clue if you don't tell them and if other customers feel the same way, the organization will be forced to change. If there are inadequate service channels to voice your concerns, use social media. At the end of the day, you have the right to get your opinion out there. Organizations that genuinely care will respond quickly and put you first.

IN PURSUIT OF EXCELLENCE

This book has gone through many iterations. From a personal perspective, the concepts and their direct connections that are discussed in it took me years to understand. The book started off as a scrap book with myriad of notes jotted down in random order that meant nothing to a casual observer. As it went through an initial storyboarding with topics brought out as headlines to create some semblance of structure, I was able to visualize its form and content. As my thoughts started to flow, I wrote down many stories spontaneously. I read and re-read it, got it proofread and during this phase many sections were re-written to make the concepts and ideas comprehensible and relatable to a wider audience. To support the book, I also had to draw out what I was trying to say on a piece of paper, and then convert them to words. That's why I say, a picture can speak a thousand words.

The book then went through rigorous reviews, finally taking shape as an acceptable manuscript. The embellishments were then added in, to make it to you in this shape for your consumption.

The story of Mercedes-Benz is no different from the evolution of this book. From its humble beginnings in 1901, followed by its merger with Karl Benz's organization in 1926, Mercedes-Benz's innovative spirit turned into real passion in the pursuit of excellence over the years. They moved to 'the best or nothing' over the years and have always closely guarded the number one position.

As I just get up from my chair after watching the Monaco Formula One Grand Prix race, and reflect once again on the 'best or nothing' attitude of Mercedes, I cannot but feel humbled by the legacy that the company has created over the last century and promises to bear well into the next.

As I write the final words of this book, I can feel the spirit of Mercedes-Benz's transformation from 'in pursuit of excellence' to 'the best or nothing' philosophy. I hope you enjoyed the book as much as I did and thank you once again for your time.

CONCLUDING REMARKS—YOUR OPPORTUNITY

If you have come this far into the book, you would have realized that there are a ton of ideas that you can take inspiration from and implement irrespective of which part of the organization you represent and make a difference.

This book is not intended to answer all questions and be prescriptive about what you need to do. It just opens doors into new horizons and sheds light on areas you could look at to improve. It gives you the belief that things can be improved from where you are and talks about the areas where you could potentially invest.

You would also realize that your improvement may in turn increase your engagement with your employees, and this in turn would have an effect in terms of their engagement with the organization.

But the biggest thing you would realize is that by taking such small steps, you can make really big changes.

The more precisely you scope out your next steps, the more achievable the results will be; while the broader you make them at one go, the more ambiguous these steps can become. Remember that success was achieved by gold standard CX organizations by taking the steady path.

Seize the opportunity! May you conquer greater heights.

Acknowledgements

An interaction with my friend, acclaimed Malaysian artist, Jega Ramachandram, inspired my creativity, and sparked my journey into putting out this book. Through the years, I discovered new meaning to experience—as a customer, employee, colleague, entrepreneur and adviser.

This book to me marks the pinnacle of that journey. I have interacted with countless individuals from my various professional experiences, leaders of industry, governments, saints, gurus and advisors. Each taught me the values of staying human. Each one taught me invaluable lessons in excellence, to go forward but to keep looking at my rear-view mirror. All my notes are as a result of paying heed to my rear-view mirror, and those are the lessons I have penned down in this book.

The book will also connect you back to your own examples around experiences that make your journey fruitful. The book elaborates on 'what?' and 'how?' through these examples.

Leaders knowingly or unknowingly leave their mark through quotes. They bless this book as well. Some have left us for greener pastures, and some stay as god amongst men and continue to inspire.

A special thank you goes out to my friends and well-wishers who have shared their experiences, asked questions, and given critique to improve my understanding.

Dad continues to bless me from above, and initiated me into the pursuit of perfection. Dad's influence continues to encourage me to learn. Mom taught me perseverance and continues to encourage me to fly higher and achieve new goals.

My wife, Jo, brother, Sridhar and dear friend, Jayaram, spent hours reviewing, editing and giving suggestions to make the book immeasurably better.

The final shape and form of this book wouldn't have been possible without support from my agent—Anish Chandy, and the editors at Penguin Random House, who have been instrumental in putting this book into your hands.

And finally, the unconditional support from Jo and my daughter, Jia, has encouraged me and supported my journey to making this book a reality.

At the end of the day, though my name finds a place on the cover of this book, I know that I am blessed to walk as a mere mortal with the support from my friends and family to whom I owe more credit. Thank you, all.

Appendix

Facts and Figures

When I wrote the book, I incorporated industry terms and concepts without explaining them separately. The objective of the appendix is to familiarize readers with some terms they may not be fully comfortable with.

I have also incorporated concepts that experts use into figures in this section to explain them.

CHAPTER 1

Customer Experience—The perception that the customer has of your brand. Your brand is created through touch points, user experience, operational experience, and, finally, advocacy as outlined in the diagram below.

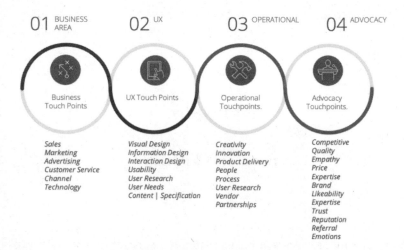

Customer Adoption—Different customers perceive change differently. Radically different changes are first adopted by innovators, followed by early adopters, and then the majority starts to accept the change, tailed by a few people called laggards. Dr Everett Rogers popularized this theory in his book *Diffusion of Innovations*, first published in 1962.

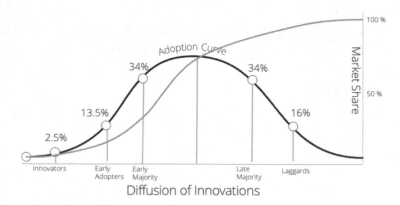

Personalities—Customer personality differs from customer to customer. Broadly, you can classify them into four brackets: aggressive, analytical, expressive and passive. Your strategy towards CX should be tailored to each personality type in order to create maximum impact.

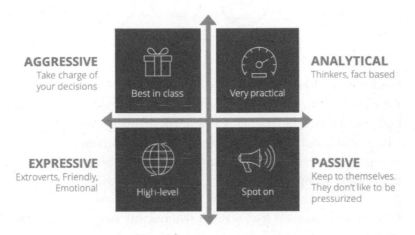

Customer Centricity—A way to foster positive customer experience for every stage of the customer.

Customer Advocacy—A customer who recommends your product or service to others. A person who seeks to convert others to use the product (Evangelist), or a customer who is keen to see you grow (Shareholder).

The book focuses on a five-step process to reach advocacy, and describes ways of achieving this throughout the book.

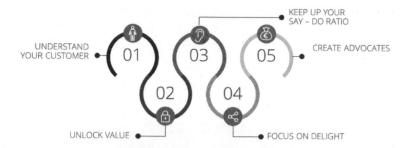

Intellectual Property—Assets you can create legally protected through patents, trademarks, copyrights, and trade secrets. Your customer experience strategy is a result of defining what works and what doesn't, and in order to reach that point, there is enough energy that goes into it. Protecting it through IP could be a good business model. For example, franchising.

Unsecured Loans—A loan granted without any asset to back it up. A car loan is secured, a personal loan is unsecured.

Credit Policy—An operational guideline that defines rules to follow to acquire and manage customers used when granting a loan to a customer.

Average Revenue per User (ARPU)—The total revenue divided by the number of subscribers to describe gross revenue generated by subscriber or customer.

Public Sector Indian Bank—A major type of bank in India where the government holds more than 50 per cent stake.

User Experience (UX)—The interaction experience a customer feels while using a system, website, app or other digital medium.

WYSIWYG—'What You See Is What You Get'. Initially used in system parlance to convey synergy between sight and intent, to outcome.

Say–Do Ratio—Reliability ratio of your promises made and fulfilled to customers.

Customer Service—The service you provide to customers before, during and after making a purchase.

Patient Experience (PX)—Everything we say and do that affects our patients' thoughts, feelings and well-being.

Unicorn—A term used to describe a valued company with a very high share holder valuation (stock price) in an investor's mind.

Champion Products—Products that do exceedingly well in your product catalogue.

Net Promoter Score (NPS)—The willingness of customers to recommend your product or service. A measure of customer loyalty.

Customer Satisfaction Score (CSAT)—A measure of satisfaction of your experience.

Customer Attrition—A term to describe the loss of customers to a company. Similar terms are customer churn, defection or turnover.

Multi-Year Payback—A business bet made with upfront investment with the expectation of return on investment and profitability over many years.

Cost Recovery Model—A model in which income is not recognized for a sale, till the cost of goods or services have been recovered in cash.

Crowd Funding Platform—Internet websites that support ventures of a person, product or entity, to provide money from a large number of people in small increments for a reward. The reward could be a product, service or just a recognition or an acknowledgement.

Champion–Challenger—An approach to test the continuation of an established way of doing things (Champion) with a different way (Challenger).

A-B Testing—In A-B testing the idea is to look at two different ways of doing something, and finding a winner. Say you have two different banners for your ad campaign, and you want to find the one that suits your customers. You divide the sample into two categories and check for acceptance.

Product Company—A company which derives its revenue by selling products to customers.

Services Company—A company that derives its revenue by providing services.

CHAPTER 2

Microfinance—A banking service provided to unemployed or low income individual or group who have limited access to other forms of financial services.

Non-Bank Financial Companies—Financial Institutions that offer specific banking services engaged in specific financial services business. The common denominator is lending.

Cash Deposit Centre—Places to deposit cash, including CDM Machines and ATMs.

Customer Persona—It's a descriptive sketch of a key segment of your audience. It's a way to better understand prospects and customers at a more personal level. Personas are used early in the process to provide you a customer description for prospecting and unifying customer segments. A typical capture format for a Customer Persona is given below to give more granularity into creating your own persona.

Customer Segments—A way in which customers can be classified into specific groups based on quantitative data. Segmentation is complex requiring quantitative research to analyse and distil into groups.

B2B—A transaction between Business–to-Business i.e. between two companies.

B2C—A process of selling products or services to end consumers.

Empathy Map—A visual way of getting insider a customer's head to capture knowledge about a user's behaviour and attitude. A typical empathy map start point is represented below. The customer is at the centre.

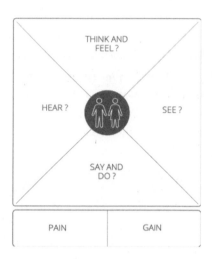

Cognitive—Mental actions or processes to acquire knowledge and understanding through thought, experience and senses.

A typical cognitive behaviour that goes on in a customer's mind for buying is represented below:

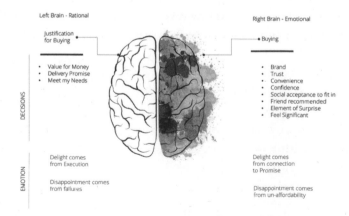

Customer Sciences—The science of gaining a richer understanding of customers in the digital era.

Acquisition—A process of bringing in new customers or clients to your business.

Customer Retention—A process of retaining customers through initiatives to engage through alternate products, services, customer loyalty or other brand initiatives.

Social Relationships—A science established to understand how social structures work in regards to social interaction or relationships between two or more individuals.

Relationship Manager (RM)—A person responsible to improve relationships with specific clients and partners.

Wealth Management Tier—A hierarchy created by personal financial advisers to create products and services most relevant to your financial needs.

Balance Transfer—A process of moving a form of debt from one institution to another or from one financial instrument to another.

Life Time Value—The present value of all future cashflows that are attributed to a customer during his or her entire relationship with the company.

Buyer's Remorse—A sense of regret from a customer after having made a purchase.

High Resolution—A relative term used to describe higher quality based on currently evolved standards. A high resolution product can be benchmarked stronger with differentiated value with a customer.

Target Segment—The process of breaking down a market into segments and concentrating your efforts into a few key segments.

Community Bank—A bank typically owned and operated for the local working of a community.

Customer Satisfaction Survey—A survey used for feedback to improve loyalty, drive growth and to reduce churn.

Agile Methodology—An iterative methodology used in project management to release benefits through the process rather than only at the end.

Sprint—A short time-boxed iteration used within the Agile Methodology.

Artificial Intelligence—A computer simulation for human intelligence in machines to mimic human thinking and actions.

Positioning Strategy—A strategy that considers choices to concentrate on an excel in specific areas using a deeper understanding of strengths and weaknesses of the organization, competition, and needs of customers.

A typical positioning map for a product to be developed is given below based on price and value.

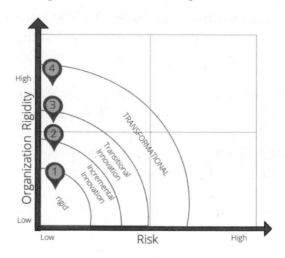

Transformation—A strategy to bring about a marked change inside the organization, product or service. Transformation exercises are often complex due to organization rigidity and risk perception of an organization.

A typical transformation journey from rigidity through incremental innovation leading to transformation is depicted below:

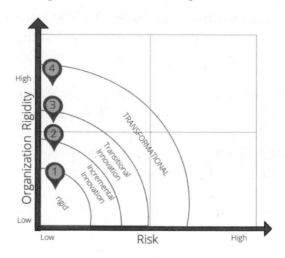

Product Restructuring—A process of introducing new features or solutions matching customer requirements to an existing product, while sunsetting a no longer relevant feature set.

Personalization—The process of converting a general product or service into a relevant proposition for your customers to make them feel it has been tailor-made to their requirements.

Quick Cash—Used in reference to ATM machines in the book, is the process of making available customized cash requirements for each customer.

Angle of Arrival—An emerging technology standard that indicates the direction of the signal sources for better tracking. Used in Bluetooth 5.1 specifications.

Angle of Departure—A direction finding feature making it possible to detect the direction of a Bluetooth signal departure. Also refer to Angle of Arrival.

General Data Protection Regulation (GDPR)—A regulation in European Union (EU) law for data privacy and protection, including its application outside EU and Eastern Economic Areas.

Immediate Payment Service (IMPS)—Introduced by NPCI, India's payment service platform for funds transfers.

Unified Payments Interface (UPI)—A system allowing for merging several banking features, and routing of payments.

Unstructured Data—Unorganized Information not presented within a pre-defined data model.

Customer Sentiment—The emotion behind the customer engagement, which could be measured in tone, context, or actions.

Machine Learning—An application of Artificial Intelligence designed to learn automatically to improve from experience without being explicitly programmed.

Product Signalling—A way in which the product can influence customer choice without explicitly saying a word.

Notepad–Telecaller—Where a Telecaller captures the feedback of a customer inside the system for a system trail and further action.

Voice Modulation—A means by which the emotion of the message the customer wants to convey is captured.

Sentiment Analysis—A means to understand, interpret and classify human emotions within voice or text data.

CHAPTER 4

Scrums—A process framework used in the context of teamwork, accountability and iterative progress towards a well-defined goal.

Squads and Tribes—A framework popularized by Spotify to describe a specific type of agile management process.

Keurig—An extremely popular and robust brewing, juicer system created for home and commercial use.

Ethnographic Research—A study of customers in their natural environment through direct observation rather than in a lab.

CHAPTER 5

ROI—Short for Return on Investment. The building blocks for creating a great ROI are outlined in the diagram below:

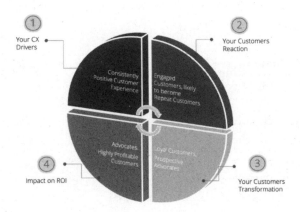

Active Customers—Customers that show promising signs of using or interacting with the product or service.

Cost of Acquisition—The total cost of acquiring a customer including incentives or promotions.

Cost to Serve—The total cost to serve a customer including cost of actual business activities and overhead costs incurred in the service of that customer.

Humanize Financial Services—A programme of converting the brand to become more 'human' towards its customers and their communities.

Key Performance Indicators (KPIs)—Key measurements that are critical for organizational success.

CHAPTER 6

Kaizen—A Japanese word for improvement signifying a concept to continuously improve all functions with the involvement of all employees.

Data Model—A logical structure for a database.

Regression Testing—A process of software testing to confirm re-testing based on partial changes made to existing functionalities.

Circle of Excellence—A term coined by Mercedes-Benz to create an exclusive programme towards exclusive Mercedes-Benz owners.

CHAPTER 7

Vision Statement, Mission Statement—While we work on our own businesses or for an organization, at the core you will find the reason and possibilities to aim for—your vision statement. The mission, values, culture surround the core. The policies and decisions are derivatives that can change to support all of the above.

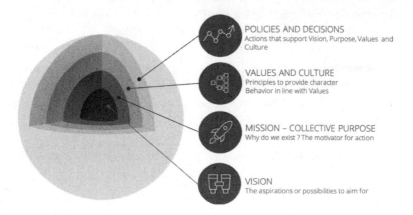

POLICIES AND DECISIONS
Actions that support Vision, Purpose, Values and Culture

VALUES AND CULTURE
Principles to provide character
Behavior in line with Values

MISSION – COLLECTIVE PURPOSE
Why do we exist ? The motivator for action

VISION
The aspirations or possibilities to aim for

Guiding Principles—These are values for a framework of behaviour and decision making.

Blue Print—Detailed Plan to execute something. The different layers of a blueprint are outlined below:

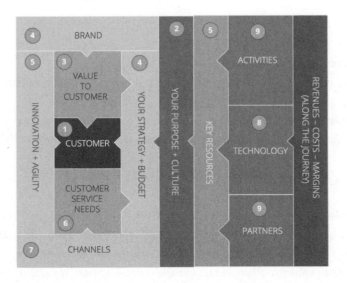

Interaction Model—A pictorial representation of how an organization interacts with a customer, overlaid with elements of a customer journey map that are outlined a little later.

Intrapreneur—A person within the company who promotes innovative product development and marketing. Organizations end up having accidental discoveries, patents and assets built over time as a result of intrapreneurial initiatives.

Mystery Shopping—A person employed to visit a shop or an outlet incognito, to assess the quality of goods or services.

Transaction Based Pricing/Subscription Model—A pricing model that enables a customer to use a product or a service for a recurring fee based on a single transaction or an interval of time.

Hosted Services Model—A lease model to move from ownership to pay for usage.

Value Train—Shifting focus of an organization from internal value to customer value.

Value Innovation—Value Innovation is the simultaneous pursuit of differentiation and low cost, creating a leap in value for both buyers and the company.

Blue Ocean—Redefining and repurposing businesses into newer market spaces to better accommodate customer interests.

Value Curves—A representation of where value is created for an organization's products and services.

Learned Helplessness—A condition where a person or an organization suffers from paralysis and conditions itself towards inaction.

Mass Error—When a mistake is repeated across a very large data set. For example, you put a wrong pricing label on a product, and it got picked up by many shoppers since it was too good to be true.

CHAPTER 8

Organizations succeed because of their teams. While responsibility is driven top down, responsiveness is driven bottoms up. The diagram is a representation of what is to follow in this chapter.

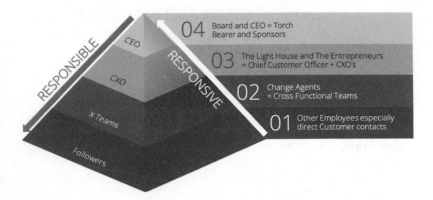

X Team—A cross functional team, created for a specific objective or resolving a problem statement within the company.

Followers—Worker bees who are the lowest common denominator in the organization.

The Torch Bearer—A term given to the CEO, who guides the direction of the entire organization.

The Lighthouse—A term given to the Chief Customer Officer, who sheds light to direct the organization towards positive customer experience.

CX Culture—Driving the culture of an organization towards customer experience

SWOT—An analysis of Strength–Weakness–Opportunity–Threat that an organization perceives of itself or its competitors.

CHAPTER 9

Elevator Pitch—The ability to convey meaning and value to a person with a very short attention span.

8 Steps to CX Transformation—CX transformation is an iterative process. The figure 8 is possibly the best representation of the process.

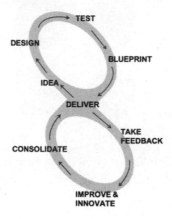

Customer Lifecycle Map—The different stages of a customer engagement with a company and their ultimate exit from the product, service, brand or business.

The illustration below is an illustration of customer moods, endorsement and exit in a customer life cycle.

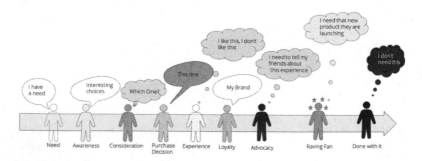

Service Design—The science around creating optimal service focus, taking into consideration actors, their interactions, supporting materials and infrastructure.

Below is an illustration of Service Design Elements and Tools:

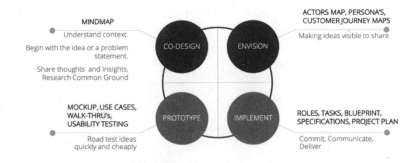

Actor Maps—An illustration of how a customer (a persona in this case) in a service design establishes relationships, for his needs and wants.

9 Moods—The 9 emotional states of a human being, with their intensities affect customer experience positively or negatively. Driving your CX strategy with these considerations can deeply benefit organizational response. A chart depicting the 21 most common emotions expressed during customer interactions is illustrated below:

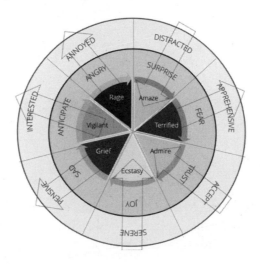

The Secret Customer—A term derived from mystery shopping, used by the author to explain how incognito customers can drive value within the organization.

Diary Study—A research method to collect qualitative information of participants going about their daily lives through a diary, log or journal.

Cultural Probes—A set of tools, artefacts or tasks are used to provoke the user, to think about their environment in new ways.

Moment of Truth—A point in time showcasing experiences of a person testing something, making a decision or facing a crisis.
An illustration of my personal moments of truth while at a Starbucks in South East Asia is depicted below:

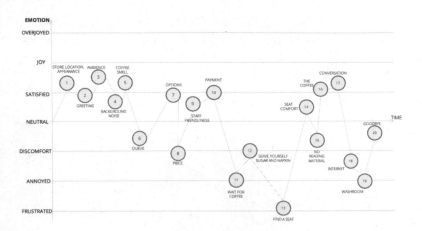

Customer Journey Maps—A diagram or multiple diagrams representing different stages, considerations, decisions and experiences that a customer goes through.

An illustration of a Journey Map Template along with what could potentially be captured is depicted below:

Stage	Aware	Consideration	Decision	Experience	Loyalty & Advocacy
Time Scale	2 Min	3 Min	5 Min	45 Min	5 Min
Customer Goals (Expectations)	I need a strong cup of coffee. Ah!! I can see a Starbucks				
Customer Thinking (in the mind)	Store is Attractive	What should I order?	I need to find a place to sit	Found a place, wait for business contact.	Need to claim free beverage next time from loyalty
Customer Insights | Pain Points	Difficult to park Car	Its Crowded / Few Payment Options	No seats. Have to wait. Don't have my preferred flavor	Nothing to Read / Slow WiFi	
Organization Insights and Actions	Can we rent space for cars to park?	Can we expand the store? / Can we improve Takeaways?	Expand Customer Options / Create separate takeaway point	Improve WiFi speed	Create Loyalty awareness campaigns
Governing Principles | Principles around the entire experience – e.g. Packaging, Receipt of Product, Payment, Setup and Use	Greet at Arrival	Ask Customer if he has a loyalty membership.	Menu and pricing is clear / Swift Payment. Keep Customer wait to under 3 minutes	Beverage and Food is warmed up to right temperature. Ensure tables are clean. Rubbish is disposed as soon as customer leaves. Steady WiFi	Greet on Leaving / Standardize loyalty across country
Guiding Principles | Business Goal | How do you guide the experience – Showcasing the brand, Speed, How do you engage, Principles around informing customers.	Starbucks Brand / Store inside Branding and standard layout.	Inform Customers of Beverage Options, Flavors. Explain menu's if asked / Capture Customer Mobile Number	Provide Receipt. / Warm the Mug, Starbucks Packaging / Starbucks branded Cutlery / Ensure consistency of beverage	Minimize disruption to customer experience	Ensure redemptions possibilities at every payment touchpoint
Defining Principles | Principles around Brand Association, Simplicity, Confidence, Clarity, Closure, Meeting Customer Expectations, Personalization, Customer Joy, Communication, Information Dissemination, and Timeliness	Brand Sign Visible. / Inspires Starbucks Standard / Buzz at store / Furniture similar to standards	Ensure Menu and Sizes are clear to understand. Display Food for quick customer choice. / Ensure speed of order to get to next customer. Meet turnaround times	Write Customer Name on Beverage / Call Customer by name when Beverage and Food is ready / Keep supplies like Sugar and Napkin topped up	Help customer identify free table quickly.	Ensure accurate deductions for redemptions
Customer Feeling | Emotions	That looks like a good store. One parking slot. Great!!	Excellent Ambience / Great Coffee Smell / Very Crowded	Staff is Friendly	Nice Coffee. Comfortable Seat. Warm Food – easy.	That coffee was free. Came from my loyalty points.
Touchpoints | Customer Doing (Actions)	Identified Starbucks store	Greeted at Store / Looked at Coffee Options / Reviewed Prices / Took Decision / Made Payment	Ordered Coffee and Cake / Wait for Coffee / Searching for Seat / Connect to WiFi	Consuming beverage and food / Friendly chat with client.	
Target Experience	Meet Starbucks Branding Standards. / Customer pleasantly surprised.	Quick Decision and Payment	Seamless transition from decision to experience	Comfortable. Customized food tailored to country palette.	Ease of Earn and Burn
Who is Responsible | RACI chart, can be an addendum to the Journey Map	ADDENDUM				
How are Pain points addressed	Parking Space	Point to seats when available	Point to popular flavors	Keep tables clean	Communicate different loyalty schemes
Recovery Principles | When things go wrong People – Process - Technology	1. Ensure customer is satisfied with food and beverage. 2. Fix any customer highlighted issues not meeting Starbucks standards. 3. Manual billing in case of system failure 4. Freebies for Starbucks errors.				
Brand Impact | Impact on Brand	Customer wants to visit again				
Technology	Which Technology Platforms and Solutions will be touched				
Minimum Viable Experience | Non Negotiables around Experience	Get same experience across all global outlets	Recognizes Starbucks Experience	Standardized TAT	Consistent Beverage Taste	Similar Loyalty programs globally
Future Enhancements | Projects, People, Process, Technology	1. Additional Payment instrument acceptance / 2. Starbucks chatbots for ordering				

RACI Chart—RACI stands for Responsible, Accountable, Consulted, Informed. A simple matrix used to assign roles and responsibilities for each task, milestone or decision on a project.

Minimum Viable Experiences—A minimum expectation of experience set by a customer based on promises, industry benchmarks, price paid, and lovability.

Voice of Customer—A process of capturing customer expectations, preferences and aversions.

Design Provocation—Using a visual medium created from an idea to forcibly cause your mind to move out of its comfort zone, to come up with radical solutions for the problem at hand.
A typical workflow for design provocation is depicted below:

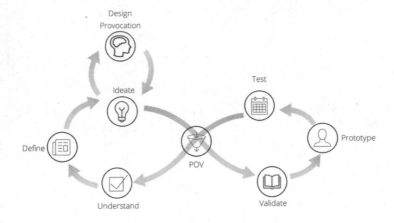

Design Thinking—A process to understand users or customers, challenge assumptions, redefine the problem statement, and design an innovative solution to prototype and test.

Focus Groups—A representative group of people brought together to participate in a discussion to provide feedback about a product, service or initiative.

Social Media Analytics—The practice of gathering data from social media sites and analysing them for taking business decisions.

Customer Service Triangle—A term coined by the author, and inspired from photography to explain the causal relationships between speed, number of channels and customer sensitivity to drive organizational responsiveness to customer experience.

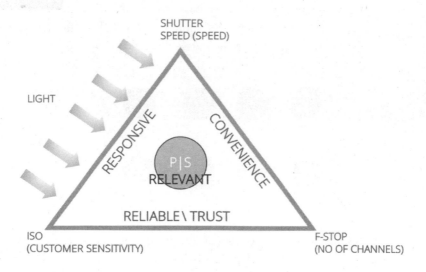

Chatbots—A computer programme created to simulate conversations with human users over the Internet using Artificial Intelligence.

Beacon Technology—A small wireless Bluetooth transmitter used to send signals to smart devices nearby carried by customers to locate or interact easily.

CHAPTER 10

First Mover Advantage—Marketing strategy associated with competitive advantage gained as a first entrant to the market.

Jugaad—Indian term translated as a non-conventional, frugal innovation or work-around referred to sometimes as hacks.

Omni Channel—A way in which you create a single customer experience for your brand.

Non-integrated channels tend to have an inconsistent fulfilment experience. In multi-channel the channels are treated in silos, so in multi-channel they are treated separately like below:

In Omni Channel you create a single customer experience irrespective of the channel of origin as depicted below:

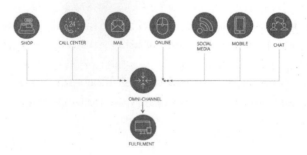

Robotic Process Automation (RPA)—With the usage of software robots (bots) or Artificial Intelligence(AI) you can capture and interpret a process and trigger appropriate responses and communicate with other digital systems. These are basic tasks executed by bots to reduce the burden of repetitive, simple tasks on humans.

AI Deep Learning/Deep Neural Learning/Deep Neural Network—An AI function that imitates the workings of the human brain for processing data and creating patterns for decision making.

Optical Character Recognition (OCR)—The conversion of images of typed, handwritten or printed text into machine-encoded text.

Computer Vision Algorithms—Getting computers to gain high-level understanding of digital images or videos.

Algo Trading—The process of executing trading instructions in an automated and pre-programmed manner.

Internet of Things—A system of interrelated devices—mechanical and digital devices able to transfer information over a network.

CAGR—Compounded Annual Growth Rate.

OECD Countries—Thirty-five member countries from Europe including Austria, Belgium, Czech Republic, Denmark, Estonia, Finland, France, Germany, Greece, Hungary, Iceland, Ireland, Italy, Latvia, Luxembourg, Netherlands, Norway, Portugal, Poland, Slovak Republic, Slovenia, Spain, Sweden, Switzerland and UK.

Connected Cars—A car that can communicate bidirectionally with other systems outside the car. The car allows Internet access and data transfer with other devices inside and outside the vehicle.

EMV Standard—Short for Europay, MasterCard and Visa. A standard incorporating secure technology used for worldwide payments done with credit, debit and prepaid EMV smart cards using contact, contactless and mobile forms.

Customer Relationship Management (CRM)—Typically used in conjunction with a software used for the same purpose.

CHAPTER 11

KPI Tree—A graphical representation modelled on a tree diagram showing you how KPIs work together.

Method—A systematic, established way of approaching or accomplishing something. The customer may see a final product but never the method. Coca-Cola has a method to achieving flavour for example.

Measure—The indicator to assess customer experience.

There are 5 categories to CX measures outlined in the diagram below:

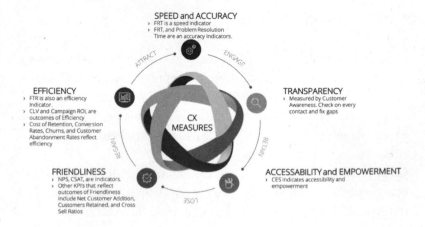

First Response Time (FRT)—The time taken between the submission of a case by a customer to the time the service rep responds to the customer.

Problem Resolution Time—Time taken to resolve a customer issue
Customer Effort Score (CES)—The effort required by a customer to get an issue resolved or a request fulfilled.

Usually collected with a service metric poll by asking the customer 'how easy was it to interact with the [company]' using the following scale to assess difficulty:

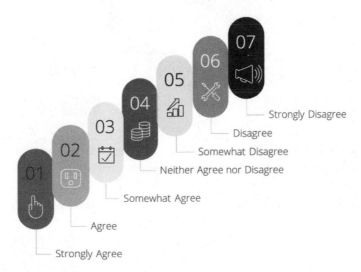

Net Promoter Score (NPS) Formula

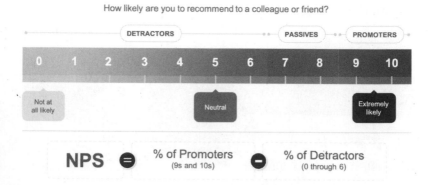

Customer Satisfaction Score (CSAT)—Obtained as an average from responses from customers on a survey conducted to assess customer satisfaction. Scale used for a series of the survey:

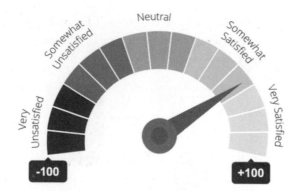

Cross Sell Ratio—The number of customers having more than one product or service to account versus a single product.

First Time Right (FTR)—A measure to assess customer effectiveness for carrying out activities in the right manner at the first instance every time. The framework for FTR is depicted by a diagram below:

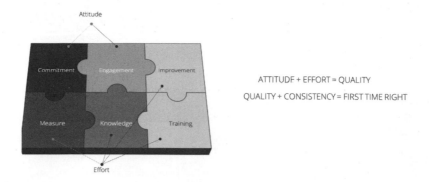

ATTITUDE + EFFORT = QUALITY

QUALITY + CONSISTENCY = FIRST TIME RIGHT

Problem Resolution Time (PRT)—Time taken from awareness of a customer issue to customer acceptance regarding resolution.

CLV—Customer Lifetime Value.

The formula for calculation of CLV is outlined below:

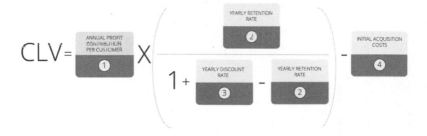

Campaign ROI—The assessment of whether a campaign was successful or not, and whether it met the outcomes desired at the beginning of the exercise.

Conversion Rate—The number of customers who positively responded to a campaign or promotion versus the total number of customers targeted. The flow of customer happens through multiple stages and is outlined in a simple illustration below:

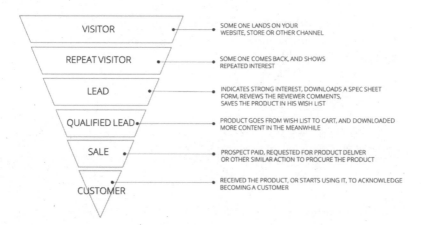

Churn Types—A diagrammatic illustration of the four different churn types:

	CONTRACTUAL	NON CONTRACTUAL	
	EXAMPLE Cancelling a Netflix Subscription	*EXAMPLE* Customer moves country, hence cancels order	VOLUNTARY
	EXAMPLE Bank decides to discontinue your Loan for credit reasons	*EXAMPLE* Retailer cancels order since it ran out of stock	INVOLUNTARY

Cost of Retention—While an organization survives because of its customers, sometimes the cost to retain a customer might exceed the lifetime value or residual value. So this measure is used to assess those circumstances.

Customer Abandonment Rates—In the online world many customers show initial interest but abandon their pursuit midway. The flow is depicted below:

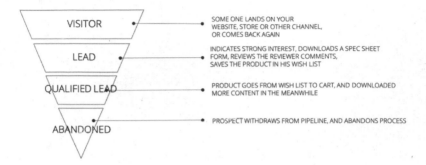

VISITOR — SOME ONE LANDS ON YOUR WEBSITE, STORE OR OTHER CHANNEL, OR COMES BACK AGAIN

LEAD — INDICATES STRONG INTEREST, DOWNLOADS A SPEC SHEET FORM, REVIEWS THE REVIEWER COMMENTS, SAVES THE PRODUCT IN HIS WISH LIST

QUALIFIED LEAD — PRODUCT GOES FROM WISH LIST TO CART, AND DOWNLOADED MORE CONTENT IN THE MEANWHILE

ABANDONED — PROSPECT WITHDRAWS FROM PIPELINE, AND ABANDONS PROCESS

Notes

Preface

1. Matt Parker, *Humble Pi*, Allen Lane, 10 April 2019.
2. Introductory video in Apple WWDC Keynote 2013, https://tinyurl.com/y6z6wb2p
3. 'Seven Customer Service Lessons I Learned in One Day from Richard Branson', Forbes.com, 9 May 2013, https://tinyurl.com/y648n9xz

Section I: Connecting the Dots

One: C for Customer, H for Human

1. 'Vodafone India's Q4FY18 revenue falls by 21.2%; Group CEO Colao to depart', Medianama.com, 15 May 2018, https://rb.gy/mkikb2.
2. 'Revenue Per User Continues to Decline for Telcos', Themobileindian.com, 16 August 2018, https://tinyurl.com/y5zvbwob
3. 'Telecom Statistics India', 2019, https://tinyurl.com/y3mpcolp
4. 'Indians Are Starting to Save For Retirement Early, But Is It Enough?' Livemint.com, 29 September 2019, https://tinyurl.com/y5jd9vh7
5. Everett M. Rogers, *Diffusion of Innovations*, Simon & Schuster, New York, 6 July 2010.
6. https://tinyurl.com/ycanhfyj
7. 'Timeline: Boeing 737 Max Jetliner Crashes and Aftermath', *Chicago Tribune*, 18 November 2020, https://tinyurl.com/y28ntx7w
8. 'Why Those Samsung Batteries Exploded', *Washington Post*, 12 September 2016, https://tinyurl.com/zrowys9

9. 'Explained: Why IndiGo is Struggling to Find Pilots to Fly its Planes', the *Economic Times*, 1 February 2019, https://tinyurl.com/yyfgvwv6

10. https://en.wikipedia.org/wiki/History_of_iPhone

11. 'The Birth of the IBM PC', https://tinyurl.com/yxuk6byx

12. https://en.wikipedia.org/wiki/Apple_III

13. 'Avengers: Endgame' Earns 2 Trillion Won for 9 Days in Korea', *the Dong A-Ilbo*, 6 May 2019, https://tinyurl.com/y5j6zu7f

14. 'Pixar only happened because of Howard the Duck. Allow us to explain . . .', DigitalSpy.com, 15 December 2019. https://tinyurl.com/y4qu7lsg

15. 'The Heated Razor by GilletteLabs—SOLD OUT', Indiegogo.com, 19 October 2018, https://tinyurl.com/y2aeuhrw

16. 'Airbus To Stop Production Of A380 Superjumbo Jet', Npr.org, 14 February 2019, https://tinyurl.com/y5h96nar

17. Ibid.

18. 'Remembering the Durable Ceramic Apple Watch Edition, Now Dropped From Apple's Lineup', Appleinsider.com, 12 September 2018, https://tinyurl.com/y7da2n5f

19. 'Apple's Luxury Watch Dream is Over', Theverge.com, 7 September 2016, https://tinyurl.com/y4nvhzfo

20. Peter Thiel, *Zero to One*, Currency, 16 September 2014.

21. https://www.peakdesign.com/pages/story

22. https://www.kickstarter.com/discover/advanced?term=peak+design&woe_id=Earth&sort=magic&ref=nav_search&seed=2637537&page=2

23. Standford Commencement Speech, https://www.zdnet.com/article/stevejobs-big-lesson-stay-hungry-stay-foolish/

Two: Get Closer to Your Customers

1. 'Chapter 3: Public sector banks: an overview and identification of weak banks', Rbi.org, https://tinyurl.com/yyjjk9fh

2. https://www.heraldsun.com.au/businessold/ing-direct-doing-without-bricks-and-mortar/news-story/7c54323f570ef0d4cf5a933f62c1beff?sv=a43c51a1906582a6560720ed5a78479

3. 'Outcasts in a Digital World', *BusinessLine*, 21 May 2017, https://tinyurl.com/y63uofsq

4. 'Robin Dunbar: we can only ever have 150 friends at most . . .' Guardian.com, March 2010, https://tinyurl.com/y2veusrw

5. 'CIPA Releases Figures on Market Share of DSLRs vs. Mirrorless', Slrlounge.com, 2017, https://tinyurl.com/y2y2u8oy

6. Malcom Gladwell, *The Tipping Point*, Back Bay Books, 7 January 2002.

7. 'A Boing Whistleblower Says He Tried to Raise Concerns About Sloppy 737 Max Production, But Was Ignored by the CEO, Board, FAA and NTSB', *Business Insider*, 10 December 2019, https://tinyurl.com/yy2bywg5
8. 'The "IKEA Effect": When Labor Leads to Love', Harvard Business School, 2011, https://tinyurl.com/y58pr2fz
9. https://en.wikipedia.org/wiki/General_Motors_EV1
10. 'Remembering the Apple Newton's Prophetic Failure and Lasting Impact', Wired.com, 2013, https://tinyurl.com/yc95vhsh
11. https://www.kearney.com/web/the-purchasing-chessboard
12. 'Opal Nugget Ice Maker, Indiegogo.com, https://tinyurl.com/mj2jz3c
13. 'Facial recognition to be used in British supermarkets for the first time', Telegraph.co.uk, 17 October 2018, https://tinyurl.com/y2b4bype
14. 'Our Virtual Try-On Is Better Than Any Makeup App You've Seen', L'Oreal Paris, https://tinyurl.com/y4qyu4el
15. 'Heineken's Launches "Ignite"—its First Interactive Beer Bottle', DigitalSynopsis.com, https://tinyurl.com/y4hy3vmm
16. 'How Pepsi Gamify the Coming World Cup 2014 Experience?' Juloot. com, https://tinyurl.com/y2jbg7pk
17. 'Shazam partners Up with KitKat to make Packaging Interactive in Latest Promotion', Campaignbrief.com, 10 May 2016, https://tinyurl.com/y6rpoby6
18. 'How Rebecca Minkoff Uses Tech to Make her Fashion Stores Stand Out', Engadget.com, 25 December 2016, https://tinyurl.com/y3nrj4rt
19. 'How Does Amazon & Netflix Personalization Work?' Vwo.com, 4 November 2020, https://tinyurl.com/y6kd3pna
20. 'Share a Coke Campaign Post-analysis', Marketingmag.com, 22 June 2012, https://tinyurl.com/yxrg2x2l
21. 'Bluetooth Direction Finding: Angle of Arrival (AoA) and Angle of Departure (AoD)', Silabs.com, https://tinyurl.com/y3hnv5jn
22. 'How Target Figured Out A Teen Girl Was Pregnant Before Her Father Did', Forbes.com, 16 February 2012, https://tinyurl.com/yyfdflzh

Three: Customer Experience in Times of Crisis

1. 'Chipotle Attempts to Recover from Coli PR Disaster: A Case Study', Medium.com, 4 August 2017, https://tinyurl.com/y34wk45x
2. 'How These Three Brands Have Survived a Reputation Crisis', Brandstruck. co, 25 October 2017, https://tinyurl.com/yxntmagw
3. 'United Airlines Shows How to Make a PR Crisis a Total Disaster', Money. cnn.com, 11 April 2017, https://tinyurl.com/ycml8wmm

4. '12 Times United Was America's Most Hated Airline', Businessinsider.in, https://tinyurl.com/y47opmrn
5. 'BP Customer Base Falls In Wake of Spill', Experian.com, 11 August 2010, https://tinyurl.com/y22xg5vc
6. 'Top Software Failures in Recent History', Computerworld.com, 17 February 2020, https://tinyurl.com/y3ofgcvv
7. 'Covid-19, An Opportunity for Indian Industry', Business Line, 21 March 2020, https://tinyurl.com/rjjaa9x
8. 'Customer Experience in Times of Crisis', Ashtonmedia.com, 21 April 2016, https://tinyurl.com/y54ycqwk
9. Gita V. Johar, Matthias M. Birk, Sabine, A. Einwiler, 'How to Save Your Band in the Face of Crisis', MIT Sloan, 11 June 2020, https://tinyurl.com/y2vckq72
10. 'Prominent CEOs Promise that They Will Not Layoff Workers in 2020', *Forbes*, 27 March 2020, https://tinyurl.com/y6xf2kyo
11. Ranjay Gulati, Nitin Nohria, Franz Wohlgezogen, *Harvard Business Review*, March 2010.
12. Joost, 'How Progressive Companies Survive and Thrive in Crisis', Corporaterebels.com, March 2020, https://tinyurl.com/y5xl99g8

Four: Going Above and Beyond

1. https://en.wikipedia.org/wiki/Red_Bull
2. 'Learn More About the Spotify Squad Framework — Part I', Medium.com, 7 March 2017, https://tinyurl.com/y2pfdhxs
3. 'United Community Bank named to Forbes List of America's Best 100 Banks', 30 January 2019, https://tinyurl.com/y2ngjctv
4. 'Retail Bank Customer Satisfaction Strained by Growth of Digital-Only Segment, J.D. Power Finds', JDPower.com, 26 April 2018, https://tinyurl.com/y2mhk68p
5. 'Harley-Davidson Suffers Eighth Consecutive U.S. Sales Loss', Rideapart.com, 29 January 2019, https://tinyurl.com/yxp6e48b
6. 'BMW i8 Coupe (2018)', Podpoint.com, https://tinyurl.com/y3fyrhqb
7. https://www.gogoro.com
8. 'How Lego Went From Nearly Bankrupt to the Most Powerful Brand in the World', Successagency.com, 27 February 2020, https://tinyurl.com/y4o5sbvt
9. 'How The Local Competition Defeated a Global Brand: The Case of Starbucks' Australian Marketing Journal, 2010, https://tinyurl.com/y2at3zfn
10. Australian Bureau of Statistics, 2008.

11. 'The Sad Decline of Barnes & Noble', Theamericanconservative.com, 21 May 2018, https://tinyurl.com/y5qydf62
12. 'Volkswagen: The Scandal Explained', BBC.com, 10 December 2015, https://tinyurl.com/yhseswyt
13. 'US Companies With the Best and Worst Customer Experience Ratings in 2016', Marketingcharts.com, 10 March 2016, https://tinyurl.com/y4gjvt2v
14. 'IT Failure at Heathrow T5: What Really Happened', Zdnet.com, 7 April 2008, https://tinyurl.com/y2wqsnmv
15. https://www.failory.com/cemetery/juicero

Five: Why Do It?

1. 'Maybank Makes it into the World's Top 500 Brands', Nst.com, 28 January 2019, https://tinyurl.com/y35xrsqb

Section II: Executing for Results

Six: The Commitment

1. 'Singapore—Statistics & Facts', Statista.com, 1 August 2018, https://tinyurl.com/y4636zn8
2. 'Here are 10 of Amazon's Biggest Failures', TheStreet.com, 13 November 2015, https://tinyurl.com/y5g3cjb2.
3. 'The Wolf of Main Street Auction at Sotheby's', News&Media, 20 April 2018, https://tinyurl.com/yy58m38l
4. 'Mercedes Benz—"The Best or Nothing" Car commercial', Youtube.com, 19 June 2017, https://tinyurl.com/yxrc2fjp

Seven: Build Your Strategy

1. 'New Sony Sensor Specs Resemble Chips Found Inside Fujifilm X-T3, Panasonic GH5S, Others', Dpreview.com, 20 October 2018, https://tinyurl.com/y4btx44g
2. 'Apple CEO Tim Cook's Feud with Blackberry Has a Quiet End', Fortune.com, 29 September 2016, https://tinyurl.com/y6lnmv4p
3. 'Apple Plans to Use Its Own Processors in Macs from 2020: Report', India Today, 3 April 2018, https://tinyurl.com/y34rjbdn
4. 'Blue Ocean Strategy', Harvard Business Review Press, October 2004, https://tinyurl.com/y3rsp98x

5.   'Four Reasons Google Bought Waze', Forbes.com, 11 June 2013, https://tinyurl.com/y4tacr3f

6.   'India's "Beauty Queen" Who Made in India to Sell in Switzerland in 1992: Biotique Founder Vinita Jain's Story', Yourstory.com, 11 November 2016, https://tinyurl.com/yyrstq5g

7.   'Patanjali Enters Big Retail with Future Group Tie-up', Economictimes.com, 10 October 2015, https://tinyurl.com/y3wnofpa

8.   'Cathay Pacific Error Sees $16,000 Flights Sold for $675', TheGuardian.com, January 2019, https://tinyurl.com/yddhedha

9.   'SIA Will Honour Erroneous Sale of Business-class Tickets at economy-class Fares in Australia', Straitstimes.com, 8 December 2014, https://tinyurl.com/y44723rl

10. 'Zappos.com's $1.6M Mistake That Boosted its Brand', Blog.Hubspot.com, 24 May 2010, https://tinyurl.com/yyrcfy39

Nine: The Second Building Block for Execution—Your Process, Methods and Tools

1.   'Self-report Captures 27 Distinct Categories of Emotion Bridged by Continuous Gradients', Pnas.org, 5 September 2017, https://tinyurl.com/yy88vnl8

2.   'Designing the Soft Side of Customer Service', Sloanreview.mit.edu, 1 October 2010, https://tinyurl.com/y63nu6p7

3.   'Scientists Have Mapped Where People Feel Emotions in Their Bodies', Curiosity.com, 31 October 2018, https://tinyurl.com/y2r4cqja

4.   Jan Carlzon, *Moments of Truth*, Harper Business, 15 February 1989.

5.   'Zero Moment of Truth (ZMOT)', ThinkWithGoogle.com, https://tinyurl.com/y55jbk35

6.   'First Moment of Truth (FMOT)', Monash.edu, https://tinyurl.com/ybx9lh6x

7.   https://en.wikipedia.org/wiki/Moment_of_truth_(marketing)

8.   https://en.wikipedia.org/wiki/Moment_of_truth_(marketing)

9.   A.G. Lafley and Ram Charan, *The Game Changer: How You Can Drive Revenue and Profit Growth with Innovation,* Crown Business, 8 April 2008.

10. Tim Brown, *Change by Design: How Design Thinking Transforms Organizations and Inspires Innovation*, HarperCollins, 16 September 2009.

11. Edward De-Bono, *Po: Beyond Yes and No*, Penguin, 14 October 2000 Intl Center for Creative Thinking,

12. 'Keep the Change Savings Program', Bank of America, https://tinyurl.com/yyxfbrlp

13. 'Design thinking in 3 steps: How to build a culture of innovation', ThinkWithGoogle.com, October 2019, https://tinyurl.com/y3dmlgg9
14. Ben Pring, Malcolm Frank, and Paul Roehrig, *Code Halos: How the Digital Lives of People, Things, and Organizations are Changing the Rules of Business*, Wiley, 7 May 2014.
15. 'United Breaks Guitars': Did It Really Cost The Airline $180 Million?', Huffpost.com, 24 August 2009, https://tinyurl.com/y6s2wxc9

Ten: The Third Building Block for Execution—Surprise with Innovation and Outperforming with Technology

1. 'The Coca-Cola Company', Britannica.com, https://tinyurl.com/yda8w76l
2. David Ebstein, Range: Why Generalists Triumph in a Specialized World, Riverhead Books, 28 May 2019.
3. Eva, Hdfcbank.com, https://tinyurl.com/yxltwuvl
4. https://www.marketwatch.com/press-release/wearable-devices-market-2019-size-industry-share-approaches-and-forecast-by-2024---marketresearch-engine-2019-09-24

Eleven: Measuring Results

1. https://www.nytimes.com/1983/07/30/us/jet-s-fuel-ran-out-after-metricconversion-errors.html
2. 'Honda Recalls 5088 Vehicles to Fix Takata Airbags', Economictimes.indiatimes.com, 29 July 2019, https://tinyurl.com/y67yflpa